AF593283

SAILING CAN BE SIMPLE

Acknowledgement is made to Stanford Maritime Press for permission to reproduce the material on pages 154, 155 and 163.

Sailing Can Be Simple

JOHN MELLOR

Souvenir Press

First published 1977 by Souvenir Press Ltd,
43 Great Russell Street, London WC1B 3PA
and simultaneously in Canada

Reprinted November 1977

ISBN 0 285 62276 5

Filmset and printed in Great Britain by
BAS Printers Limited, Over Wallop, Hampshire

Contents

1 The Basic Idea

Undoubtedly one of the biggest problems facing the newcomer to sailing is the somewhat esoteric nature of the game. Like Hi-Fi and photography it shimmers with strange and hidden mysteries, jealously guarded, perhaps even exaggerated by its many acolytes. To a race of beings designed for living on the land, the sea and all its appurtenances present an alien, confusing and sometimes even frightening front. Add to this a new terminology, a strange language and the ever-present feeling of instability when actually afloat, and we have all the ingredients for a classic witches brew, from which rises a swirling fog of confusion and mystique, vigorously stirred by those in the know.

This book is designed to sweep away that veil of mystery and lay bare the salient and important bones of sailing—simple sailing that will get you afloat quickly and safely, with a firm grasp of the fundamentals of sailing and seamanship so that you will derive the maximum satisfaction and pleasure from your sport. For to the majority of people it is a sport, not a disease or a way of life, or an all-consuming ego trip, or a path to glory. A sport, that will give them and their family and friends (not forgetting you) many hours of healthy, exciting, lazy and satisfying pleasure.

To begin with, I shall not confuse you with technicalities, but will concentrate on the fundamentals of sailing, safety and seamanship. We will then move on to basic coastal navigation, simple weather lore, elementary maintenance and so on, so that we cover a solid, basic and practical grounding in getting your boat into the water, taking her sailing, and getting home again in one piece. And if that sounds elementary, it is. It is also a fundamental ability that many who can reel off screeds of detailed information on astro navigation, the use of trenail fastenings in carvel-built sixty footers and all the rest of it do not have. Such details will come later, when we have thoroughly covered the basics. There is no need at this stage for anyone to know the difference between clinker planking and double diagonal building, or the intricacies of the wishbone schooner rig. The chances of your boat being anything other than a small bermudan sloop are very small, so we shall confine ourselves to that. If you have a ketch, then there is no need for me to tell you what it is. If you haven't, there is no need, at the moment, for you to know.

So, what is sailing? Well, we can go even more fundamental than that—what is a boat? Quite simply, it is a floating container in which we can travel on the water. To make it move we fit it with a propellant, such as a pair of oars, an engine or sails. For our purposes we are going to take the sails. Originally, way back, boats were rowed; then some bright spark probably realised that if he stood up in the boat while the wind was behind him he would go faster. It was not a great leap in the dark for mankind for him to realise that if he held a large sheet of something up he would go even faster. And doubtless it didn't tax his imagination too much to hang this sheet on a vertical pole to save him having to stand up with it for hours on end. Thus we have a sailing boat. No cunningham holes, crosscut spinnakers, tallboys, ghosters, etc. perhaps, but, nevertheless, a sailing boat.

Over the years this elementary sail was refined and developed until it was discovered that one could actually sail into the wind with it. How and why, no-one knew. But it did not stop them doing it; and it is not going to stop us. There are many excellent text books on the whys and wherefores of sailing into the wind, for those who really want to know. We shall not concern ourselves with it at this stage. It is sufficient to know that it can be done, to a certain extent.

In figs 1a and b we see an original, simple sail alongside the refined

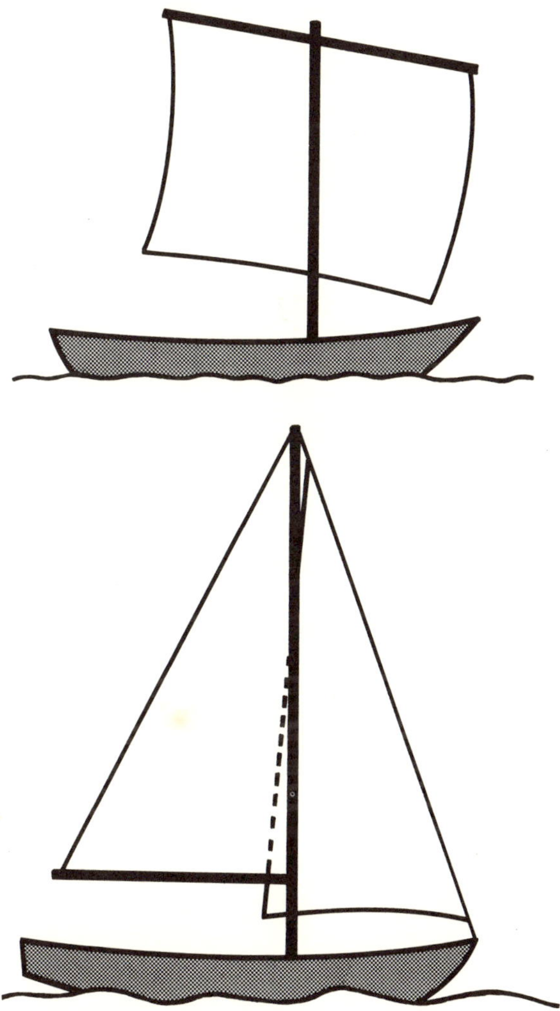

Fig. 1a

version of our small bermudan sloop. The mast remains basically the same, but the old square sail has been split into two and tapered to a point at the top. The sail at the front of the boat is known as the foresail (being to the fore) and the one at the back the mainsail (this is arguable,

Fig. 1b

but for our purposes we shall say it is because it is the most important). Now, in the photo, we can see that both these sails pivot about their front edges, the mainsail being attached to the mast and the foresail to a wire running from the front of the boat to the top of the mast. Both the sails are thus free to flap in the wind, so in order to fill them with wind and make the boat go, we have a rope attached to the rear corner of each sail with which we can pull the sail into the wind and stop it flapping, exactly as we would a sheet hanging on a washing line. This rope, for some reason lost in antiquity, is known as a sheet.

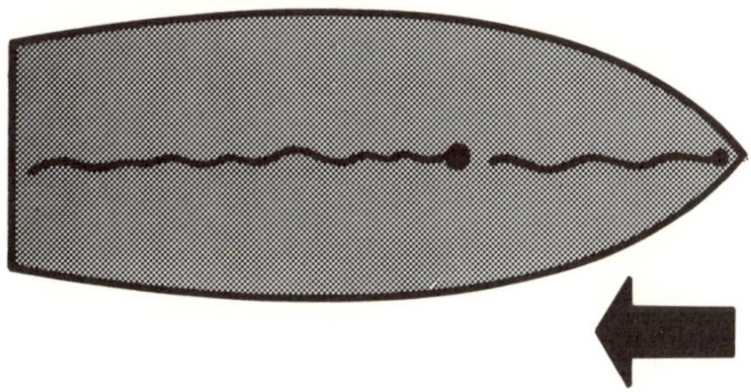

Fig. 2a

In figs 2a and b we look down on the boat from above. We can see that with the wind blowing from right ahead the sails merely flap. The photo shows the boat as the wind would see it. So we cannot sail directly into the wind, as the sails need to be full of wind in order to drive the boat. In figs 3a and b the wind has shifted round sufficiently to fill the sails when they have been pulled as close as possible to the centreline by their sheets. In your boat the wind probably has to be around 45 to 50 degrees to one side of the centreline before the sails will fill properly and begin to drive the boat through the water. This is as close to the direction of the wind as you will be able to sail, and it is known as sailing close-hauled.

You will notice that the foresail is aligned with the mainsail at roughly the same angle to the centreline. This is so that it can direct a flow of wind over the lee side (opposite the wind) of the mainsail in

Fig. 2b

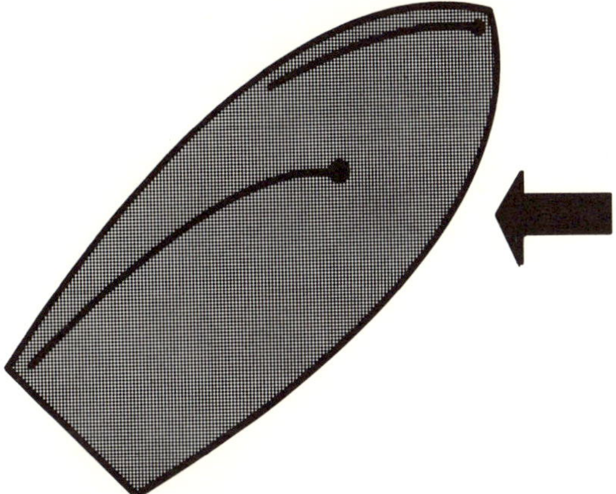

Fig. 3a

order to increase the latter's efficiency. Both the sails are positioned by the sheets holding them against the pressure of the wind. Thus we sail to windward, steering the boat so as to keep the wind at the same angle to the centreline all the time. This is generally done by referring to a small flag, known as a burgee, at the top of the mast. The burgee will show you the angle of the wind to the centreline. (See fig 4.)

Having positioned our boat at the requisite 45 to 50 degrees to the wind and hauled in the sheets till the sails fill and cease flapping, various things will begin to happen—most of them very worrying to the beginner. First the boat will start moving—that is the good news. As she does so, you will notice two particularly important things. The tiller (a piece of wood we use to control the angle of the rudder, which steers the boat) will tend to pull over to leeward (away from the wind). This will try to move the rudder and swing the boat into the wind. (See fig 5). A firm, steady hand will be required to counteract this and keep the boat moving straight. This tendency of the boat to swing into the wind is known as weather helm and is a design factor built into the boat to ensure that, should you let go of the tiller, she will swing head into the wind where the sails will flap and stop driving. The boat then stops. Thus you will find that a light, steady pressure will be required on the tiller at all times to keep the boat running straight.

Fig. 3b

Fig. 4

The other important thing that you will notice, unless the wind is extremely light, is that the boat will heel over away from the wind. This can be very worrying to the novice, but rest assured the designers know all about it. There are two ways of preventing the boat from heeling right over and capsizing, due to the pressure of the wind on the sails. One is to put a heavy weight underneath the boat, which will constantly exert a force to pull her upright. This generally takes the

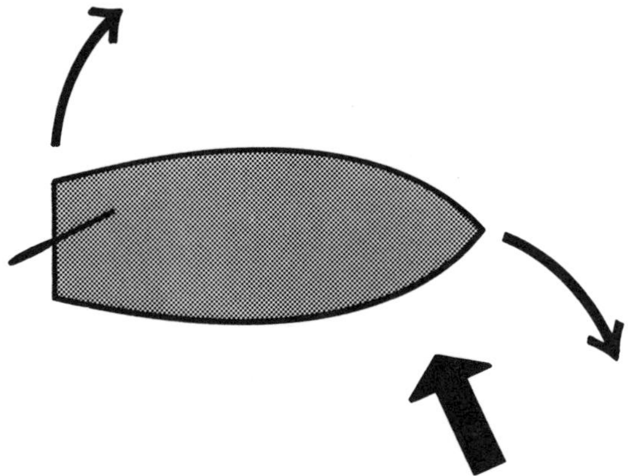

Fig. 5

form, in cabin boats, of lead or iron on the bottom of the flat area of boat under the water known as the keel. (See figs 6a, b and c.) This keel can form part of the boat herself, or be a separate plate bolted to the bottom of the boat. It prevents the boat being blown by the wind sideways through the water. (See fig 7.) In small racing dinghies the keel is generally made of wood and can be lifted clear of the water

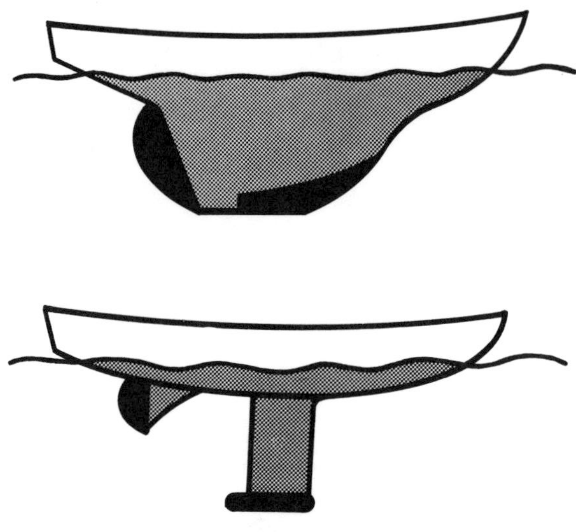

Fig. 6a

Fig. 6b

Fig. 6c

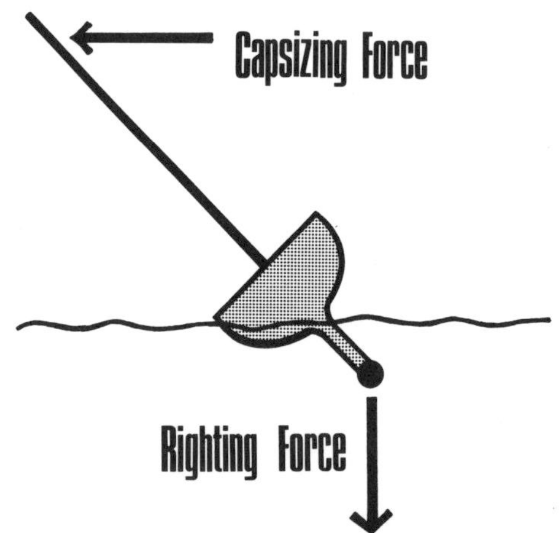

Fig. 7

through a slot in the bottom of the boat for ease of handling ashore. It is called a centreboard and is used solely to prevent the boat being pushed sideways. To prevent her capsizing, the crew sit on or hang over the windward side (nearest the wind) of the boat. This is very strenuous and not to be recommended to the serious cruising man, who is far better off relying on a lump of lead to do the job for him. It is worth noting also that cabin boats stabilised with a heavy keel are virtually uncapsizable, as the further they heel, the more effective the keel becomes in preventing them heeling further. If the wind becomes so strong that the decks are nearly underwater then not only will you be very uncomfortable, but the boat will not sail very efficiently, and you will have to reduce the amount of sail you have set. This will decrease the heeling effect of the wind and we will look at it more closely later. For the moment we will simply appreciate that it can be done.

The third thing of interest that will occur when we get moving is that the burgee will lie closer to the centreline than the 45/50 degrees that we mentioned earlier. This is quite normal and is simply due to our forward motion through the water tending to try and align the burgee with the centreline. Push the tiller slightly to leeward (or just ease your hold on it so that the weather helm takes it) and let the boat swing slowly and gently closer towards the wind. Watch the front edge of the foresail carefully. When you see it begin to lift or flap you are too close to the wind. Any further and the wind will be too close to the centreline to fill the sails. Pull on the tiller slightly to swing the boat away a little, until the sails are just filling nicely. You will soon get to know the best angle for your burgee.

And that, stripped of the details and the mystique, is how we sail to windward. There is nothing magical about it—we simply place the boat so that the wind is blowing from about 50 degrees off the centreline, haul in the sheet till the sail just stops flapping, and away we go. A light pressure on the tiller to keep her going straight against the effect of the weather helm, confidence in the ability of the lump of lead or iron at the bottom of the keel to prevent us from capsizing, knowledge that the flat area of that keel will stop the wind from blowing us sideways, and we are sailing. Keep an eye on the burgee to check that we are all the time as close to the wind as we can get, and get into the habit of easing the pull on the tiller from time to time so that she will swing gently closer to the wind. Watch the leading edge of the foresail for any sign of lifting or flapping, whereupon you pull back against the weather helm to steady her before she swings right into the wind. Keep the sails just filling nicely without taking the boat too far away from the wind.

If you are now sailing peacefully closehauled into the sunset, be sure to place an order for the next chapter, when we shall see how to sail in other directions so that you can get back. This will be followed by nautical terminology, rigging, manoeuvring, reefing and coping with bad weather, safety, knots and seamanship, basic coastal navigation, simple weather lore, elementary maintenance and a final round-up of all that has gone before.

Some of you will probably have noticed that many of the statements I have made in this chapter are not strictly correct. They have been made for the specific purpose of simplifying and clarifying the understanding, at this early stage, of the points we have covered. The strictly correct definitions and terminology will creep in as we progress and the basic techniques become thoroughly understood. At this stage they serve only to confuse, so please don't write and tell me the difference between a keel and a centreboard—I know!

2 Sailing

In the last chapter we left you sailing cheerfully closehauled into the sunset with the wind around 50 degrees to the right of the centreline. You had hauled hard in on your sheets so that the sails were full of wind and as near the centreline as you could get them. They were just filling nicely, with the foresail not quite lifting or flapping, and you held the tiller with a light steady pressure to counteract the weather helm. Your beady eye was checking the burgee regularly to make sure you were holding the boat at the correct angle to the wind. All was well.

Well, a chapter on starboard tack (closehauled with the wind on the right-hand side of the boat) is long enough for anyone. And anyway, we want to get more over to the right, or we won't get to where we want to go. Now, if we can sail closehauled with the wind on the starboard side (right) then it follows that we can sail equally well closehauled with the wind on the port side (left). The process is exactly the same, with the exception that we place the boat with the wind on the port side. We haul in the sheets and steer the boat so that the sails are just filling. We are then on port tack. Fig 8 (a–c) shows the boat on port tack and on starboard tack.

In fig 9 we see that if we need to move directly into the eye of the wind we can do so by the simple expedient of zig-zagging, first on port tack, then starboard and so on, just like a road winds up a mountain too steep to be climbed direct. Changing tacks at the end of each zig is simply a matter of pushing the tiller down to leeward (away from the wind) so that the boat turns towards the wind. The tiller is held over

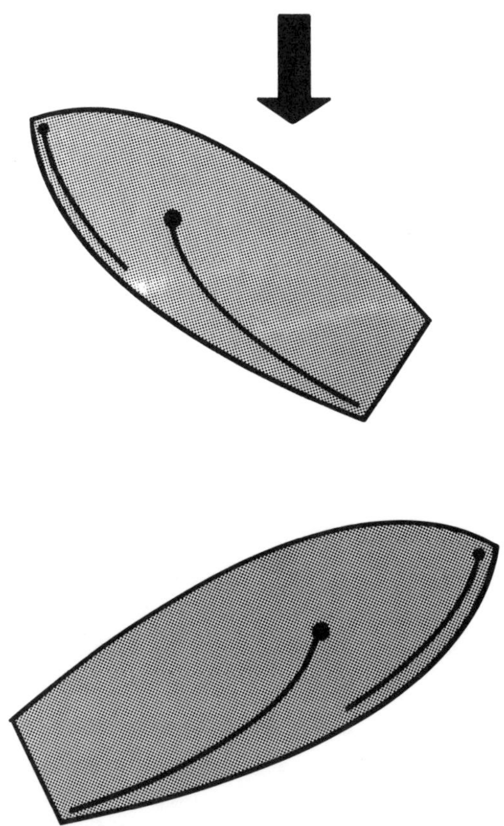

Fig. 8a

while the boat swings into the eye of the wind, and continues to swing until the wind is around 50 degrees the other side of the centreline. The boat is then steadied on the course and the sails hauled in again by their sheets, close to the centreline. We then continue as before but with the wind on the opposite side.

We have seen that when sailing closehauled we haul the sails in tight and steer the boat so as to keep as close to the wind as we can. If we want to sail away from the wind, however, we reverse the process. We point the boat in the direction we want to go and let out the sails until they begin to flap. We then haul them in again just enough to

Fig. 8b Port Tack

Fig. 8c Starboard Tack

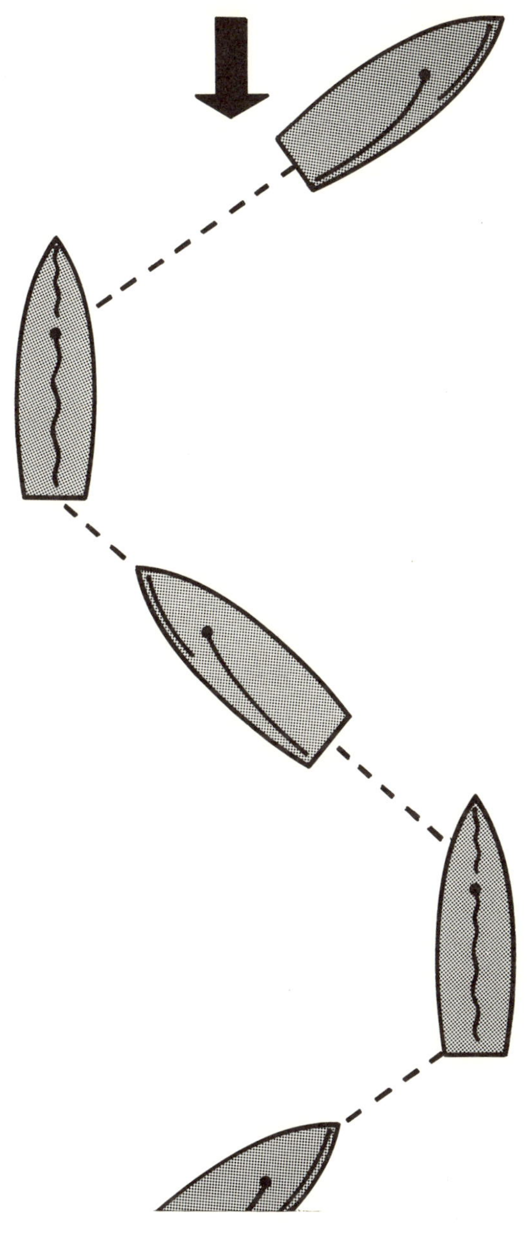

Fig. 9

stop them flapping. We hold to the fixed course and vary the position of our sails whenever the wind shifts, in order to keep them just filling nicely. If we want to alter course, we do so, then adjust the position of the sails to suit the different angle of the wind. Sailing away from the wind is known as reaching. See figs 10a, b and c.

Paradoxically, with modern sails, the most difficult point of sailing is running with the wind right behind you. This is because the bottom of the mainsail is generally attached to a long piece of wood known as a boom. With the wind directly behind you, the sails have to be let right out on their sheets until they are at right angles to the centreline, and the wind. See figs 11a, b and c. In this situation it does not matter which side of the boat the sails are (as long as the wind is absolutely

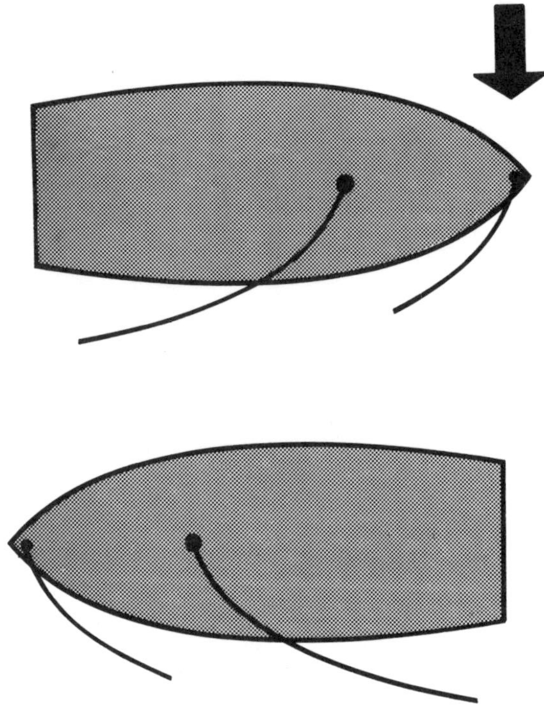

Fig. 10a

Fig. 10b

Fig. 10c

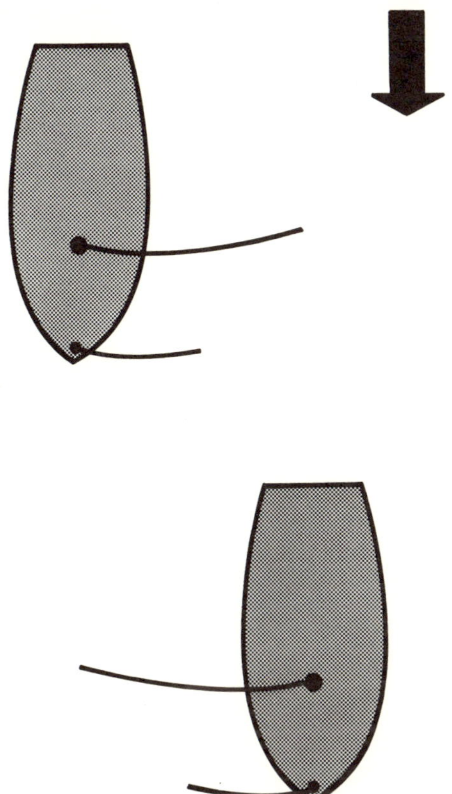

Fig. 11a

dead behind you), and, in fact, it generally pays to have one either side so that they do not shield each other. See figs 12a and 12b.

So far, so good. The problem arises if the wind suddenly shifts to the same side as the mainsail. There is then the danger of it getting behind the sail and blowing it right across the boat to the other side. This is often embarrassing, and sometimes dangerous if the wind is strong. A heavy boom flashing suddenly right across the boat can do a lot of damage. So it is vital to keep a very sharp eye on the burgee when running, to ensure that the wind does not get behind the mainsail. A simple alteration of course is all that is required in order to bring the

Fig. 11b Running on starboard tack.

Fig. 11c   Running on port tack.

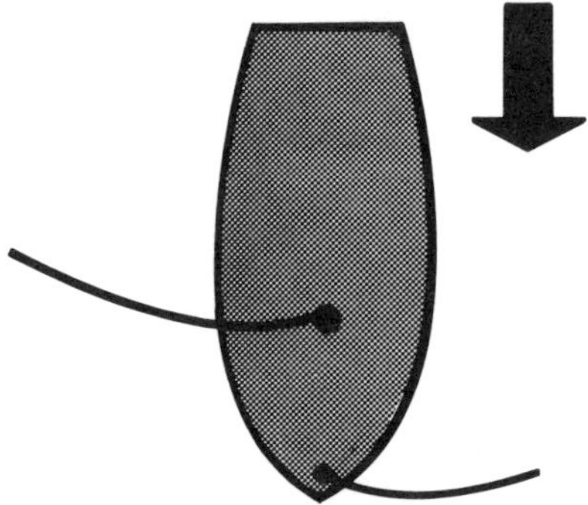

Fig. 12a

wind astern (behind) again. Just push the tiller over to swing the bow (front of the boat) into line with the burgee. See fig 13.

There will be times, of course, when you want to alter course when running. If the alteration is going to bring the wind round so that it continues to fill the same side of the mainsail, there is no problem. Simply put the tiller over to bring the boat pointing in the new direction and haul in the sheets until the sails just stop flapping. Then carry on sailing. If, however, the alteration will bring the wind round to blow on the back of the mainsail, then it will be necessary to shift the mainsail over to the other side of the boat before it blows over of its own accord. This process is known as gybing, and consists of hauling

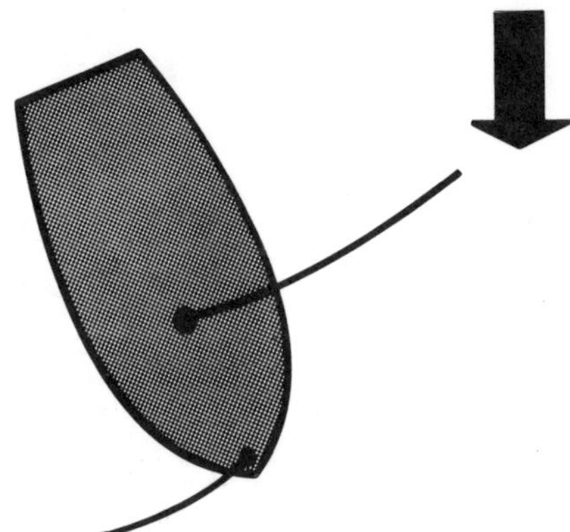

Fig. 13

Fig. 12b

in the sheet tight until the mainsail is held firmly on the centreline. Course is then altered. With the mainsail pinned in firmly to the centre of the boat there is no danger that it will flip violently across. When the new course is reached, the mainsail is eased out again until it begins to flap, then trimmed in to just fill nicely. The foresail is also trimmed in to fill nicely and away we go. See fig 14.

And that, basically, is sailing—making a boat move through the water by the action of the wind on the sails. Everything else is a development, modification or sophistication of this, and if the fundamental facts that we have covered so far are thoroughly digested, the rest will follow on easily and naturally. Let us look back over what we have done and apply it in a rather more practical manner.

Let us look at the sheets—those lines that control the angle of the sails. In figs 15a, 15b and 15c we see that there is a bit more to them than a simple piece of rope. When the mainsail is full of wind it can be very difficult to haul in, so we make the mainsheet a tackle with a purchase of something like four to one. This enables us to haul it in with a quarter of the effort. One end is attached to the boom (the long piece of wood to which the bottom of the sail is attached) and the other to a point at the stern (back end) of the boat. The hauling part of the tackle is led to a cleat, a piece of wood round which we tie the sheet to hold it in its desired position. In a small dinghy this sheet is held in the hand so that it can be released quickly to avert a capsize.

The foresail sheet is split into two, so that one can be used on each side of the boat. These are led through fairleads or blocks, and then to a winch on each side of the cockpit, which is used to haul the sheet in tight. When tacking or gybing (to bring the wind from one side of the boat to the other), one foresail sheet is released and the one on the other side of the boat hauled in when the boat has altered course to bring the wind to the other side.

While on the subject of tacking and gybing, remember that a boat will not stick to the water as a car does the road, but will tend to slide.

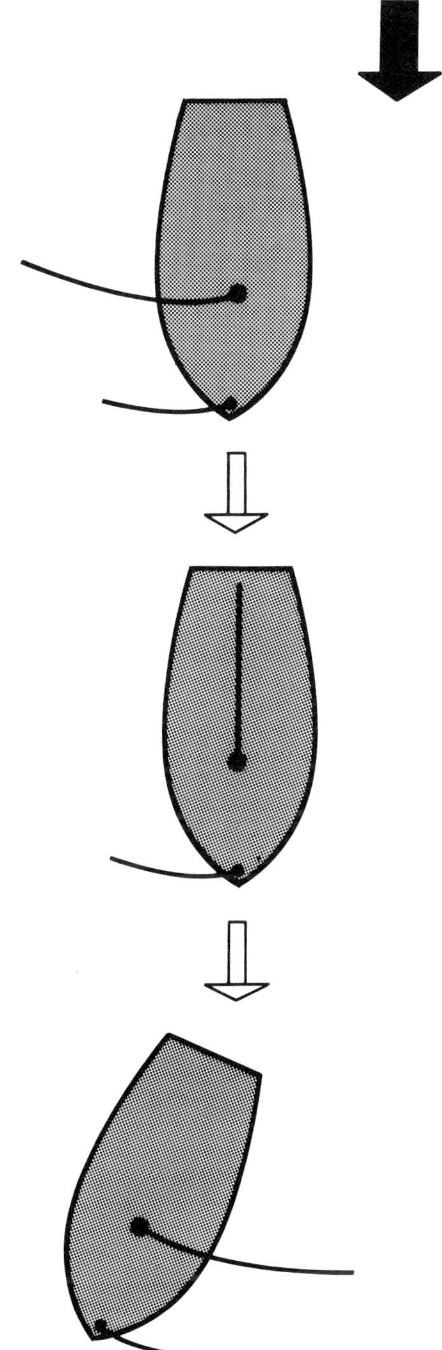

Fig. 14

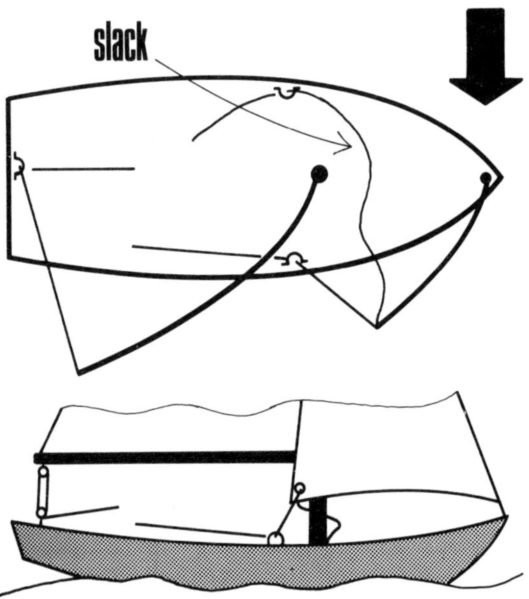

Fig. 15a

So, generally, a little opposite tiller is required to stop the swing just before you reach the course you want. Remember that corner you took a bit too fast the other week, when you lost the back end of your car and had to correct? Same problem. Remember also that a tiller works the opposite way to a wheel. If you put the tiller to port (left) the boat will go to starboard. Very confusing that, isn't it? So don't try and remember it; just remember that the stern will swing to where you put the tiller. And the boat will pivot about a point roughly a third of the way back from the bow (front end). You are not, in fact, steering the front end, as you do a car, but the back end. The simple appreciation of that fact will save you a lot of embarrassment, not to mention expense if you go the wrong way in a tight situation.

We mentioned earlier that when sailing closehauled (as close to the wind as we can) we haul in the sheets so that the sails are as near as possible the centreline of the boat. This is not strictly true. It is possible to sheet in the sails too tightly and kill their drive. In strong

Fig. 15b *Foresail sheet leads through fairlead to winch beside cockpit.*

Fig. 15c *The mainsheet.*

winds the very strength of the wind automatically prevents you from oversheeting, so you can haul in as tight as possible. In light winds, however, give them just a little slack. If they are too tight, you will feel the boat go dead. Ease them off just a shade and bear away (swing the boat away from the wind) till they are just filling. On all other points of sailing, the sails should be trimmed so that they are almost, but not quite, beginning to flap at the leading edge. This leading edge is known as the luff. Don't ask me why.

In fig 16, I give the theory of how sails work, as we understand it. If you find it confusing, ignore it. It is necessary for the designing of Twelve-Metre sailplans and for boring girls in the Club bar, but it is not necessary for sailing. You can drive a car perfectly well without knowing why an internal combustion engine works, can't you? If you are interested in this theory, mug it up after you have learnt to sail. Not before.

More important is to be able to keep track of the wind direction. This is one of the most difficult things for the beginner; not helped by all the nonsense written about feeling it on your face or the back of your neck. I have been sailing all my life—dinghies, small keelboats, cruisers, ocean racers, walloping great schooners, day sailing, hot racing, the lot; and I've tried it all—the cigarette smoke, the back of the neck, the wet finger, multiplying the square root of the burgee angle by 1.4 times the logarithm to the base E of the boat speed minus the number I first thought of bearing in mind my astrological birth sign, and all the rest of the twaddle. And it is twaddle. For a small cruiser man, your guide to the wind direction is your burgee. If it blows back almost along the centreline of the boat, you are closehauled. The wind, as it affects your sails, blows along the direction in which your burgee is lying. To alter the direction of the wind relative to your sails you use the tiller to swing the boat around underneath the burgee. Think of the wind as a great big arrow pointing along the direction of your burgee, and swing your boat around beneath it accordingly.

This way of noting the wind direction is especially useful when tacking and gybing. Tacking is the action of changing from sailing closehauled with the wind on one side, to sailing closehauled with the wind on the other side. During the process of tacking, the wind, relative to you, swings from one side of the boat, through right ahead, to the other side. If you think of the wind as a huge arrow pointing along the axis of the burgee, you will see it swinging across the centreline of the boat as you go round. When it arrives in the new

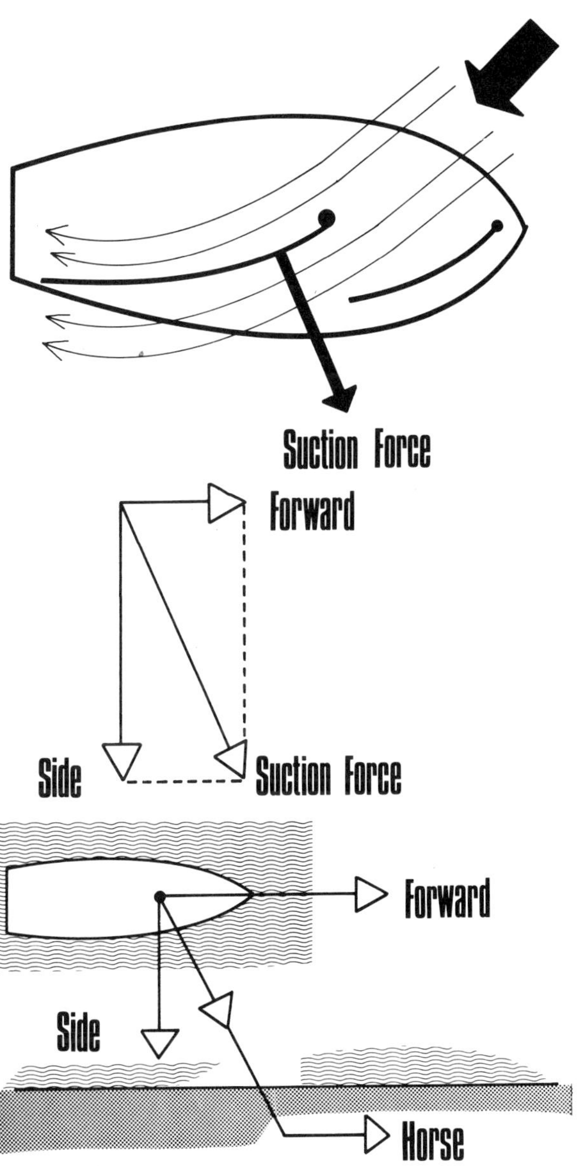

Fig. 16

The wind blowing round the lee side of the mainsail has further to travel than that on the weather side, and as the status quo has to be preserved, this lee side airflow is forced to travel faster in order to keep up with its weather compatriot.

Nothing, however, is free in this world of ours, and the increase in speed is paid for with a decrease in pressure exerted on the sail. Thus, the pressure on the weather side of the sail is greater than that on the lee side, creating a suction force (as shown in the diagram) that acts at right angles to the line of the sail.

This force, if resolved according to the parallelogram of forces, can be considered to act as two separate forces at right angles to one another (see second diagram)—in this particular case, one acting forward and the other sideways to the boat. The sideways component is cancelled (almost—more of this later) by the effect of the keel, and the forward one drives the boat.

The action is similar to that of the horse walking along a canal towpath, towing a barge, as in the third diagram.

correct position (about 45 degrees off the bow) you steady up on the tiller, trim your sails and sail away. As you gather speed, the burgee will lay back closer to the centreline, drawn there by your forward speed.

It is just the same with gybing. In this process you are swinging the boat round to bring the wind from one side of the stern, through right astern, to the other side. Watch that mythical arrow in the sky, swing your boat round underneath it by pushing the tiller to where you want the stern to go, and you will always know precisely where the wind is blowing from, and how it will affect your sails. Remember when gybing that the action of the wind suddenly impinging on the mainsail from the opposite side will tend to swing you round very quickly. So be prepared to counteract this with a little opposite tiller.

Well, by this time we should be sailing fairly confidently. We know how to set the sails at the correct angle to the wind, how to steer, tack, gybe, how to trim the sails and how to keep track of the wind direction. In the next chapter, we will see how our sails actually get on to the mast, how the mast doesn't fall down, and all the practical details of how the boat is rigged to enable us to sail the way we have just described. At the same time, we will cover the necessary nautical terminology so that we can call all the various bits by their correct names, which are invariably more concise than 'the bit of wire that holds the mast up at the side'.

3 The Boat

In figs 17a and 17b, we see photos of a boat on her mooring without sails and with sails. We know where the sails go—how do we get them there? Let us take the mainsail first. The boom, to which the foot of the sail is attached, is fixed permanently to the mast, at a suitable height to keep the sail as low as possible (to reduce the capsizing effect) without knocking our heads off. The fitting, a sort of universal joint which allows the boom to swivel, is called a gooseneck, possibly because a goose's neck swivels in a similar manner. The foot of the sail is attached to the top of the boom in various ways, the two most commonly used being shown in fig 18a. The two lower corners of the sail are fixed separately by means of metal eyelets fitted into the sail. The front corner, known as the tack, is lashed or bolted to the gooseneck fitting, and the rear corner (the clew) lashed to an eye in the end of the boom, and also round the boom itself in order to prevent it from lifting out. See figs 18a, b, and c. This clew lashing is generally called an outhaul, as it hauls the sails out, and is often adjustable. Different boats have different methods, but the basic principle is the same.

The sail is then hoisted to the top of the mast. It will be attached to the mast along its leading edge, known as the luff, in the same way that the foot is attached to the boom, and is hoisted by means of a rope or wire known as a halliard. This halliard is fastened to the top of the mainsail by various means, the commonest being shown in fig 19. The top corner, or head, of the mainsail is normally reinforced strongly with a metal plate or similar, known as a headboard, into which a hole is let for the attachment of the halliard by means of a knot or shackle.

Fig. 17a

Fig. 17b

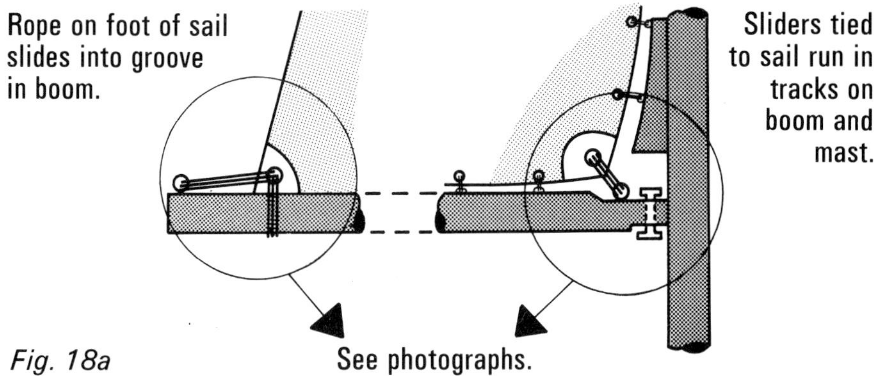

Fig. 18a

By hauling on the halliard, the sail is hoisted up the mast, nice and tight, and the halliard secured to a cleat. As with the foresail sheets, there may be a winch to help you tighten the luff (leading edge). With a wire halliard, this winch may contain all the halliard, and have a ratchet pawl to prevent it running out, thus dispensing with the need for a cleat.

Sometimes the gooseneck slides up and down in a track on the mast, in which case a small tackle is provided to haul down the boom tightly after the halliard is secured. This is called a tack tackle, as it hauls on the tack of the sail. The only other thing we have to do, before the sail is hoisted, is fit the battens. These are short lengths of wood, fibreglass, aluminium or whatever, that slide into pockets in the after edge of the sail to keep it stiff. This after edge is called the leach of the sail. See figs 20a and b.

The mainsail can then be hoisted, taking care that the mainsheet is slack so that the sail can swing freely in the wind. If you have a boom vang, a small tackle or winch attached as in fig 21 to prevent the boom lifting too high, attach it now and haul it down tight. Our boat will then look like fig 22. Halliard, outhaul, tack tackle and boom vang should all be fairly tight; the stronger the wind, the tighter they should all be, to prevent the sail billowing out too loosely.

Fig. 18b

Fig. 18c

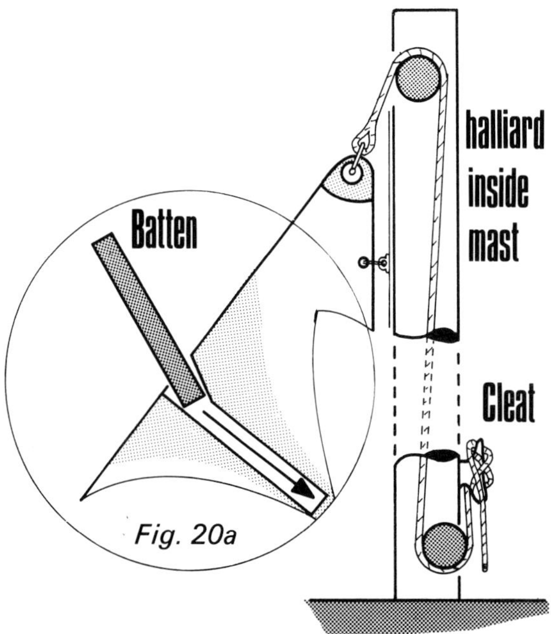

Fig. 19

Now we come to the foresail. This sail is more commonly called a jib, perhaps because it sticks out of the front of the boat like the jib of a crane. Basically it is set in exactly the same manner as the mainsail, with the exception that it generally does not have a boom fixed along its foot. The tack (front lower corner) is attached to a fitting on the bow by means of a shackle or lashing through the eyelet, and the luff (leading edge) secured to the forestay (wire holding up the mast at the front) by means of various sorts of clips. The halliard is tied or shackled to the eyelet in the head of the sail, and the sheets attached similarly to the clew. The sail is then hauled up as tightly as possible by means of the halliard, which is then secured to a cleat, generally on the mast. As with the mainsail, a winch is often used to assist one in hauling it tight.

And there we have the boat, rigged and all ready for sailing, in fig 23. The only difficulty one is likely to experience in all this is getting

Fig. 20b

the sails upside down or the wrong way round. Believe me, I have seen experienced sailors do it. Most sailors have the three corners of their sails clearly marked—clew, tack and head—and this solves the problem completely, obviating any need to search along the edges for clips, sliders or battens, or measuring the angles of the corners to decide which is which. The problem is further simplified by always packing jibs away in their bags heads first, leaving the tack (front

Fig. 21

corner) on top. This then comes out first and can be immediately attached to the stemhead fitting (see fig 24). In strong winds this gives immediate invaluable control over the sail while one is setting it.

Taking the sails down is simply the reverse of putting them up (setting them). Slacken off sheets, undo halliards and lower the sails. Unclip the jib from the forestay, remove the sheets and stow both, if dry, in the sailbag, remembering to put the jib in head first and leaving

Fig. 22

Fig. 23

Fig. 24

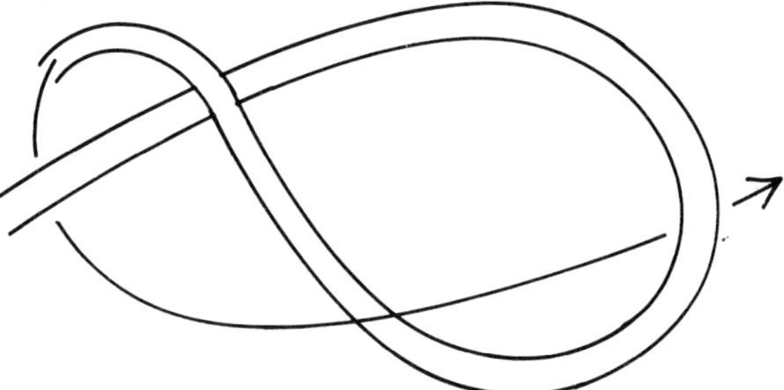

Fig. 25a

the tack on top. You will find that your sheets have figure-of-eight knots tied in their ends. See figs 25a and b. These are to prevent the ends of the sheets from running away through the fairleads or blocks through which they have been led. Obviously, one unties these in the jib sheets before stowing them away. The one on the end of the mainsheet can be left in as this sheet is not removed from the boat.

Stowing the mainsail is slightly different, as we do not generally remove it from the boat. It is normally lashed firmly to the boom. Lower the mainsail. You will then probably find that the boom has dropped on your head and is now lying sprawled across the deck. Clearly this is not a very satisfactory state of affairs, so we have a simple arrangement to prevent it. While the sail is set, of course, the sail itself holds up the boom. To hold up the boom when the sail is down we have a rope or wire called a topping lift. See figs 26a and b. By taking the weight of the boom on the topping lift before lowering the mainsail, we prevent it from dropping painfully onto our heads. When the sail is down we position the boom firmly (parallel with the deck for smartness) either by resting the end in a crutch, or simply by securing the end of the topping lift to a cleat, then hauling down tight on the mainsheet. The sail is then bundled and rolled neatly and tightly on top of the boom and lashed into place with suitable short lengths of webbing or similar. See fig 27. Remember that on your mooring you may get very windy conditions—you will be on the mooring when it is too windy to sail for instance—so make sure the mainsail is rolled and lashed as tightly as you possibly can. If it comes adrift, in a very short time you will have no mainsail—so keep it really tight and use plenty of tiers, about 18 inches apart.

How are we doing? Sails handed (taken down), sails set, sails stowed, sailing the boat in all and sundry directions, tacking and gybing, what the various bits are called and look like. What more do we have? Quite a lot, actually—enough to keep me writing non-stop for the rest of my life! However, we have covered the essential core of the subject; the rest will come naturally as we expand our experience

Fig. 25b

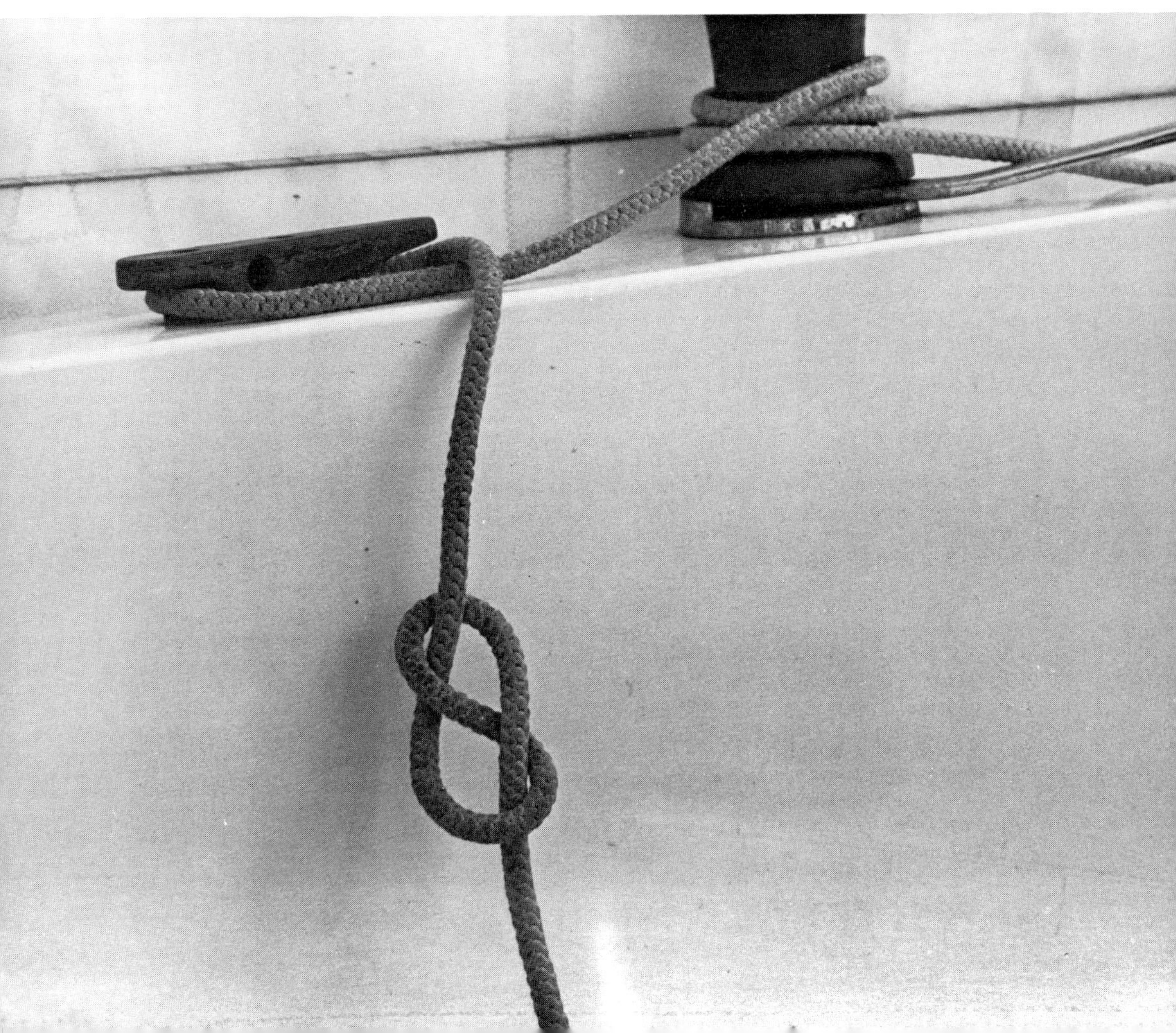

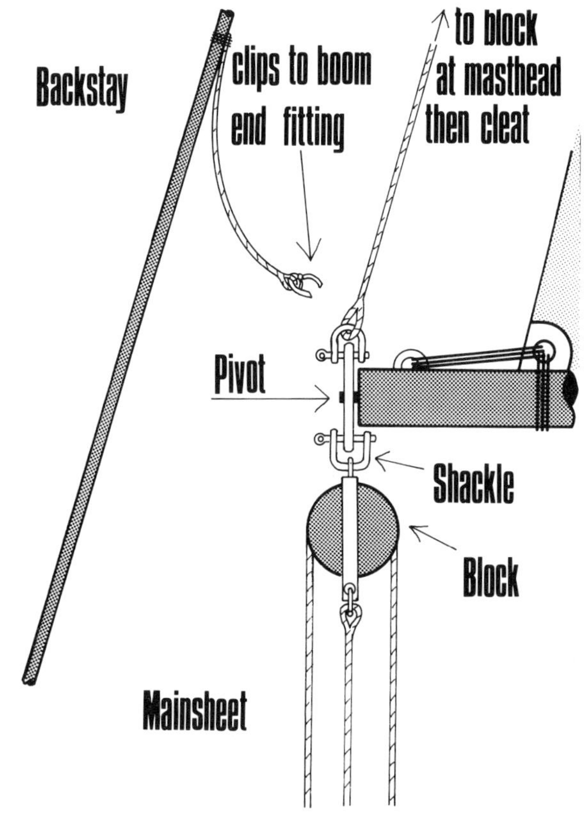

Fig. 26a

through the rest of the book. One small but important point must be made before we move on to see how we prevent the mast from falling down, and take a look at a few more bits and pieces that help us to sail our boat. Clearly it makes a lot of sense, when hoisting and lowering sails, to hold the boat pointing directly into the wind (head to wind). This gives the sails maximum space to flap around freely without filling with wind and causing us to sail off who knows where. (Usually in circles, uncontrollably, until we crash into something.) So check the wind directions before setting sail, to ensure that the sails will be free to flap as they go up. If they are not, move the boat till they are. We shall look at this problem more closely in the next chapter.

Now, how do we stop the mast falling down? How does one stop a flagpole, or telegraph pole from falling down? Ideally, we step the mast in the very bottom of the boat, so that it comes up through the deck and is supported there. In many boats this is done. In the majority of small cruisers, however, space below decks precludes it. So we step the mast on the deck, or on top of the cabin. Some sort of pole or girder or bulkhead (internal wall) is placed under the step so that the weight

Fig. 26b

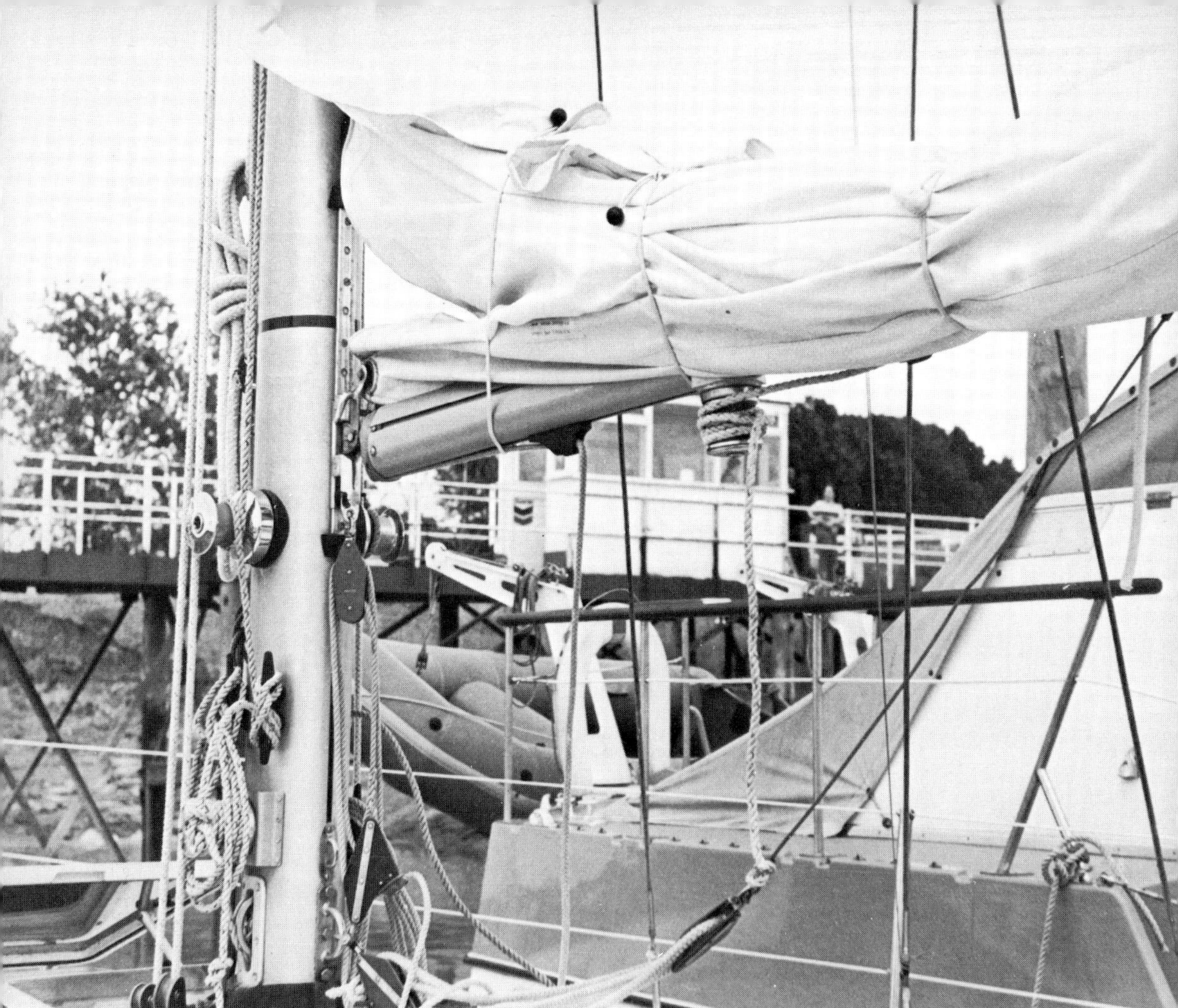

Fig. 27

and the forces generated while sailing are transmitted through to the keel (the backbone at the bottom of the boat). The mast is then stabilised by wires running from the top (or near it—the precise positioning involves a lot of complex theory, which we do not need) to the sides of the boat. See fig 28. Ideally in a small cruiser, four wires are used—the forestay on to which we clip the jib, the backstay which goes down to the stern, and a wire down to each side of the boat.

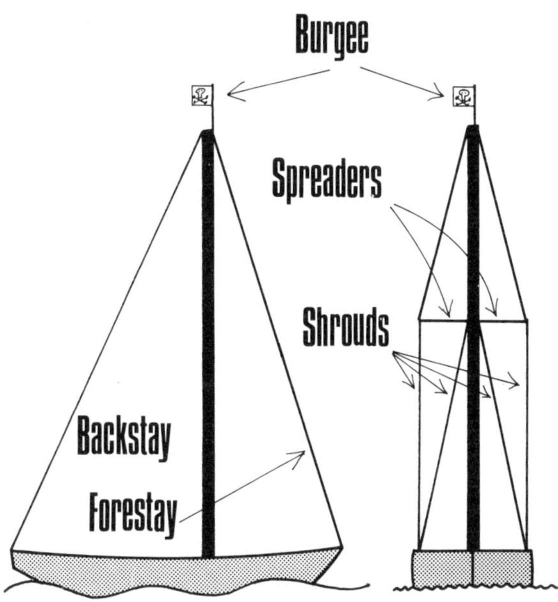

Fig. 28

(Generally there are two—one leading slightly forward of the mast, the other leading slightly to the rear). These side stays are known as shrouds. Some boats, because of the shape of their mainsails, do not have backstays, in which cases the after shrouds are led further back, to counteract the tendency of the mast to fall forward. They cannot, of course, come back too far or it would not be possible to let the boom right out when running before the wind.

Some means of adjusting the tension in these stays is provided, generally bottlescrews or lanyards (rope lashings) are fitted at the bottom of the stays where they are secured to the chainplates. The correct tensioning of these is a highly skilled job and should be left to expert riggers. If, however, you have to do them yourself, you won't go too far wrong if you wind them till they pluck with a fairly low twang. Do, however, if you can, get them set up by an expert, especially if your rigging is at all complex, as all sorts of weird stresses and strains can be set up in the mast by incorrectly tensioned rigging.

ON THE QUARTER
ABEAM
ON THE BOW
PORT
ASTERN
AHEAD
STARBOARD
ON THE QUARTER
ABEAM
ON THE BOW
MAINSAIL
and JIB
Head
Cringles
forward
Luff
Leech
Clew
Foot
Tack
WINDWARD
WEATHER SIDE
AFT
AMIDSHIPS
FORWARD
LEE SIDE
LEEWARD

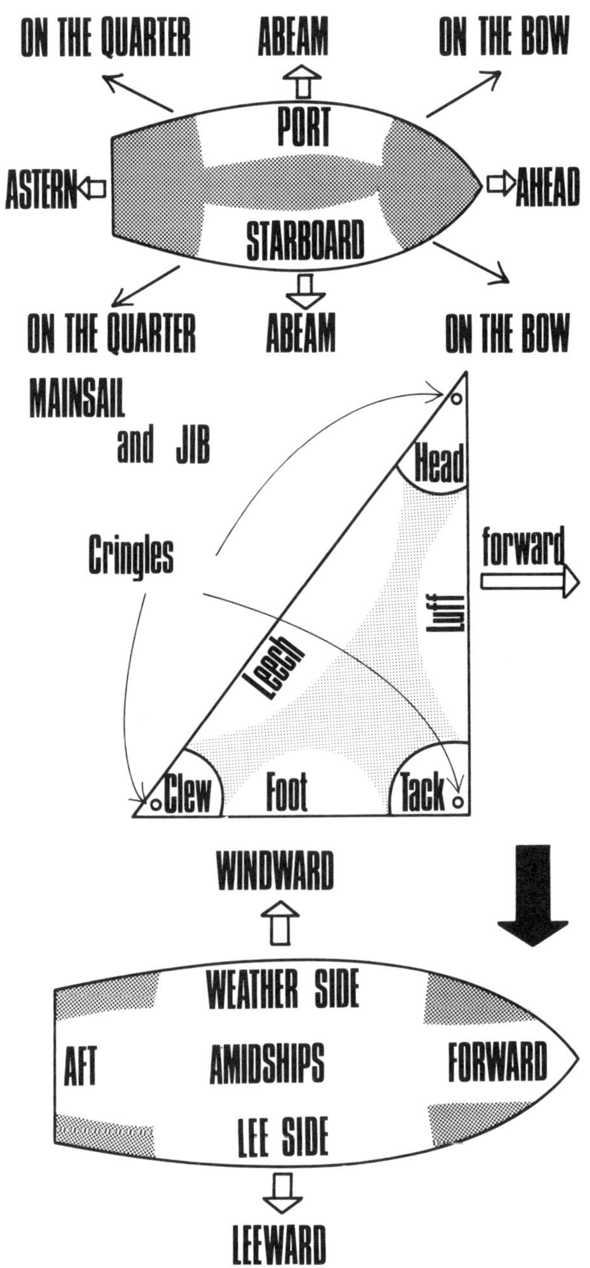

Fig. 29

As regards the angle of the mast—just set it more or less vertical. If it leans sideways at all, you will sail faster on one tack than the other. If it leans forward or back it will affect the amount of weather helm the boat will carry. It will also affect how close to the wind you can sail. But there are many other factors which can influence these, and the whole thing can get most confusing. Best to go and chat up a local expert—most of them will delight in demonstrating their skill at 'tuning' a boat. Watching and listening to them will teach you more in two minutes than a year of book study, as it is very much a matter of feel. The same goes for fine adjustment of sails.

Now that we have learnt to sail and rig the boat, so have a bit more idea of what it is all about, let us acquire some more technical jargon. Fig 29 shows all the parts of the boat that will concern us at this stage. Some of the terms we have already discussed: some we have not, because they have not been necessary. The next chapter will be on manoeuvring, mooring, anchoring and so on, so a little more of the nautical mumbo-jumbo will come in handy to prepare us for it.

All boats will differ slightly in the layout of their equipment, but the actual objects will be more or less the same. As some Chinese philosophical sailor might have said—a boat is a boat is a boat. It is important not to get bogged down with too specific details, or, if your boat does not have that specific type of fitting, you will be lost. More confusion is caused among novice sailors through learning particular techniques, and studying particular equipment, than anything. It is far easier to remember principles than techniques; and if you know the principles thoroughly the techniques will be no problem. But I mean practical principles, not theoretical explanations.

In the next few chapters we will look at the practical principles of manoeuvring, mooring, anchoring and so on. In the meantime let us take a break, and I'll tell you a story.

4 On sailing to windward

Beating to windward. A phrase that evokes visions of mighty clipper ships thrashing through the gale-ridden and ice-laden waters of Cape Horn in the Southern mid-winter. Reefed to the lower tops'ls, green water pouring through the well-deck as men fall from the yardarms like flies and the Captain brandishes pistols on the poop to prevent faint-hearted mates from reducing sail. An image calculated to put anyone off sailing for life.

But it is not all like that. There are balmy evenings in late summer when the prow cleaves phosphorescent furrows through a calm and moonlit sea. When the warm wind breathes tranquillity into aching bones; smiling dolphins leap ahead and point the way as stars twinkle with a gaiety never seen ashore; and contentment creeps over the sailor who gives thanks for the joy of being at sea.

Somewhere in between those two is what usually happens. Sometimes it rains, and sometimes the sun shines. Sometimes it is calm; sometimes it blows. To the man bitten by the sailing bug it is all the same. Just different facets of the fascination that is sailing. Especially, perhaps, to windward.

Sailing to windward is, I have generally found, considered to be perhaps the darkest of all the esoteric secrets of the sailor. Ask any weatherbeaten, experienced sailor how he sails to windward and he will invariably reply: 'By feel'. While this may be true, it is neither very explicit nor very helpful to the beginner. However, behind that simple, laconic statement lies a wealth of truth and experience, useful even to us at this early stage. Let us have a closer look at what the expert means by 'sailing by feel'.

An old timer storms to windward. The Skipper has a lot of weather helm to hold, but otherwise he lets her sail herself.

Somewhere, seemingly lost within the mists of time, I set foot for the first time on a boat. It was a very small racing dinghy and I was a very small twelve-year-old. And it was quite windy. Up till then my hobby had been birdwatching.

Anyway, off we went, my friend and I, me crouched at the front end clutching nervously on to a jib sheet. We were sailing on a marine lake, enclosed by a sea wall, and when we reached the wall and went about the boat didn't. That is to say, it failed to swing round through the wind, in order to sail off close-hauled with the wind on the other side. It ended up pointing into the wind with the sails flapping, and drifted onto the wall. My friend, my heroic friend, leapt onto the wall in order to push us off; which he did, most admirably. The only trouble was, he forgot to jump back in the boat.

So there I was, all alone in this extraordinarily strange machine, drifting off into the middle of the lake. 'Sail her solo!' Peter shouted, optimistically. So, putting two and two together, I grabbed the jibsheet and mainsheet and hauled them in tight. I then grabbed the tiller and she took off like a motorbike. My moment of glory lasted, I judge, about five seconds, before she keeled over gradually and gracefully. The mast and sails hit the water a bare moment or two before I did.

Well, I was duly rescued and instructed in the finer art of righting a capsized dinghy. But the most important lesson I had learned, viewing the incident in retrospect, had been during those few moments of glory, when I sailed her 'solo'. When I sat grimly on the deck, clutching those sheets and the tiller, and that boat sailed. I remember vividly to this day the feeling as she took off, and the feeling as she slowly but surely keeled over and capsized.

While she was sailing, she was like a well-tuned sports car, roof off, hair in the breeze, flying down the open road at just the right speed; exhaust burbling contentedly, engine roaring happily, gauges and instruments relaxed and reading right, tyres glued to the tarmac. Everything was right and everything felt right, just as in that sports car. All the effort, all the driving force of the sails, was directed into pushing that boat forward, calmly and efficiently, and I could sense it. Just as one can sense when a car is going well.

So how did I capsize? you might ask. A good question. The answer is that, in my ignorance and near-panic, I pulled too hard on the tiller, causing the boat to bear away too far off the wind. At the same time I kept the sheets in hard as for sailing closehauled. This had the same

Skippers of both the open boat in the foreground and the little cruiser hold their tillers against the weather helm, and concentrate on looking ahead.

sort of effect on the boat as driving that sports car we mentioned round a sharp bend at the same speed that was just right for the open road—too fast. And I am sure most of you have had the latter experience. What happens in the boat is much the same as happens with the car. The sails, or engine, are applying too much power for the particular conditions, and the machine is incapable of transmitting all that power into forward motion. The excess spills over, as it were, pushing both boat and car sideways. The car spins off the road and the boat capsizes, and the feeling experienced by the driver is much the same in both machines.

Instability as the boat heels excessively, and the car begins to lift the inside wheels; strain and tension as both machines try desperately to hold their courses, the car on the line of the bend and the boat upright; the overall impression that things are beginning to run away from your control. I am sure most of you know the feeling.

The remedy is much the same in both cases, and in both cases it must be applied early. Namely—to reduce power before things get out of hand. Slow down the car before the corner; ease off the sails of the boat as you begin to bear away. Or, if you bore away unintentionally while trying to sail close-hauled (a common enough error), simply bringing the boat back towards the wind to the proper course will reduce the strain, as would straightening out the car. As you do this, with either car or boat, you will feel the strain lessening, the machine relaxing and settling back into the groove.

If you go too far the other way with the boat and sail her too close to the wind, the sails will begin to flap and lose their drive and the boat will feel dead, as would the car if you turned off the engine.

And that, basically, is what sailing by feel is all about. I am sure it was not long after your first drive that you began to operate your car by feel, and you will find the same with your boat.

I have exaggerated somewhat here in order to illustrate the point. If you sail your small cruiser too far away from the wind when close-hauled, you will not experience the same strain and instant retribution that you would with a small racing dinghy, or a sports car at speed. The strain is there, however, and the analogy should help you to feel it. As you sail by your burgee angle, look for the feeling of the boat when the burgee tells you she is sailing correctly, and compare it with the feeling when the burgee tells you she is not. Feel the shivering of the sails and the deadness of the boat when you are too close to the wind, and compare it with the liveliness when she is right.

It won't be long before you can pass the unofficial test of the windward sailor—half a mile with your eyes closed. But make sure someone is watching, to see that you don't hit anything!

5 Manoeuvring Principles

When we learn to drive a car we have first to be taught how to make the thing move, and the names and functions of the important parts. After this we go on the road to put it all into practice, and we find there is a little more to it than simply operating the wheel, pedals and gear lever. We have to start and stop, go round corners, park and manoeuvre past other vehicles and so on. It is just the same in a sailing boat. In the first four chapters we learnt how to sail the boat through the water, how to rig it and the names and functions of the important parts. Now we shall consider how actually to maoeuvre the boat on the water, how to sail away from our mooring, go over to the beach for a picnic and return safely to the mooring. In this chapter we shall take a look at the principles involved, before going into the actual practical procedures.

But do not be put off by the word 'principles'. I do not use it to mean a complex mass of theoretical equations and mathematical proofs; I use it simply to infer an understanding of how various factors affect the way a boat behaves on the water. In the same way, before we can drive a car properly we must understand the effects of such things as cornering, braking, hills, wet roads and so on. If we understand the effect a shallow bend has on our car, then we can work out the effects of all other sorts of bends, without having to learn a technique for every type of bend we are ever likely to meet. Similarly, if we understand the effects of wind and tide on our boat's behaviour when approaching a mooring, we can, with a little experience, work out how to cope with all manner of combinations of tide and wind, without having to remember about 10,000 different techniques for 10,000 different combinations of wind and tide. I always believed at school that if I could understand a thing I had no need to remember it as I could always work it out, This saved me a tremendous amount of wasted effort, and it is an excellent principle to apply to sailing as there is such a tremendous variation and number of factors that can affect a boat's behaviour on the water.

There are two very basic and extremely important factors that influence the handling of a sailing boat, and if we can understand the effect of these we will be well on the way to handling our boats competently in all sorts of conditions. These factors are the wind and the tide. As we have already discussed the effect of the wind in the earlier chapters, let us continue with that.

The wind has a twofold effect on a sailing boat. First, it is deflected by the sails to produce a driving force that makes the boat move forward. Second, it blows directly against the flat area of the sails, thus tending both to blow the boat sideways and to tip it over. We will discuss the tipping-over effect in a later chapter on strong winds. As far as manoeuvring is concerned our problem is the tendency to be blow sideways, as clearly this will influence our ability to sail in a straight line.

This sideways drift is known as leeway and is counteracted to a large extent by the boat's keel, as we mentioned earlier. Without a keel a boat would drift sideways so fast that it would never get anywhere: even with a keel it still drifts to a certain extent. The deeper the keel, the less the boat will drift: the more the windage (sails, rigging, cabin tops etc) the more the boat will drift. Balancing these factors to produce a boat most suited to a particular task is the job of the designer, and clearly it is a Peter and Paul situation. The more space he puts in a boat, the higher the cabin and the more the windage. The shallower he makes the boat, to enable it to sail in small harbours and so on, the less will be the resistance to leeway. The lower he makes the cabin tops, the less room there will be inside, and so on. This problem, inevitably, is greatest in the small sailing cruiser, where the designer has literally to try and put a quart into a pint pot, so that the children have somewhere to sleep, the cook somewhere to cook and so on. On top of all this he has to make it sail reasonably well, not only to give us greater pleasure, but to make the boat safe. We will look at these questions more closely in the later chapter on buying a boat.

The other thing, after design, that affects leeway is the point of sailing. Because the wind pressure on the sails is greatest when we are sailing to windward, that is the time when we experience most leeway. When we are sailing into the wind, the total wind speed acting on our sails is the speed of the actual wind plus the speed of the boat. When we are reaching, with the wind on the beam, the total wind speed is simply the speed of the actual wind, while running downwind the total speed is that of the wind minus the speed of the boat. (These calculations are approximate and serve to illustrate the variance of leeway with the point of sailing—the absolute truth is very little different, aerodynamically complex and serves only to confuse). Thus we can see that leeway is greatest when closehauled, considerably less when reaching, and (because the wind does not blow from the side) non-existent when running.

How do we calculate this leeway and cope with it when sailing? If, for instance, we sail in a straight line pointing at the beach where we want to have our picnic, with boat closehauled, we will not get there. We will end up some way down wind of the beach and will have to go about and sail back to it on the other tack. If we are reaching we will find ourselves having constantly to alter course slightly towards the wind in order to keep pointing towards the beach, as we drift downwind. Clearly then we must aim some way upwind of our destination and crab our way sideways towards it.

How far do we aim off? Well, I'm sure many of you will have experienced the unpleasant sensation of driving a car over an exposed bridge in a strong wind. To counteract the tendency of the wind to blow the car sideways we have to steer into the wind. The car, however, continues to move straight along the bridge, despite the fact that the wheels are turned to one side. The effect is basically the same although the boat, not being as firmly attached to the water as the car is to the road, is affected to a much greater extent. Anyway, most of us manage to make our cars go in a straight line over the bridge, so how do we do it?

We do it quite simply, without realising it probably, by lining up the nose of the car with the end of the bridge. Assuming we do not skid, as long as we keep the nose of the car in line with the end of the bridge we will travel towards it in a straight-line, regardless of where the wheels are pointing. The same basic principle applies to the boat, with the exception that whereas with the car we only aim off the wheel, with a boat we have to aim off the boat itself. This is because the boat's hull running through the water is equivalent to the car's wheels running along the road. Thus it would be of little use trying to line the boat's bow up with the beach. The boat's bow must aim off in the same way as the car's wheels, so we must find something else to line up with our destination.

If we look now at fig 30 we see that if the wind is blowing from the bottom of the picture such that we are sailing closehauled pointing in the direction of the solid arrows, leeway (exaggerated here for clarity) will actually cause us to move in the direction of the pecked arrow. Now if we superimpose our car on the diagram, the wheels will be pointing in the direction of the solid arrows while the body of the car will point and move in the direction of the pecked arrow. Thus we can see that, with a boat, instead of lining up the bow with our destination we line up some object on the leeward side. In the diagram an object on the port bow would appear to be necessary, but in practice, if the destination is more than a few yards away, any object on the leeward side will be found perfectly adequate. As long as we remain in the same position and steer our boat so as to keep an object on the leeward side in line with our destination, we will move towards it in a straight line, as indicated by the pecked line in the figure. When we say

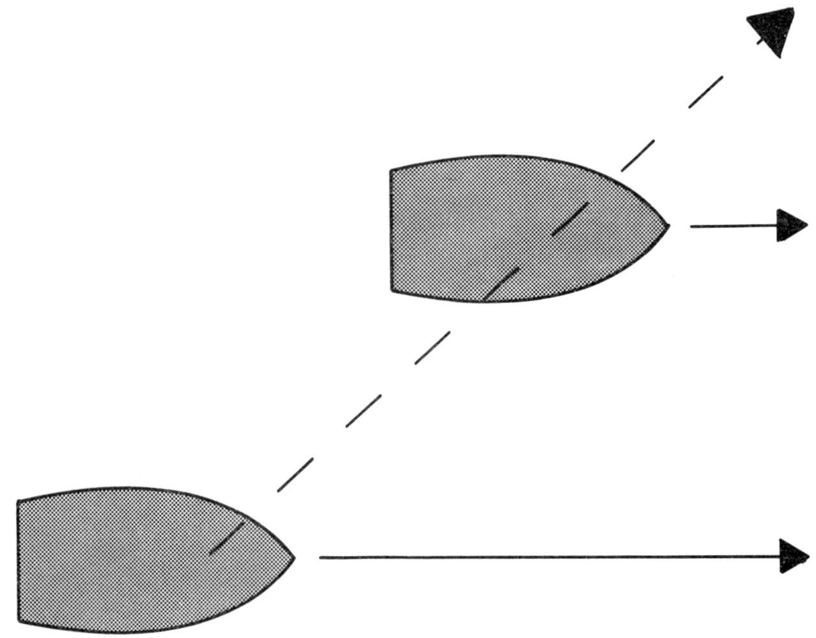
Fig. 30

leeward side we mean the leeward side of the helmsman's eye, so any convenient object between you and your destination, such as the mast, a shroud, a guardrail stanchion or whatever, will do.

Initially we have to guess how much to aim off. It is not likely to be much—negligible when reaching and perhaps five or ten degrees when beating. As we sail along we watch how the destination moves in relation to the object we have lined up with it. If it moves to the right in the example of fig 30, then it means we are drifting to the left, downwind, and we must aim off to windward a bit more until it steadies in line with our object. If it moves to the left of our mast, or whatever we are using, it means we have aimed off too much and we must bear away a little off the wind (to the left) until it remains in line. So we simply alter course in the same direction the destination has moved.

The same technique is used for avoiding things we do not want to hit, such as other boats, buoys etc. We line the object up with the mast, shroud or whatever is handy and watch it for a while. If it remains in line we will hit it, just as surely as we will arrive at the beach if we keep that in line. See fig 31. So we must alter course to avoid it. If the other boat or buoy moves from the mast towards our bow then it will pass clear ahead of us; if towards the stern it will pass astern; but allow a good margin, and if it is another boat sailing, make a bold alteration so that he can see clearly what you are doing.

There are various regulations governing the avoidance of collision between two boats and we will deal with them fully in the chapter on

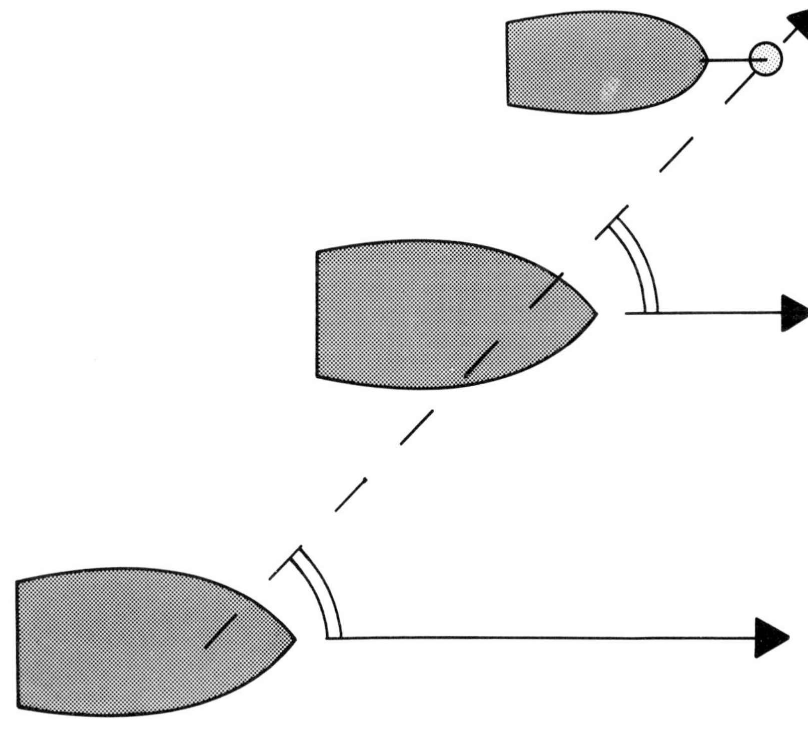

Fig. 31

safety. For the time being it will be enough to say that all power driven vessels must give way to sailing boats; sailing boats on port tack (with the wind on the port side) give way to those on starboard tack; and if on the same tack, a reaching or running boat gives way to a close-hauled boat. A vessel overtaking another one, whether power or sail, must give way. A vessel that has right of way must hold his course and the vessel giving way must do so boldly and in good time so that his intentions are clear.

Before going on to the tide there is one other effect the wind has on us that can be important in close quarter situations, such as tacking near a buoy or river bank. Look at fig 32. We see that when a sailing boat (or any boat for that matter) turns, its stern drifts out of the turn quite considerably, just like a racing car cornering. This is not often a

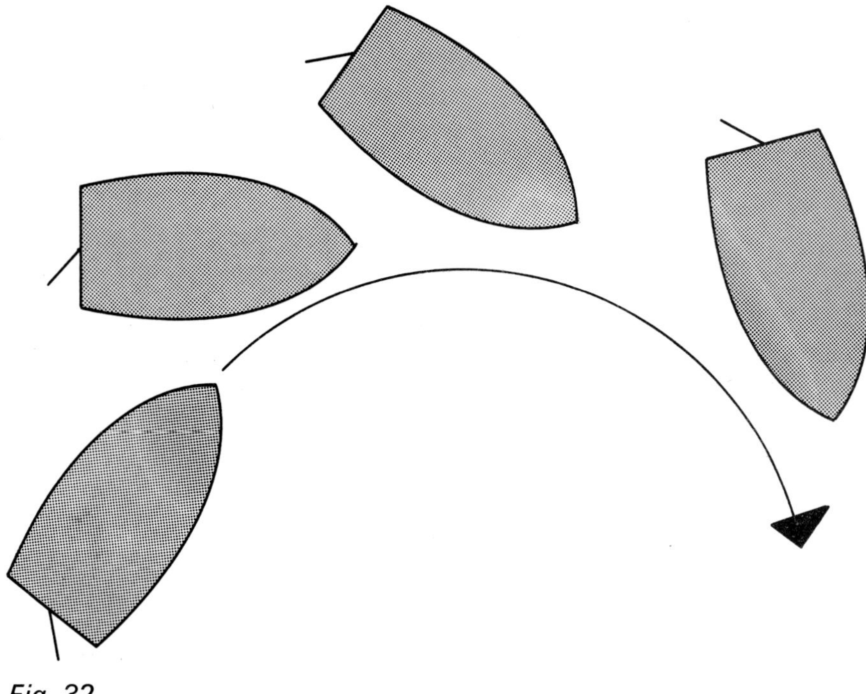

Fig. 32

problem, as such, but it must be borne in mind when manoeuvring near other objects.

Now, what about the tide? First though, what is the tide? We will be going into it in more detail in the next chapter when we look at anchoring, and also in the navigation section, but in the meantime let us consider it as a movement of water over the globe, caused by the gravitational pull of the moon and the sun. As the positions of sun and moon vary, so does the direction and speed of this water flow vary. Roughly speaking, in any particular part of the world, the tide rises for a period of about six hours then falls for six hours, the highest point being known as High Water and the lowest point Low Water. As the tide rises it flows up the beaches, into the harbours and estuaries, and is said to be flooding. This is the Flood Tide. Six hours later, roughly, it reaches High Water, pauses for a short while, then falls for a period of six hours, during which time it is said to be ebbing, as it flows out of the harbours and so on. This is the Ebb Tide. For the moment that is all we need to know. Our problem, when manoeuvring, is to allow for the way this tidal flow will carry us back and forth as it runs in and out—as it floods and ebbs.

The speeds of tides vary tremendously, depending on the area and the circumstances, anything from zero to ten knots or more (a knot being a nautical mile per hour. A nautical mile is about 2000 yards, a little longer than a land mile), but around two or three knots is a reasonable average when the tide is running at its strongest (half-way between Low and High Waters). Clearly then this tide will have considerably more effect on our boats than leeway has. Although much stronger, however, the effect is basically the same, and we allow for its effect in the same way—by lining up our destination with some part of the boat and steering so as to keep them in line. The aim-off, of course, will be greater than it generally is for leeway, and it will not always be to weather of the direct line.

How do we assess the tide—its direction and speed—in order to make our first tentative aim-off? Leeway is relatively easy, as we

Fig. 33 Boats will lie back from an anchor or mooring in the direction of the tide, but beware of boats moored fore and aft. The true tidal direction is shown by the dinghy in the foreground—the only boat not secured at both ends.

know the drift is always to leeward and is not very great. The tidal drift is rather more difficult as its strength and direction vary throughout the day, from place to place in the harbour as it is deflected round corners and obstacles, and of course, relative to us, it will vary with the direction in which we are steering.

Well, if we open our eyes and have a good look round we will see

Fig. 34 The direction of the tide can easily be seen by the way it sweeps past a buoy.

that there are a number of things that will tell us what the tide is doing. Moored boats, so long as they are moored by the bow only, and boats at anchor will generally, unless the wind is very strong or they have a tremendous amount of top hamper that will increase their windage, lie bow to the tide. A close look at buoys, beacons and so on will show the tide sluicing by, piling up on one side of the object and sweeping away from the other. See figs 33 and 34. And if we simply point our boat at our destination and begin sailing we will very soon discover which way the tide is carrying us. If we line up the mast with our destination and the mast begins moving to the right of it, then the tide is carrying us to the right and we must alter course to port to counteract it, until the two remain steadily in line.

A combination of tide and leeway, of course, will resolve itself automatically into a drift one way or the other. This is the situation we will generally meet in normal circumstances, and we simply assess the drift that we see and allow for it in the manner previously described. Because of the greater drift that we generally experience from the tide, we must be especially careful when avoiding other boats, buoys, spits of land and so on. If they are on a steady bearing we must alter course boldly and in plenty of time so that we have sufficient run to be sure that the bearing is moving fairly quickly, such that they will pass well clear. The tide will always vary slightly from place to place, so we must always allow plenty of room to cope with any last minute changes. Similarly the wind may drop a little, which means the tidal influence will become relatively greater. It is a good policy, whenever possible, to pass moored objects, boats, buoys etc, down tide as this will avoid the ever-present danger of being swept down on to it at the last moment, when it is too late to take avoiding action.

The overall picture then is of a (literally) very fluid environment in which our boat is free to drift at the mercy of wind and tide. By setting and adjusting sails we can make the boat sail forward through the water, but we must make allowances for the fact that she will also drift sideways a certain amount. And when the tide is running, we also have to be aware that we will be carried in a certain direction by the moving sheet of water on which we float. It is very rare, in fact, for a sailing boat actually to move forward in a straight line, and I think this is one of the most important concepts that the sailor must grasp. The business of sailing consists of balancing all these influences in such a way that the overall effect will be to take you in the direction you want to go, and this direction will very rarely be forward. We must be constantly aware of our surroundings, always checking the wind and tide, the position of nearby objects which we need to avoid, while all the time sailing to keep our destination in line with some part of the boat. The secret, once you have the awareness of what is happening, is quite simply practice.

Well, that is how we sail about the place. Now let us have a look at stopping and starting. The moments of leaving and approaching a mooring are times when we have to be especially careful to consider the effects of wind and tide. The two main things we must consider are their effects on us while secured to the mooring, and their effects on us during the interval between casting off and beginning to sail properly. This is the time when we are most at their mercy and least able to control them.

Let us imagine we are sitting on our boat out on its mooring, preparing for an afternoon sail. Somehow we must get from being tied on to the mooring with our sails stowed, to being out on the water sailing, and it is not quite so simple as backing a car out of the garage. Let us consider the tide first. Unless the wind is very strong or the tide almost slack, we will almost certainly be lying with our bow pointing into the tide. Now, clearly we do not want to start sailing until we have let go of the mooring, yet equally we do not want to let go of the mooring until we have some sails set with which we can control and manoeuvre the boat. What we must do then is set our sails in such a way, while still moored, that they will flap freely without driving us through the water. If the wind is blowing from the same direction as the tide (from ahead or nearly ahead), then we can simply hoist both sails with no problems as they will lie fore and aft in line with the wind, and flap freely without producing any drive. To allow for the inevitable swinging of the boat we must ensure that the sheets are loose, so that the sails are free to swing loosely without filling if the boat swings away from the wind a little. When the sails are properly set we can cast off from the mooring simply by hauling in the jib to one side till the back of it fills with wind, and then letting go the mooring. See fig 35.

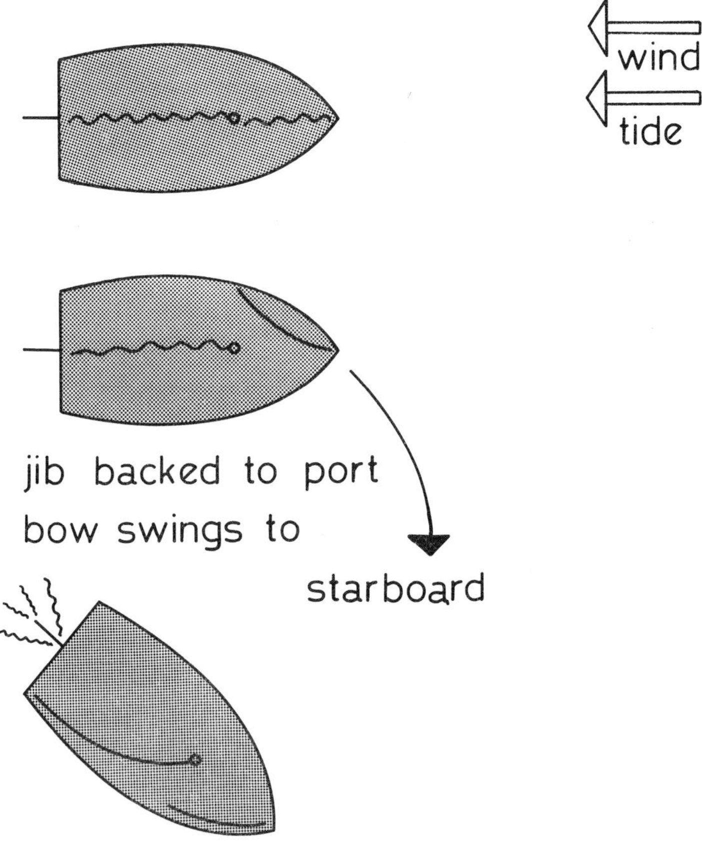

Fig. 35

This is known as backing the jib, and it will cause the bow of our boat to blow away from the wind. As soon as it has blown away sufficiently for our sails to fill, or when she has blown round to point in the direction we want to go, we can let the jib go and sheet in both the sails to the correct position and sail off. As you can see from fig 36, the wind does not need to be from directly ahead. As long as it blows from fairly

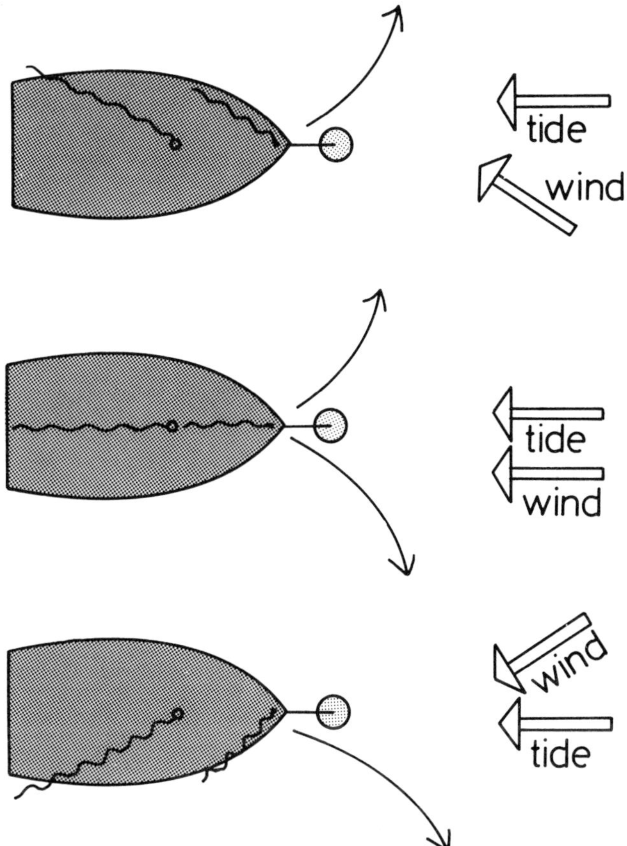

Fig. 36

well for'ard of the beam, there will be no danger of the sails filling and driving us around while still moored up.

If the wind is from astern, however, the situation is a little different. Obviously we cannot set the mainsail as it would fill immediately with wind and drive us forward over the mooring, due to the fact that it cannot be swung out further forward than the shrouds. Also it would be extremely difficult, in all but the lightest of airs, to get it up without tearing it. We can, however, safely set the jib, making sure that the

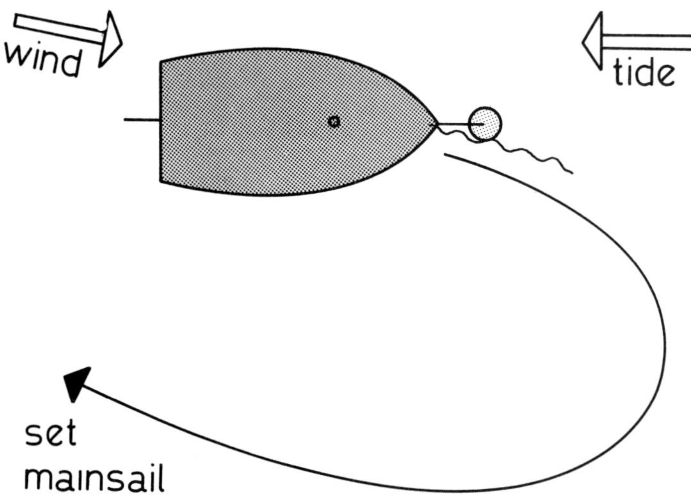

Fig. 37

sheets are free to run right out, as it will blow right for'ard and flap freely. See fig 37. We can then unlash the mainsail, attach its halliard, and get it ready for hoisting. This done, we can cast off the mooring and let the tide drift us clear before hauling in on the jib sheet and sailing off. As soon as we are moving steadily we can round up into the wind and set the mainsail. This needs to be done fairly quickly, before we stop and begin drifting and being blown about, so preparing it before we slip the mooring is important. The faster we are going under the jib before we round up, the longer the boat will continue into the wind under her momentum, and the longer we will have to set the mainsail. Once the mainsail is set, we can simply steer away from the wind, and sheet in both sails when the wind has drawn far enough round. If we have almost stopped by the time the mainsail is set, we can back the jib to cast our bow off in the direction we want to go.

With the wind on the beam, and the tide ahead, it is tempting to think that we can safely set both sails, and looking at a theoretical diagram would seem to confirm this. In practice, however, it doesn't work. We find that the wind is constantly shifting slightly and this causes the boat to swing around on her mooring. We might get the sail halfway up, but then the boat will swing her stern into the wind, the mainsail will fill, and we are in trouble. It is always best to treat a beam wind as a stern wind and just set the jib. Watch your burgee for a while before deciding what sails can be set. See how the wind varies, then set only the sails you are certain will not fill with wind and drive the boat before you have slipped the mooring. Even with the wind from ahead it is no problem to cast off under jib alone and sail away till you can safely round up into the wind to set the mainsail. See fig 38. Remember though that most boats will not sail properly, if at all, to windward with only a jib set, so round up into the wind and set that mainsail as soon as possible. Until it is set, you have only partial control over your boat.

There are, of course, many other varied combinations of wind and tide that you will experience, but it would take a library of encyclopaedias to list them all. Even then I could guarantee that the

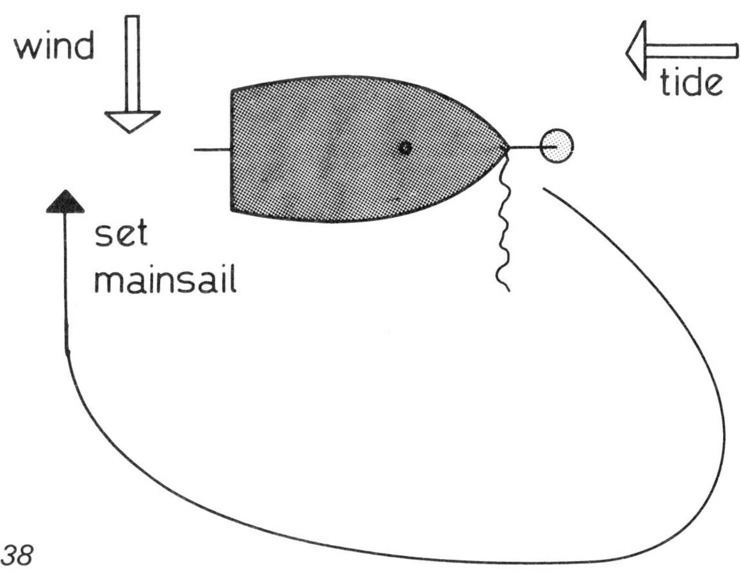

Fig. 38

moment you stepped into your boat you would meet the one I hadn't listed! The purpose of this chapter is to show the principles involved, so that you can assess each situation yourself when you come across it. And the basic principle is to set only the sails you are certain will not fill with wind and drive you round and round the mooring like a merry-go-round—a familiar sight in harbours up and down the country every year! Equally, you must be able to set full sail as soon as possible, as your manoeuvrability is very limited when only under jib. So look at your burgee over a period of minutes to check the wind direction and how it is varying. Look over the side of the boat to see which way the tide is flowing, and how fast. Look around you to see if the proximity of boats or bank oblige you to sail off in a particular direction. Then make your plans accordingly.

Remember you will need space to turn (see fig 32) and space to go head to wind while you set the mainsail, so don't cast off blindly then look for the spaces, look for them before you leave the safety of the mooring. Then you can cast off in the right direction, sail straight to the space, turn into wind and set the mainsail. Remember also that if you prepare the mainsail for hoisting before you slip, it will take only a matter of seconds to get it up and set. So think out what you are going to do, prepare it and carry it out. You'd be amazed how many people don't; and they are the ones you see on the mud, sailing round their buoys, or cuddling up a little too close to someone else's boat!

So far, so good. The next problem arises when we decide it is time to go home for tea. We have got to get ourselves tied back on to that buoy. It is no good just charging up and grabbing it, we must think of the same factors that we considered when slipping the buoy. There are two basic things we must do when returning to pick up a mooring. We must arrive and stop close enough to lean over and tie up to it, and we must do so with no sails set that are likely to remain filled with wind and drive us around the place when we need to be stopped.

The first question we must consider is: in what direction will we lie when we have secured to the buoy? The chances are we will lie to the tide, but we can check quite simply by looking at how nearby moored boats are lying. Make sure they are moored only by the bow, or anchored, and that they are influenced by the same tide as we will be. They might be in a back eddy, or nearer the bank where the tide flows more slowly. If in doubt, all we need do is sail close past the boat, look at how the tide is flowing past his buoy, then sail past our own buoy and compare them. If they are close to us, and of similar shape, they will almost certainly lie more or less the same as we will.

Having worked out how we will lie on arrival at the buoy we can then decide which sails we can safely leave set on arrival. If we go back to fig 36, and see that all the nearby boats are lying to wind and tide, we know that we can sail right up to the buoy with all sails set. All we have to do now is work out how to slow down and stop. What we do in this instance is to sail closehauled to a point just down wind and tide

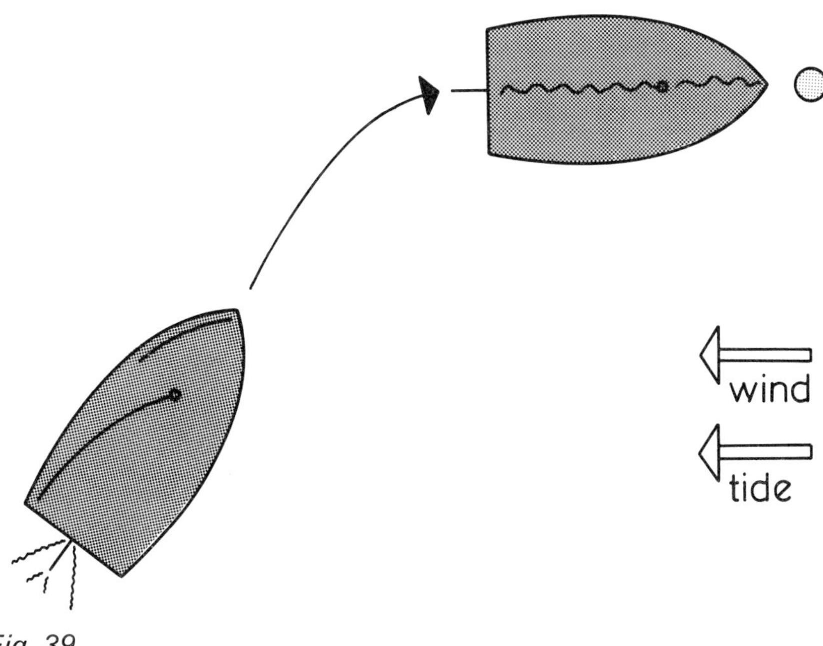

Fig. 39

from the mooring, then luff up head to wind. As the boat runs towards the buoy head to wind, the combined effect of the tide and wind against her will slow her and stop her. If you have judged the distance she will run correctly, and luffed up at the right place, she will stop right by the buoy. This judgement can only come from experience, so get out there when there's nobody about and practice. See fig 39.

With the wind and tide in opposition, as in fig 37, it is actually easier. We know that we must approach into the tide, as that is how we will lie on arrival (most likely—check nearby boats), which means coming to the buoy downwind. We must therefore approach under jib only. The advantage here is that we can come in on a straight line and

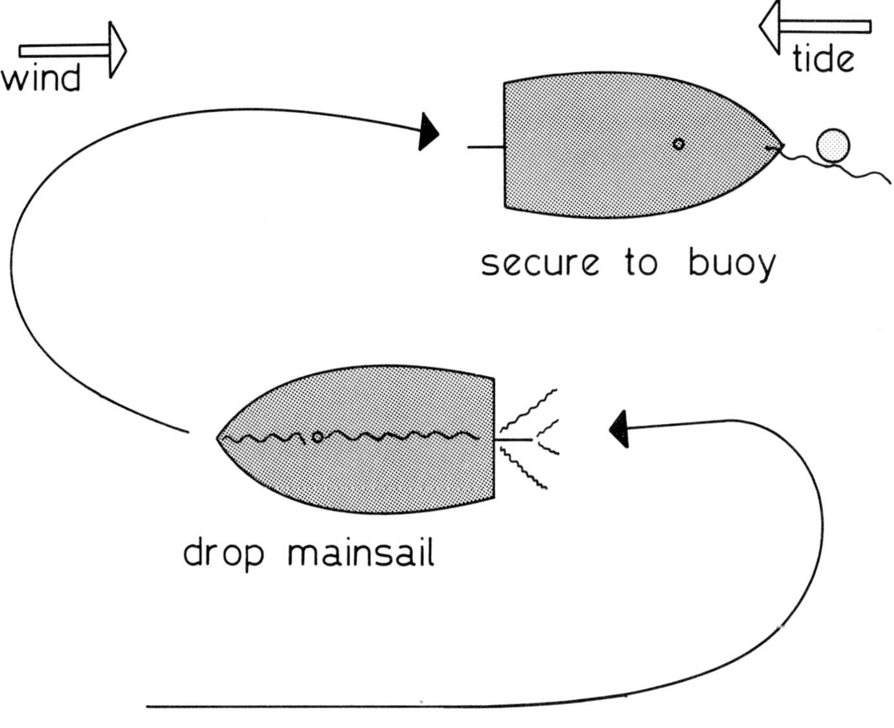

Fig. 40

simply ease the jib off to slow us down. If we are too slow we can haul the jib in a bit and so on. So we simply approach the buoy heading directly into the tide, and playing the jib to slow us down. See fig 40.

As with slipping from the mooring, if you are in any doubt as to whether the mainsail can be carried safely, then don't carry it. And also as with slipping a mooring, the secret lies in thinking out your approach carefully and thoroughly. The actual mechanics of tying to and untying from the buoy we will deal with in the chapter on seamanship.

6 Tides and Anchoring

After securing to and slipping from a mooring, the next most frequent manoeuvre we are likely to indulge in is anchoring. Although basically similar to mooring, insofar as our anchor and line is in effect a sort of portable mooring that we carry around on board our boat, there is one very crucial difference. Whereas the likelihood is that an experienced Harbour Master or Boatyard has selected the spot for your permanent mooring and laid it there, when you anchor you have to select the spot and lay the anchor yourself. The actual mechanics of anchoring is fairly simple, very much simpler than laying a permanent mooring, but the problem of where to anchor is much the same as that of where to lay a mooring. And this is what we shall consider first.

In the last chapter we discussed how the tide affects us in the horizontal plane—how it sweeps into harbours on the flood and out on the ebb, carrying all before it. Before we can anchor we must consider how the tide behaves in the vertical plane, because as it floods into a harbour or along the coast, it also rises in height. This is caused by the gravitational attraction of the sun and moon drawing it up, the effect being neatly balanced by a fall in the water level in other parts of the world. As the tide rises from its minimum at Low Water to its maximum at High Water, so it spreads up the beaches and into the harbours, exactly as a river that overflows its banks spreads over the surrounding meadows. After a short pause at High Water it then begins to fall, ebbing down the beaches and out of the harbours as it goes, until it reaches Low Water, pauses, then begins to rise again.

What happens roughly is shown in fig 41. On any particular day the

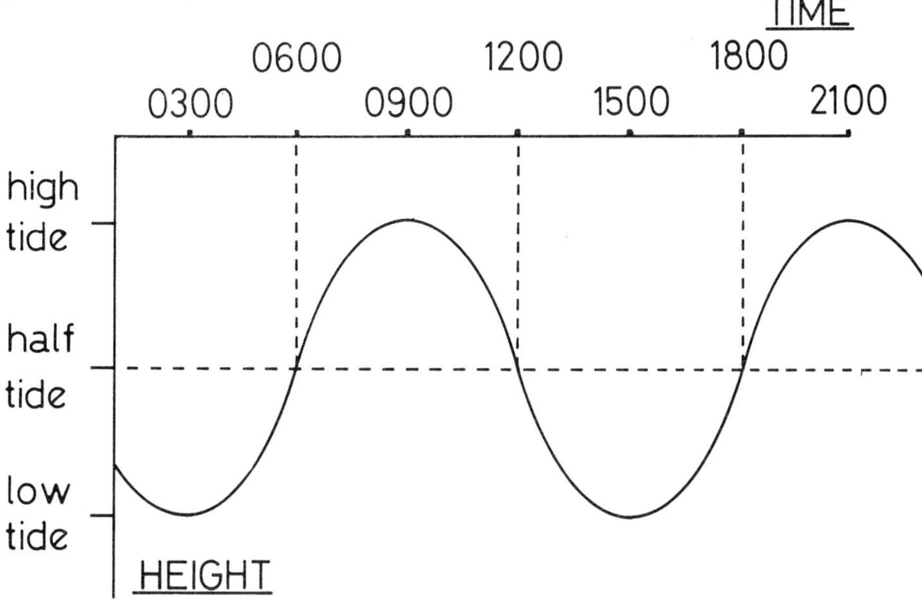

Fig. 41

tide will be at its maximum height at a certain time. This is known as High Water or High Tide. It then falls for about six hours, steadily increasing its rate of fall to a maximum at half tide (three hours later—when it also is ebbing at its maximum speed). The rate of fall and the speed of the ebb tide then slow gradually until Low Water when both stop. There is then a short pause before the tide begins flooding again up to the next High Water. The speed of the flood stream and the rate of increase of the tidal height both increase up to half tide then decrease steadily to High Water.

Now the reason all these timings are 'roughly' is because conditions in the Universe are constantly varying. Because of the progression of the earth around the sun and the moon around the earth, the time of the tide is different each day. So is the height. And these differences are not constant, simply because the tracks of the various bodies through the heavens are not constant. However, we can make a reasonable working approximation, sufficiently accurate to give us a basic formula to remember. The precise times and heights of High and Low Water each day are calculated by astronomical methods and we can find them tabulated in Tide Tables, generally on sale at local chandlers, boatyards and so on.

For our purposes now, it is sufficient to know that the time of High Water (and Low Water) is approximately one hour later each day (24 hours). So if today's High Water is at four o'clock in the morning, the next Low Water will be not quite at ten o'clock (six hours later), but nearer a quarter past. The next High Water (remembering there are two High Waters and two Low Water each day) will not be six hours later at four o'clock in the afternoon but more like half past. The next Low Water will be around a quarter to eleven and not ten o'clock, and the following High Water not twenty four hours after today's but more like twenty five—namely five o'clock in the morning. Even this is an approximation as the actual daily progression is nearer fifty minutes than the hour. However, if we want to work out times and heights of the tide we do it from the Tide Tables, as we shall see. Remembering that the tide is roughly one hour later each day is quite accurate enough for the purpose of understanding more or less what is going on.

Now, as well as varying its time each day, the tide also varies its height. This variation, again, is caused by those heavenly bodies, the sun and the moon, wending their own little ways around the place with no inclination to adhere to any simple, logical, man-made formula. The basic problem is caused by the moon. This little chappie takes approximately a month to circle the earth while the earth takes a whole year to make its way round the sun. This means that during the month the moon takes to get round the earth, the earth moves relatively little in relation to the sun. As the tides are caused by both the sun and the moon pulling on the oceans, we find that twice a month the two of them are in line and pulling together (when the moon is in line between the sun and the earth and when it is in line beyond the earth). At these times the maximum pull is exerted on the water and we have the highest tides, which are known as Spring Tides. These tides occur once a fortnight a couple of days after the New Moon and Full Moon.

In between these Spring Tides the heights gradually drop away as the moon moves out of line with the sun, until about midway between the Spring Tides, when the moon is pulling at right angles to the sun, we have the lowest tides, known as Neap Tides. Now, at Neap Tides, becauses the minimum pull is being exerted by the sun and the moon, the height of High Water, as we have just seen, will be at its lowest, before starting to creep up again to the next Spring Tide about a week later. What we must also realise is that the height of Low Water is at its highest. The reason for this is that when the pull on the water is at its minimum (at Neap Tides), creating low High Tides on one side of the world, the amount of water pulled up and away from those places having Low Water is less. Thus the water does not drop as much as it does at a Spring Low Water and the Low Water height at Neaps is therefore greater.

Similarly, at Spring Tides the pull is at its greatest, creating the highest High Tides and pulling more water up and away to give the lowest Low Tides elsewhere. Anyway, all we need to remember is that, as the tide goes up and down twice during the day to give two High Waters and two Low Waters, so it does during the month, to give two Spring Tides and two Neap Tides. The Spring Tides, which occur a couple of days after the New and Full Moons, produce the highest High Tides and the lowest Low Tides. Neap Tides, which occur midway between the Springs, produce the lowest High Tides and the highest Low Tides. In between, there is a gradual change from one to the other.

As the Spring Tide has to produce a much greater movement of water than the Neap Tide (from a lower Low to a higher High) it follows that the actual speed of the tidal stream at Springs must be greater than that at Neaps, and this is so. Thus at Spring Tides we have the highest High Waters, the lowest Low Water and the fastest streams. At Neap we have the lowest High Waters, the highest Low waters and the weakest streams.

Although of no importance to us at this stage, it is interesting to note that besides the daily variation and the monthly variation, there is also a yearly variation in the height of the tide, creating the biggest Spring Tides of the year in the Spring and Autumn. These are known as the Equinoctial Spring Tides as they occur near the periods of the Vernal and Autumnal Equinoxes. These periods also tend to be times of bad weather and many experienced cruising yachtsmen will not put to sea during the Equinoxes.

However, our business at the moment is anchoring, and what concerns us is the daily variation in the height of the tide. The reason it concerns us is that when we anchor we must know how far the tide is going to fall before we leave, so that we can be sure we will not ground on the bottom as it goes down. We must also know how high it will rise while we are anchored so that we can make sure we have sufficient line out to reach the bottom if it is to rise higher than it is when we arrive. But first, let us have a break from the tide as we have covered quite a lot of ground. Let us take a look at the other factors we must consider when selecting a place to anchor.

Take a look at fig 42. There's a nice sandy beach at the top there, and we want to anchor off it for lunch, then spend the afternoon swimming and sunbathing. How do we go about it? Well, we don't just charge in and sling the anchor over the side.

Our first requirement is shelter—shelter from the wind, shelter from the waves, and if possible shelter from the tide, especially if it is running fast. There are two reasons we seek shelter when anchoring. One is comfort and the other is safety. If we have big waves lolloping up and down in the anchorage, or a howling wind roaring across the deck, not only will it make life on board most uncomfortable, and getting ashore in the dinghy wet and hazardous, but it will increase

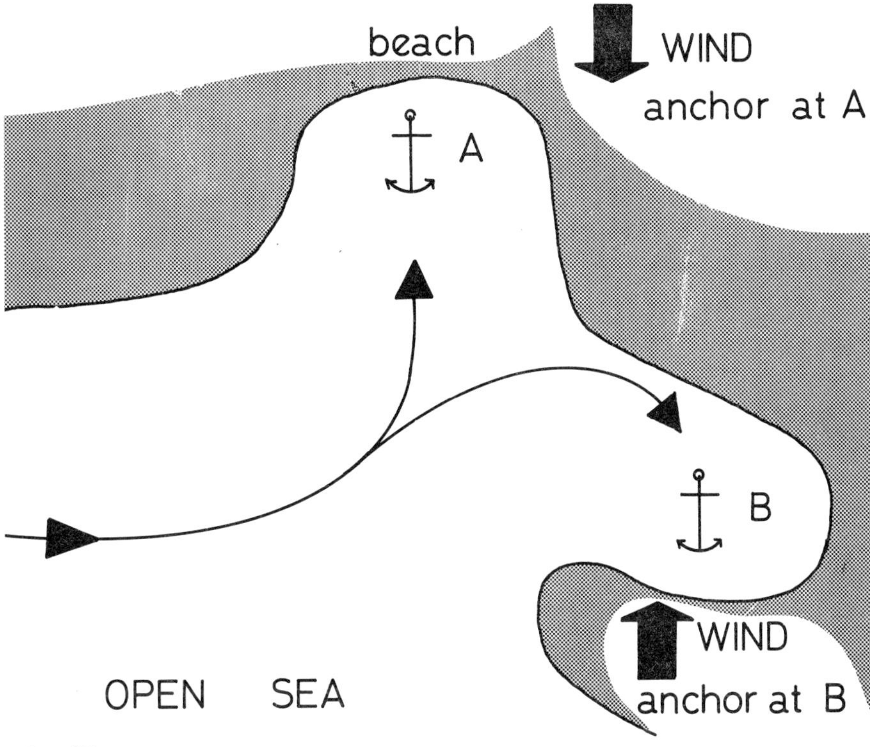

Fig. 42

tremendously the risk of dragging our anchor. We remain anchored basically because the anchor digs into the bottom and holds us. If big waves, strong winds or very fast tides put a lot of extra strain on the anchor it can pull out of the bottom and drag. The boat, of course, will then cease to be held securely to the bottom and will be blown or carried away till it meets a rock or beach, upon which it will be pounded to pieces. So we can see that the selection of a sheltered spot to anchor is most important.

In fig 42 the spot just off the beach marked A will be nice and sheltered only if the wind is blowing off the land, from the beach across the water. With the wind blowing off the land the waves will have no time to build up high before reaching us at A, and any high ground behind the beach will break up, divert and generally reduce the force of the wind itself. Also, in a small enclosed bay like this the tide will almost certainly be fairly slack, as the main force of the stream will run across the mouth of it to the open sea, or from the sea if it is flooding.

If, however, the wind was blowing off the sea into the bay with any force, it could be extremely dangerous to anchor at A. The further away the next piece of land across the sea, the bigger the waves will have built by the time they reach us at our anchorage. The wind will also blow straight in with full, unobstructed force, creating a very grave danger of dragging the anchor. If, for example, the bay faces across a stretch of water reaching fifty miles or so before the next land, the waves rolling into our anchorage could very easily be fifteen feet high! And we don't anchor thirty-foot boats in fifteen-foot waves. Even if we only have half a mile or so to the opposite side of an estuary, a strong wind could easily build up two- or three-foot waves, which would be quite sufficient to make life most unpleasant, and getting ashore in the dinghy quite dangerous.

So the simple answer for us is to find a place to anchor that is well snugged up in the lee of the land. In fig 42, if the wind blows from the top of the picture, we can safely and comfortably anchor at A. If the wind blows from the bottom of the picture, however, unless very light and calm, the anchorage at A would be untenable and we must go and anchor at B, where we will be in the lee of that spit of land below it.

The next thing we must know is whether the place we have picked is clear of obstructions—obstructions on the bottom that could foul our anchor, and obstructions on the surface that could foul the boat. In the first category come such things as wrecks, moorings (for buoys or other boats) and other boats' anchors and lines. Wrecks and moorings are generally shown on charts, but as we have yet to learn about charts we must ask. We simply ask the Harbour Master, the local chandler's shop, the local boatyard, or even a local sailor, whether the bay we have picked is clear of submerged obstructions. If we have joined a Club (we shall discuss this point in a later chapter) then, of course, there should be plenty of people to ask.

Assuming the bottom is clear, all we have to worry about is the temporary obstruction, such as another boat anchored there already. The simple answer to this one is to keep well clear, as we can never be certain in which direction his anchor lies. As we shall see when we get

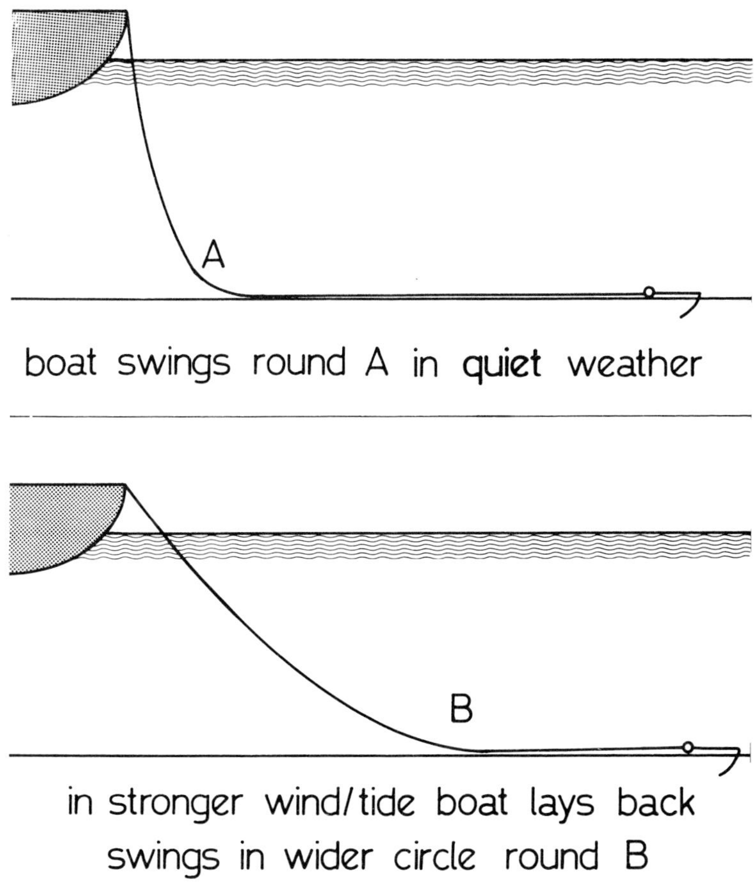

Fig. 43

on to the mechanics of anchoring, it will not necessarily lie out straight ahead of him. We must also place ourselves in such a way that if we swing when the tide turns we will not bump into any neighbours, and the space required for this is generally automatically sufficient to take care of any danger of fouling. Have a look at figs 43 and 44. You will see that even in quiet weather we will swing in a circle with a radius of something like two boat lengths, and in stronger winds or tides this

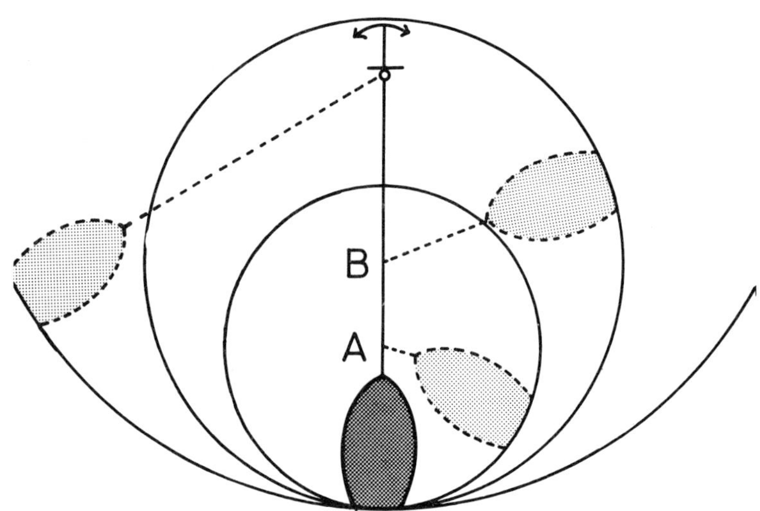

Fig. 44

could be considerably larger. We may not swing at all, of course, if we lie to the wind (very likely in a bay like this) and it does not change, but it is seamanlike to allow for the possibility of swinging. Try it out in a few open spaces first and you will soon get an idea of how your boat behaves. Anchoring in a tight spot is a very skilled art, so until we are sufficiently skilled and confident to do it, we must stick to the wide open spaces. See figs 45 and 46.

The answer for us to begin with is simply to keep well clear of other anchored boats, buoys and moored boats that will have chains

Fig. 45 A typical, fairly crowded anchorage. Make sure you have plenty of space to swing, and don't anchor in the main channel, where you will obstruct passing boats.

reaching along the bottom in all sorts of directions, and land, until we have learnt to judge just how boats lie when anchored, and how they swing. And just before we leave this question, watch out for large, diamond-shaped signposts on the shore. If they are painted red, and there is one on each side of the bay, don't drop your anchor between them as they almost certainly signify a submerged cable. If you foul one of those with your anchor you're in real trouble.

Fig. 46 A nice empty anchorage. Assuming there is sufficient depth of water and no obstructions, there is plenty of room. Note the distance between the two boats already there, and the mooring buoy astern of them. Keep clear of that as there will be ground chains holding it.

Well, we've found a sheltered bay and the Harbour Master has assured us there are no wrecks or other submerged obstructions in it. We arrive off the mouth of the bay and see one other moored boat, but there is plenty of room for us to one side of him. Incidentally, if you're not sure of the space, you could always sail past the boat already anchored, tell him you are not very experienced and ask him where you can anchor without fouling him. Fellow yachtsmen are generally very friendly and most helpful, and he will have the advantage of knowing precisely where his own anchor is. If in doubt, don't be ashamed to ask. Nobody will take the mickey out of you, but they will be most annoyed if you charge in and throw your anchor on top of theirs!

Let us suppose no obstructions and plenty of room for us to anchor. What must we think of next? Well, is the water deep enough to float us? We can find that out quite simply by sailing in and checking the depth in the place we have chosen, with either an echo-sounder or a leadline. An echo-sounder is an electronic instrument that sends pulses to the sea bottom and back. It calculates from the time taken for these pulses to return how deep the water is, and generally displays it on a dial. Echo-sounders are fitted in the bottom of the boat (except for the dial!) and before we use one we must check whether it reads the depth below itself, the depth below the keel or the depth from the surface. They can be adjusted to read any of these, so we must be sure which value ours reads before we use it. The easiest way to check is to compare it while on the mooring with the reading from a leadline.

A leadline is simply a piece of rope, usually about ten metres long, with a weight on the bottom, that is marked at various depths. We lower it over the side until it touches the bottom and read off the depth indicated at the surface. So there is no great problem in finding our depth when we arrive. The real problem is finding how much it will change while we are there. You will remember that the tide is constantly going up and down, so although there may be plenty of water when we arrive, if the tide is ebbing at the time we could easily find ourselves aground within a couple of hours, and it will be a long time before we can get off again as we shall have to wait for the tide to continue to Low Water then come back up again.

Before we can work out how much the tide will change we must understand two things. First, the height of tide given in the Tide Tables is not the depth of water you will find in the sea. The height of the tide is measured from an arbitrary line known as Chart Datum, which is approximately the lowest point to which the tide ever falls. The sea bottom, of course, does not follow this line, being sometimes above it and sometimes below. If we look at fig 47 it will become

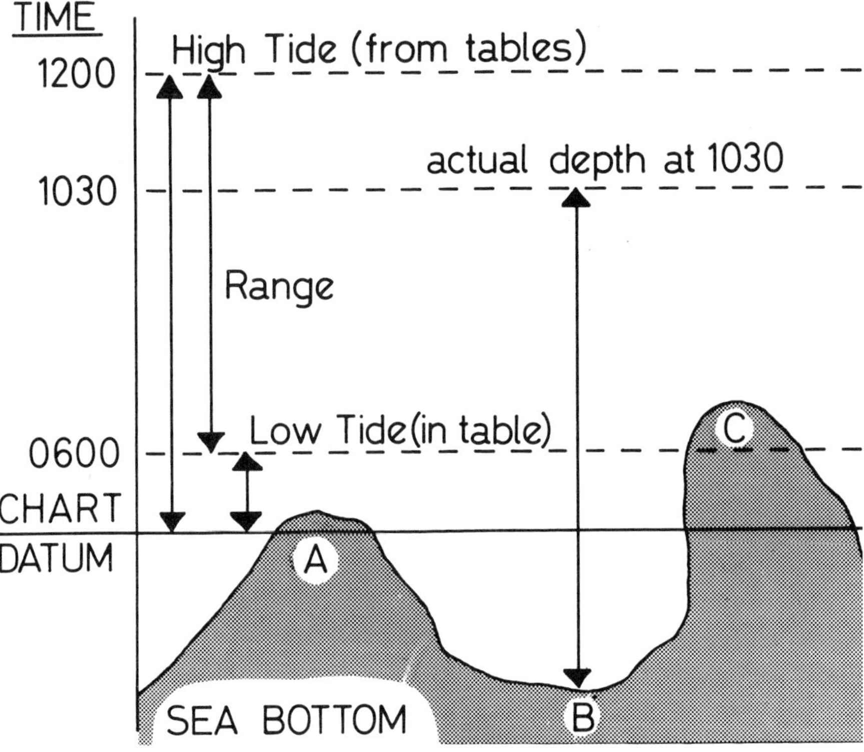

Fig. 47

clearer. At point A the bottom is above Chart Datum so the actual depth will be less than the tidal height. At point B the actual depth will be greater, while at point C not only will the depth be less than the tidal height, but at Low Tide the bottom will show above the surface, as a sandbank, rock or whatever.

How the bottom varies in relation to Chart Datum is, of course, marked on charts in the form of soundings (depth below Chart Datum), so the navigator, armed with a chart and the local Tide Tables, can always calculate the actual depth in any place at any time. We do not want to get involved in the complexities of chartwork at the moment, however, so let us see how we can work out our depths just from the Tide Tables and the reading on our echo-sounder or leadline on arrival at the anchorage. If we are using an echo-sounder which reads depth below the keel, we must first add our draft (depth of keel below the surface) to all our readings, in order to get the depth below the surface.

If we arrive at the anchorage dead on High Water, we know that the depth will decrease steadily for the next six hours as the tide falls to Low Water. So what we must find out is whether it will fall so much during our stay that we will ground. If we arrive dead on Low Water, we know the tide will rise for the next six hours, so our problem is to know how much it will rise so we can be sure we have sufficient line out to the anchor to hold us in the deeper water later. The chances are, of course, that we will arrive at some time in between, so, as Tide Tables give only the heights and times of High and Low Waters, we need some means of working out the heights at intermediate times. There is a simple formula that provides us with this means, known as 'The Twelfths Rule'.

We said earlier that the speed the tide falls or rises increases up to half tide, then decreases, the maximum rate of change being at half tide, three hours after High or Low Water. Now, fortunately for us, it does this at a steady rate and we find that in the first hour after High Water the tide falls one-twelfth of the total distance it must fall to Low Water. This distance, of course, is the difference between the height at High

Water and the height at Low Water, and is known as the 'range' of the tide. In the second hour it falls two-twelfths of the range, and in the third hour three-twelfths of the range. We are now at half tide, with the depth falling at its fastest rate. From this point on the tide begins to slow down and it slows at the same rate it increased up to half tide. Thus in the fourth hour (first hour after half tide) it falls three-twelfths again, in the fifth hour two-twelfths and in the last hour one-twelfth. We can see this in fig 48.

After a short pause at Low Water, the tide begins to rise again and it does so at the same rates it fell: namely, one-twelfth of the range in the first hour, two-twelfths in the second and so on. So from a knowledge

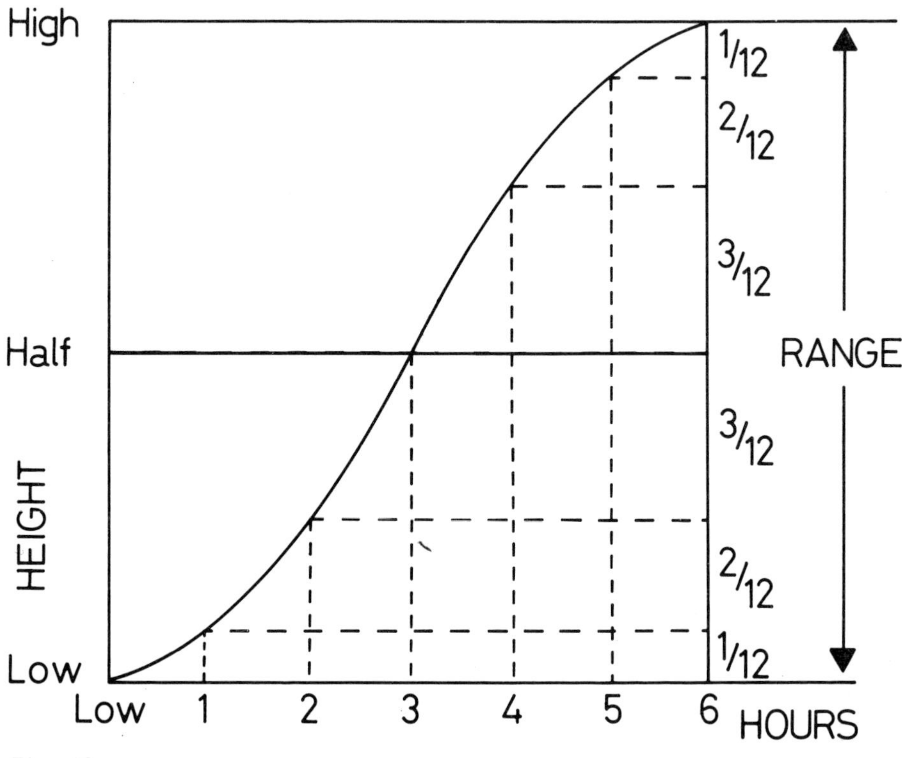

Fig. 48

of the times of High and Low Water, and their heights, we can calculate the range (difference in the heights of High and Low Water), divide it by twelve to get one-twelfth, and thus work out how much the depth will change each hour between High and Low Water. Let us have a trial run into our anchorage.

The first thing we must do is look up in the Tide Tables for the day in question and find the times and heights of High and Low Water spanning the period during which we intend anchoring. Let us say that we will arrive at the anchorage at twelve midday, and High Water is at 0800, height 3.9 metres, followed by Low Water at 1400, height 0.3 metres, and the next High Water is 2015, height 4.0 metres. The first range then is 3.6 metres (HW – 3.9 minus LW – 0.3). The second range we find is 3.7 metres over a period of six-and-a-quarter hours. This complication is the variable Universe rearing its ugly head again, but we get round it simply by approximating. So we'll call it 3.6 in six hours as that will be easier to work with. There are so many unpredictable factors that will affect the height and time of the tide anyway, such as strong winds, very high or low atmospheric pressure and so on, that it is a waste of time (and can be dangerous if we rely on it) trying to be too accurate with our tidal calculations. Because of this possibility of variation we always give ourselves a good margin of depth anyway, and this takes care of all the approximations we make.

If we now divide the range by twelve we get 0.3 metres, and this is our basic unit of calculation—the twelfth. Remembering our Twelfth Rule we can say that the tide will fall one-twelfth in the first hour (0.3 to make the height now 3.6), two-twelfths in the second hour (0.6 to make the height now 3.0) and so on. We can draw up a table as in fig 49 giving us the heights and times of the tide throughout the period that concerns us.

Now, if we arrive at the anchorage at 1200, we can say to ourselves: 'Two hours before Low Water—the tide will fall one-twelfth in the last hour and two-twelfths in the next to last, making a total of three-twelfths of the range still to fall to Low Water. That is 0.9 metres. Now

From Tide Tables:

HIGH WATER –	0800	–	3·9 m
LOW WATER –	1400	–	0·3 m

TWELFTHS RULE gives us:

HW	0800	3·9m
	0900	3·6m
	1000	3·0m
half tide	1100	2·1m
	1200	1·2m
	1300	0·6m
LW	1400	0·3m
	1500	0·6m
	1600	1·2m
half tide	1700	2·1m
	1800	3·0m
	1900	3·6m
HW	2000	3·9m — if this height differs from 0800 HW we must rework from 1400 LW to 2000 HW

Fig. 49

if we are to remain until Low Water and our boat draws 1.2 metres (depth from waterline to bottom of keel), then we must anchor in a minimum depth of 1.2 plus 0.9, that is 2.1 metres, in order to avoid grounding on the bottom at Low Water. In practice we would give ourselves a good safety margin and select at least three metres as the minimum anchoring depth. If there were any waves about causing the boat to bob up and down (even passing boats could make us bob up and down a foot or more) we would allow even more. We now know that if we sail into the bay until the depth has shallowed to three metres or so, depending on the conditions, and drop our anchor, we will have sufficient depth of water right down to Low Water.

The other aspect we must consider is whether we are to remain beyond Low Water. We must always (as we shall see in the next chapter) have about three times as much line out to the anchor as the depth of water (five times if we are using nylon line), in order to avoid the risk of the anchor pulling out of the bottom. Thus we must know how deep the water will get before we leave so that we can be certain we have sufficient line out. If we arrive at 1200 and anchor in 3.0 metres of water (that is two hours before Low Water) then, as long as we stay no longer than two hours after Low Water, when the tide will have risen again to more or less the same height it was two hours before, we will have no problem. Paying out three times as much line as the depth on arrival (3×3.0 m$=9$ m) will cope with all changes during that period, as the depth will not be increasing at all.

If however, we decide to stay until 1700 (three hours after Low Water) then the depth will increase by a further three-twelfths of the range (3×0.3 m$=0.9$ m) during this last hour before half tide, and will thus be 3.9 metres when we leave, where it was only 3.0 metres when we arrived. Thus, instead of paying out three times three (nine metres) of line, we must pay out three times 3.9 (11.7—call it twelve) metres if we are to stay until 1700. Fig 50 should make this clear visually.

And that, basically, is how we work out the depth problem. Seems complicated? It's not really—it has a certain logic to it as in the Twelfths Rule. Remember that your basic unit of change is one-twelfth of the range (difference between height of High and Low Water) and it speeds up to half tide, then slows down to full tide, whether it is going up to High Water or down to Low Water. In the first hour it changes by one-twelfth, in the second two-twelfths and in the third three-

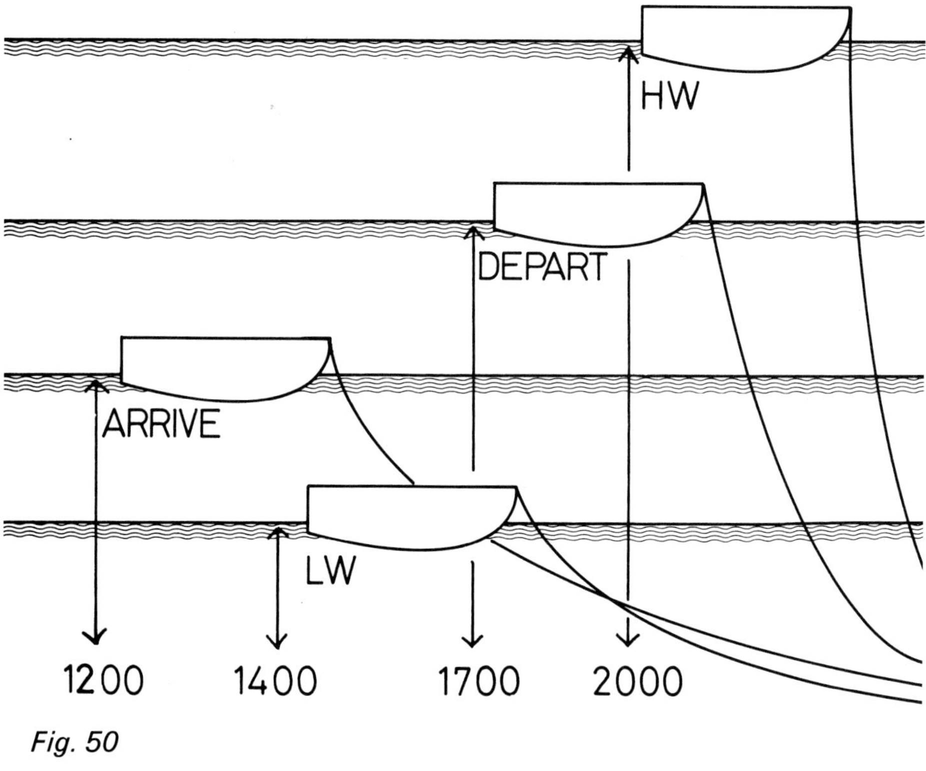

Fig. 50

twelfths. It then slows down, changing three-twelfths in the fourth hour, two in the fifth and one in the last. Then off it goes again. The secret is to keep it simple. Approximate the figures so that they calculate easily, then allow a good safety margin.

In the next chapter we will look at the mechanics of actually putting the anchor over the side, which is a good bit simpler than the tidal calculations.

7 Boathandling

We now know where to anchor, when to anchor and in what depth of water to anchor. Now let us take a look at the actual process of anchoring.

If we look at fig 51 we see that the object of the exercise is to end up with the anchor firmly dug into the bottom and secured to the boat by a warp (line) approximately three times as long as the depth of water.

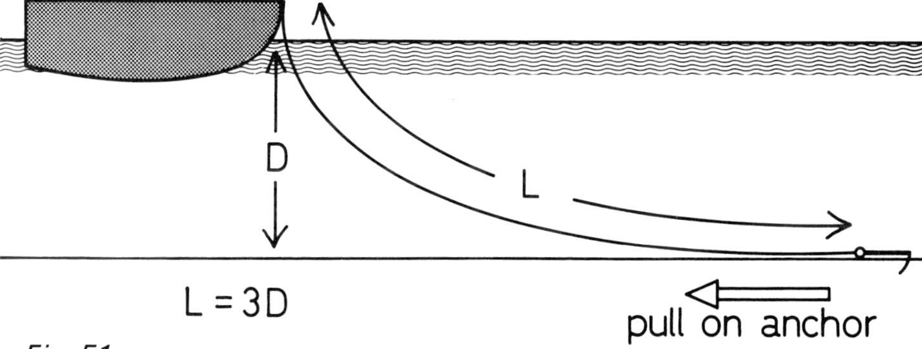

Fig. 51

This length of warp ensures that sufficient lies along the bottom to maintain a horizontal pull on the anchor. Thus all the strain of the boat pulling on the warp will tend to dig the anchor in further, and not lift it out.

We anchor a boat using either chain or nylon, both of which absorb shocks, the nylon by stretching and the chain by lifting. See fig 52. Nylon, due to its light weight, will not lie on the bottom like chain, so

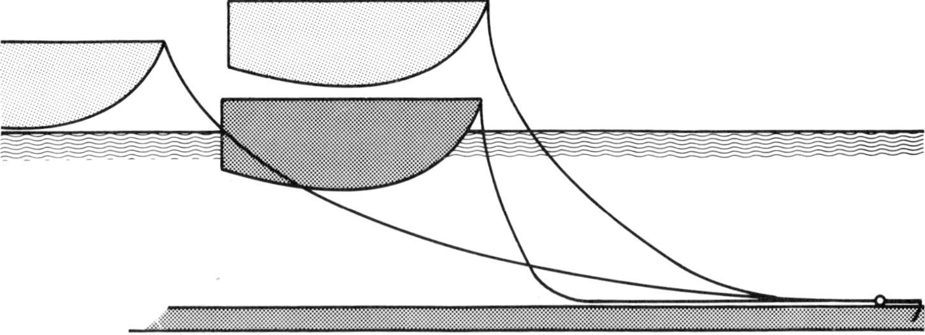

Fig. 52

we have to pay out *not three times the depth but five times*, in order to ensure a horizontal pull on the anchor. See fig 53. Nylon creates problems as it requires far more room to swing than chain, and is more likely to drag due to the difficulty of keeping it on the bottom. This can be overcome to a certain extent by attaching a couple of fathoms (1 fathom = 6 feet, or approx. 2 metres) of chain between the anchor and the nylon warp, but for really secure anchoring for any period of time (overnight, for example) chain is advisable.

How do we do it? Well, having selected our anchorage, as we saw in the previous article, we approach the actual spot where we want to

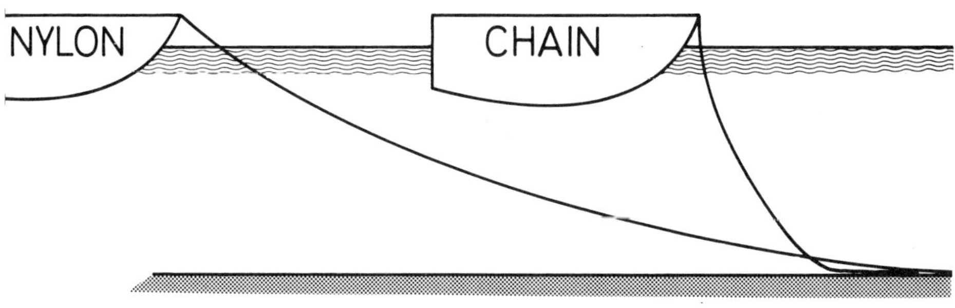

Fig. 53

drop the anchor just as we would a mooring (see chapter 5). Then, as the boat comes to a stop in the right place, we drop the anchor over the bow and pay out the warp as the boat falls back away from the spot under the actions of wind and tide. It is most important that we pay out the warp as we drop back so that it lays itself out along the bottom, as in fig 51. If we simply drop it all over the bow with the anchor, we

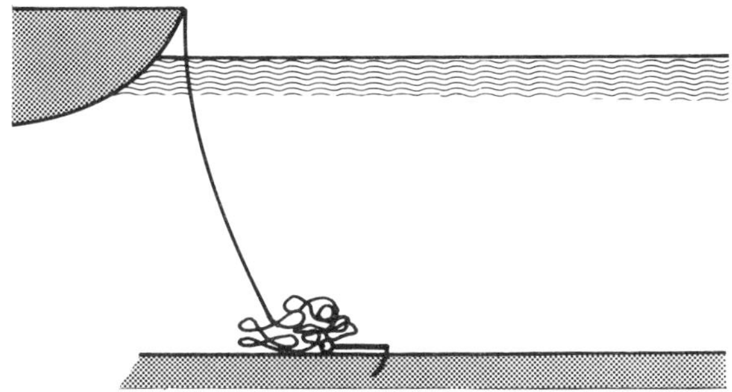

Fig. 54

will end up as in fig 54, with a big heap of tangled chain on the bottom, which is sure to catch round the anchor and lift it clean out of the bottom the moment we lay back on it. Fig 55 shows the process, which is known as a Dropping Moor to distinguish it from fig 56, where we see a Running Moor.

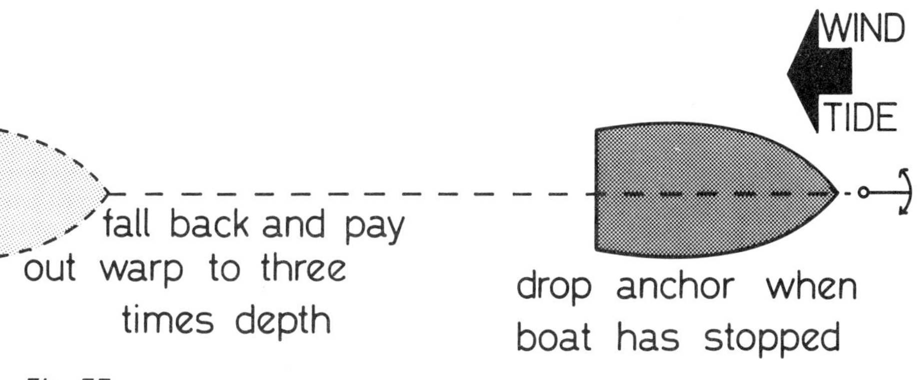

Fig. 55

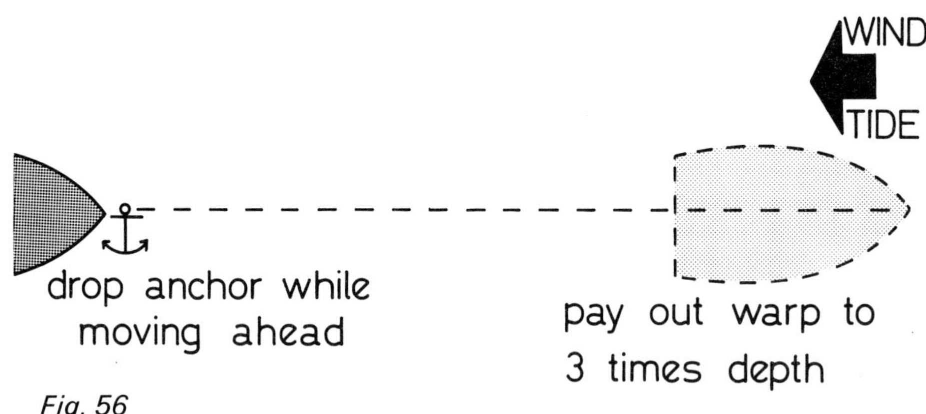

Fig. 56

The Running Moor is another way we can anchor, and it has the advantage that dropping the anchor in the correct place is somewhat easier as we do not need to be stopped. In this method we approach the anchorage in the same way, but we slow down so that we are still moving when we get to our spot. We then drop the anchor over the side as we go, paying out the cable as we run on past the anchor. If all goes well, and it is important not to be going too fast for this, we should be more or less stopped when the right amount of cable has been paid out, and we can then secure it round the mooring cleat or bollard on the foredeck. We do this by taking a turn round the bollard or cleat, then turning it up in figures of eight round the horns. See fig 57.

Fig. 57

And that, basically, is anchoring. The approach is the same as the approach to a mooring, insofar as we must balance the forces of wind and tide so that we arrive stopped in the right place, with our sails set so that they will flap freely without driving us around in embarrassing circles. Once the anchor is set we can hand the sails and open the cocktail cabinet, having first had a good look round to check our position against the shore or other boats. Then we must keep an eye out to make sure we do not drag away from our position, remembering that we will move around a certain amount on the end of the chain. See fig 58. Figs 59 and 60 show how we prevent chain from damaging the hull when moored or anchored.

Raising the anchor to sail off again is much the same as slipping the mooring. We must first ascertain which sails we can set and we then

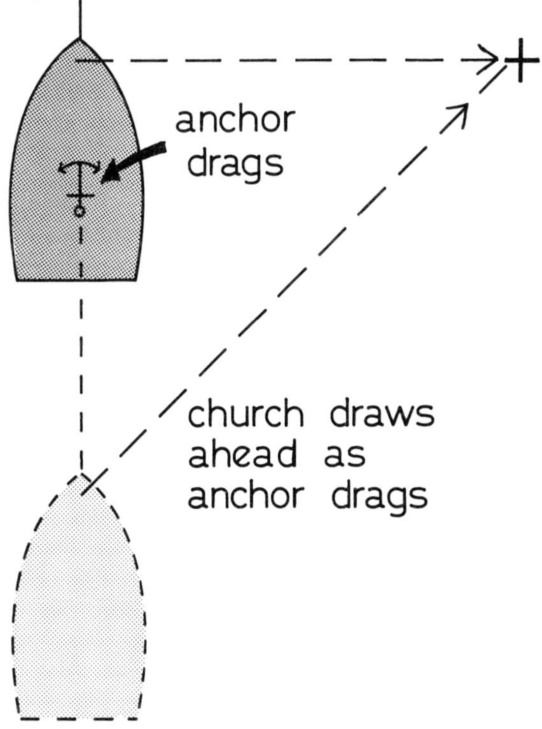

Fig. 58

Fig. 59 Hoisting the buoy close up to the bow prevents the chain chafing the hull.

haul in the anchor warp. As the anchor breaks free we can back the jib and sail off on whichever tack we want (if lying to the wind), or simply sail away by hauling in the jib (if lying to the tide with the wind astern).

In berthing alongside a wall or jetty we adopt the same basic principles as for picking up a mooring or anchoring, with the BIG difference that when we arrive alongside we cannot swing with the slight variations of the wind. This makes the question of which sails to set extremely important, especially when we also realise that a mainsail boom, or jibsheets, swinging about against or over the top of the jetty could so easily catch on something. The problem is really only overcome by handing our sails before we get to the jetty, and this

Fig. 60 Plastic pipe on the chain, and a bow fender, will prevent the mooring chain or anchor chain from scratching the hull.

means that we must be able to judge our approach speed and our slowing down very accurately indeed. If we arrive at a buoy too fast we can always go round again. If we arrive at an anchorage too fast we can go round again. If we approach a mooring or anchorage too slowly we can haul in the sails at the last minute to increase our speed, or back the jib, sail off, and come round again.

With a wall, however, our escape route to one side is cut off, and there will be many times when the escape route away from the wall is impossible due to the directions of the wind and the tide. The problem with berthing alongside a wall, basically, is that we cannot choose which direction we will lie when we arrive. This makes berthing

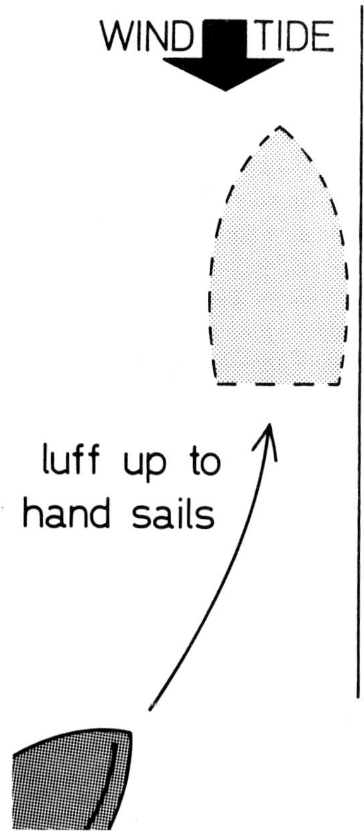

Fig. 61

alongside under sail, in all but the most favourable conditions (wind and tide parallel with the wall), very difficult for all but the most experienced of sailors. My advice, if you have an auxiliary motor, is to hand the sails well clear and approach under power. Approaching under sail, you must hand all sails the moment you estimate you have sufficient way on to reach the berth under your momentum. Have plenty of fenders over the side and a crew member standing by with a stern line, so he can jump ashore with it and slow you down if necessary. And make your approach into the tide and wind if you can, so that they will slow you down. The trouble is that you are likely to find the wind blowing onto or off the wall, and the tide doing all sorts of strange things, swirling round in eddies and so on.

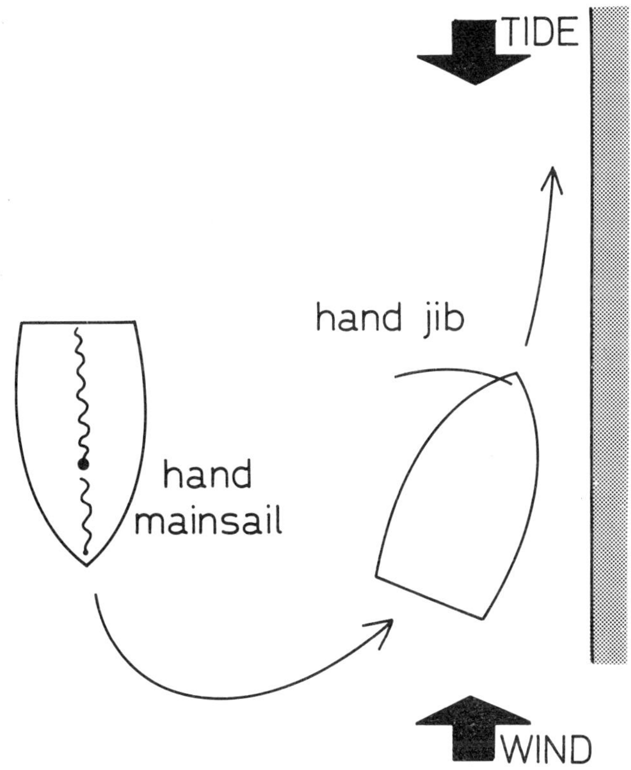

Fig. 62

In figs 61 and 62 we see techniques for berthing under sail when the tide is straightforward and running along the wall. If the wind blows off the wall (fig 63), we must get the bow close to the wall as soon as we have handed the sails and a line ashore before the wind begins to blow us off. In fig 64, get plenty of fenders over the side and do not swing parallel to the quay too far off, or the wind will blow you on, building up speed as you drift so that by the time you reach the wall you are drifting sideways rather quickly. Hand the jib a good way off to reduce speed, and swing parallel to the wall fairly close while travelling as slowly as possible.

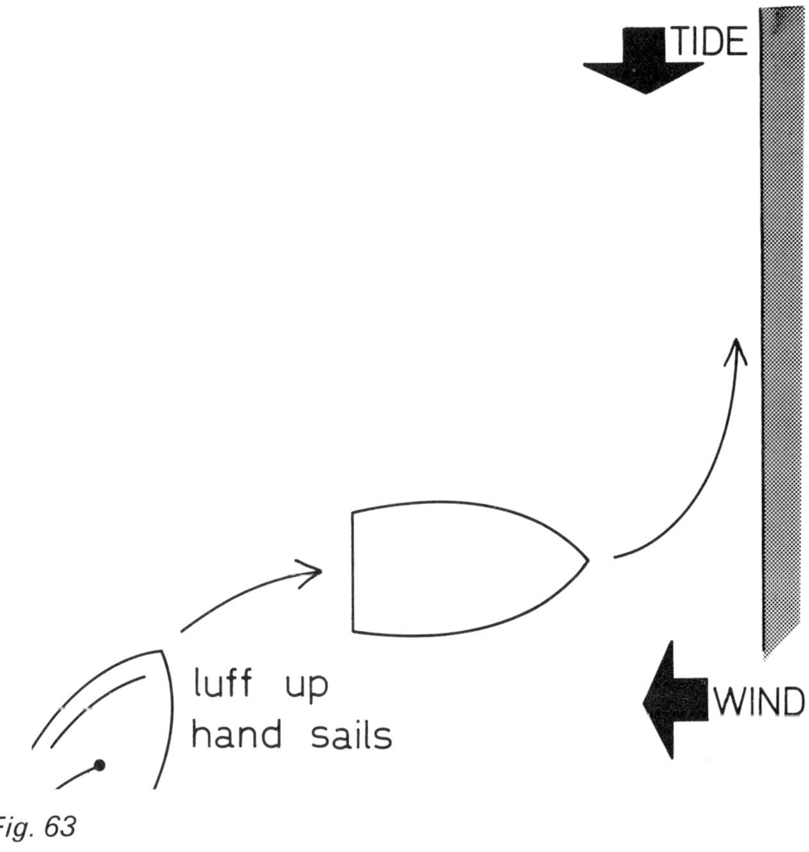

Fig. 63

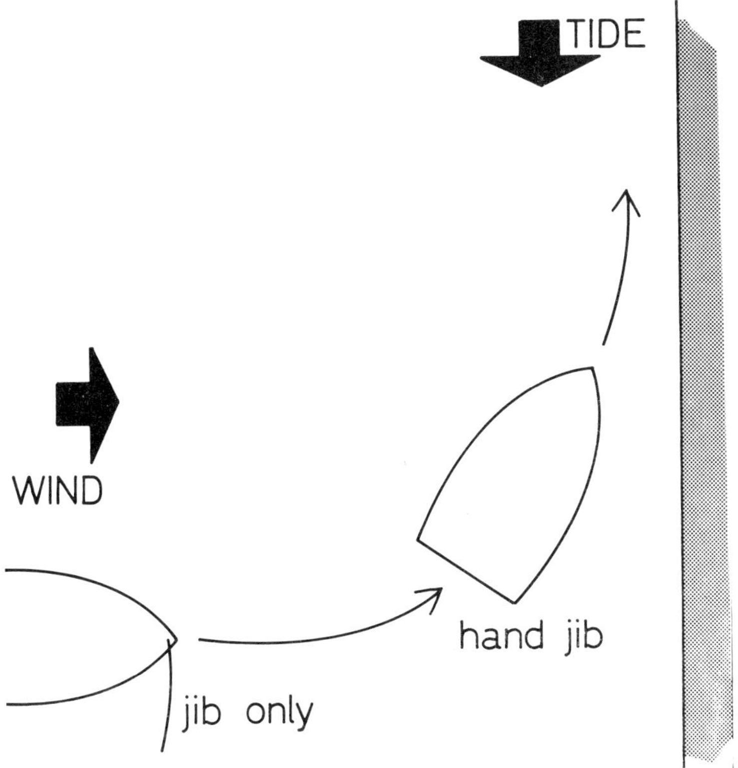

Fig. 64

Leaving an alongside berth when the wind is along the quay we can hoist the sails, back the jib and sail off closehauled. If the wind blows off the quay we simply cast off the lines, hoist the jib as she blows clear and sail off. If the wind is blowing on to the quay the manoeuvre is a more delicate one. We must haul ourselves clear of the wall and head to wind so that we can set the sails. This can be done by taking the anchor off in the dinghy, and dropping it some way to weather of the jetty, then hauling ourselves off with it, whereupon we can sail off just as we would leaving an anchorage. But do lay it a good way off—use the full

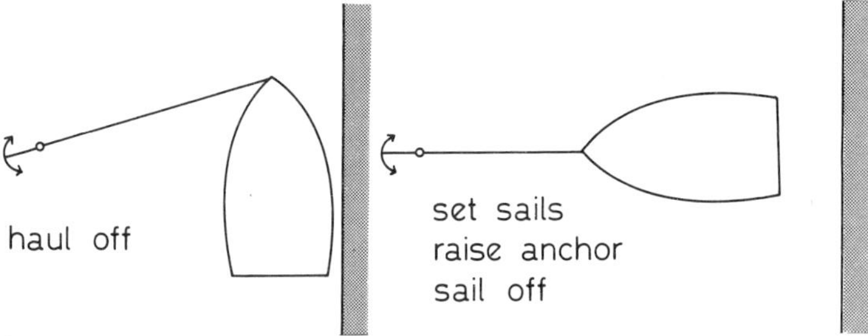

Fig. 65

length of your anchor warp, so that you can haul yourself well clear and still have enough warp out to hold you anchored. See fig 65.

If there are too many obstructions to anchor, we can achieve the same effect by taking a line to a buoy, post or jetty and hauling off with that. Or we can ask a friendly passing motorboat to give us a pluck off.

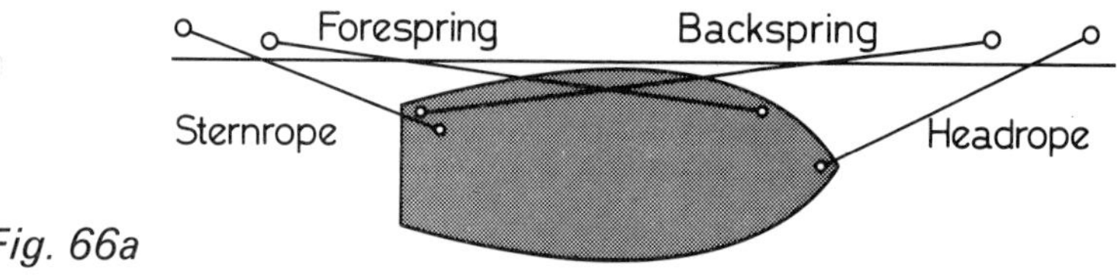

Fig. 66a

Anyway, how do we actually tie the boat up when we do get alongside? Have a look at figs 66a and b (opposite). The lines that hold us into the jetty are the head and stern ropes, and they should always be slightly slack so as to allow for any pitching movement of the boat. See fig 67. The springs (Fore and Back) prevent us moving along the

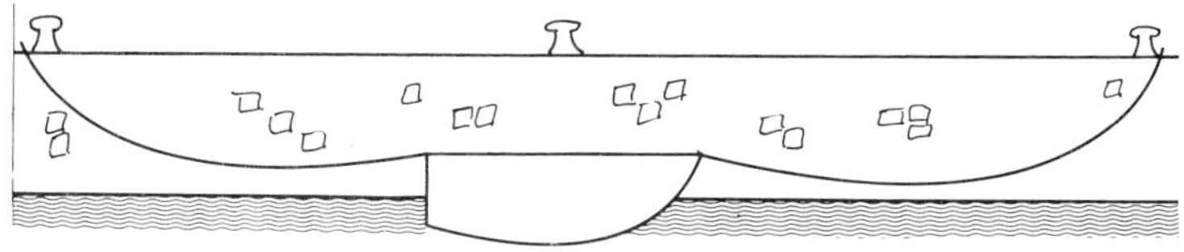
Fig. 67

Fig. 66b *Moored in a marina. Note the springs. Stern rope goes to the buoy astern of the boat.*

wall, and they should be as long as possible to that they lie as near as possible parallel to the wall. Then the pull they exert will be more or less along the wall, which is where we want it. These lines should be fairly taut, as their length and direction will allow them to cope with any pitching. If the tide is likely to rise or fall during our stay alongside, then the lines must either be adjusted from time to time to cope with the varying distance from boat to top of the wall, or they can be left sufficiently slack to begin with to stretch as far as the boat will rise or fall. This will entail knowing how much the tidal depth will alter, and we calculate this in exactly the same manner as we did for anchoring. The further from the boat the lines can be secured, the less need will there be for leaving slack in them. It should be clear from fig 68 that the boat with the longer headrope can fall further before the line tightens than can the one with the short line.

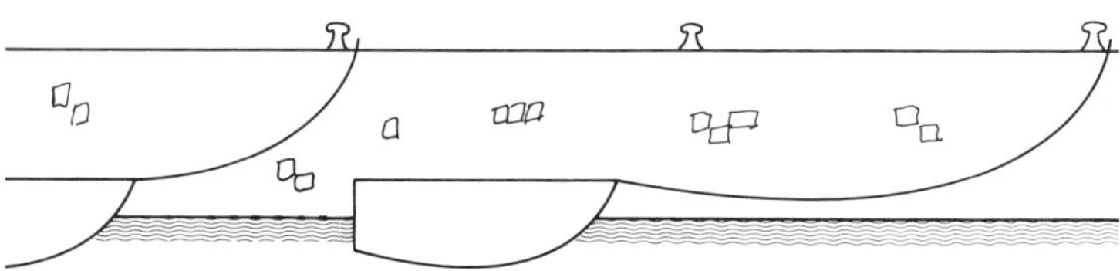

Fig. 68

And that is how we secure a boat to a wall or jetty. The actual knots we use we will cover in the Seamanship section later. In the meantime let us take a look at two other manoeuvres, one of which is quite likely to concern us at some time during our sailing life, and the other which I sincerely hope will never concern any of you at any time. The first is getting off the mud after we have run aground, and the second is recovering a man overboard.

The first thing to appreciate about running aground is that if we do it on a flood tide all we have to do is keep ourselves where we are (prevent ourselves from drifting further on into shallower water as the tide rises) and wait until the tide floats us again as it rises. If, however, we are unfortunate enough to run aground on an ebb tide, we are in trouble. We have to get ourselves off again extremely quickly if we are not to stay there for the next six hours! So let us consider the ebb tide grounding first, as everything we say will also apply to grounding on the flood but with less urgency.

If we look at fig 69 we see that a boat will generally ground towards the after end of the keel, as this is normally the deepest part. If,

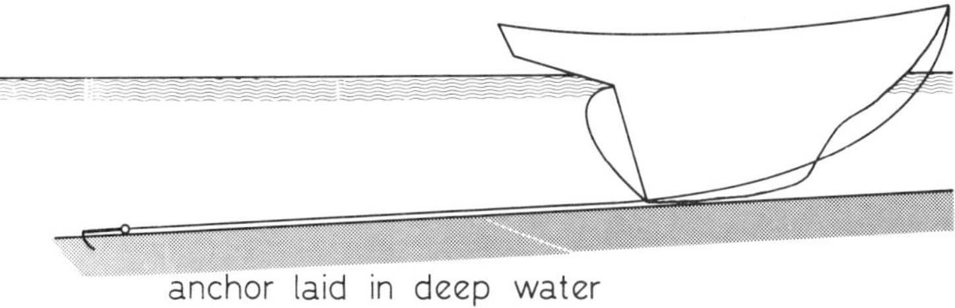

Fig. 69

therefore, we can get a lot of weight (like all the crew) right for'ard in the bow there is a chance that this leverage will lift the stern clear of the bottom, and with the rudder hard over there is just a chance we can swing her round and sail off before the tide has dropped to any appreciable extent. We can also reduce the boat's draft (depth) by swinging out the main boom and getting all the crew to hang on to it so as to heel her over. But in my experience these measures have little effect, and the best thing to do is to carry out the anchor in the dinghy towards deep water, drop it at the full extent of the warp, then haul her off as we did from a wall with the wind blowing on. If this is done immediately we go aground, and we then swing off the boom, or pile into the bow, as we are pulling her off, there is a good chance we will be successful.

The same remedy is favourite for grounding on a flood tide, as if we heel her over, or weigh down the bow, with nothing to hold us towards the deep water (such as the anchor laid out), even if that floats her, the chances are she will simply carry on sailing up the bank each time she comes afloat.

The man overboard situation is one which I hope none of you will ever meet; but knowing how to handle it will probably save a life if you do lose someone over the side. Many people have many ideas on how to recover a man overboard, but the simplest and most easily remembered and executed is fairly certain to be the most effective. The traditional method is as follows:

1) Immediately throw a lifebelt (see fig 70) to the man, preferably one with a smoke flare attached in daytime or a light at night. In fact, I would say that a smoke float or light on the lifebuoy is likely to contribute more than anything to success, as your biggest problem is seeing him. You'll never believe how difficult it is to see a man and/or lifebuoy even on a fairly calm day. At night, you've virtually no chance without a light. If you can get a lifebuoy to the man so that he can grab it and it has a light or smoke float on it, your problems are almost over.

Fig. 70 A lifebuoy with light attached fitted into a neat holder on the stern pushpit.

2) Having done this successfully you have only to circle round and go back to him, sailing up alongside him as you would a mooring buoy. If you do not see him immediately, gybe round in a circle straightaway and you are bound to return to a point very close to him. Call out and listen for his shouts, and get everyone in the crew looking out. Other than this, the real secret is practice. Practice gybing round to pick up a lifebuoy thrown over the side until you are certain that a straight gybe will bring you back to where it went over. That is the simplest, and therefore, to my mind the best way to pick up a man overboard.

Actually getting him aboard, from the water on to the boat, is often the most difficult part of the whole process. An average man in soaking wet clothes is extremely heavy, and if he has been in the water for a while he will quite likely be too exhausted to help himself. So an absolute must is a boarding ladder that hangs over the side of the boat and reaches two or three rungs below the surface. The chances are that, with a little assistance, he will be able to clamber aboard without too much trouble. We will look at this question of a man overboard again in the chapter on Safety, and we will look at it in a more positive vein—namely, how to prevent it. For that, inevitably, is the best solution of all.

Before we leave manoeuvring, however, there is one more aspect I would like to discuss, and that is the question of varying our speed. When we manoeuvre our cars about in confined spaces, or busy roads, we are constantly varying our speed, sometimes even stopping, in order to avoid collision with other cars. On the face of it this would not seem to be possible with sailing boats, or even necessary, but with harbours as crowded as they are these days it is often very necessary. It is certainly perfectly feasible, so let us have a look at it, as the ability to vary our speed and stop when necessary gives us considerable control over our boat when manoeuvring in crowded waters.

If you remember, in Chapters 1 and 2 we discussed the importance of setting the sails at just the right angle to the wind, in order to produce the maximum drive. When sailing closehauled this maximum drive is created when the boat is pointing as close to the wind as possible without the sails beginning to flap. Sailing off the wind, it is attained by letting the sails out as far as they will go without flapping, while keeping the boat on a set course. These two methods are, of course, identical, except that in one the angle of the sails to the wind is adjusted by swinging the boat and keeping the sails fixed, while in the other we swing the sails and keep the boat fixed. The end result is the same.

In Chapter 5 we discussed how to remove the drive from the sails altogether, by allowing them to point directly into the wind and flap freely, so that we could stop for anchoring, picking up moorings and so on. This we achieved in the same manner, either by swinging the whole boat to point into the wind, or by slackening off the sheets so that the sails would swing and point into the wind. Either way we prevented them from billowing out and driving us forward.

Now, if we think about it, any stage in between these two extremes (maximum drive and no drive) will produce a reduced amount of drive, and therefore less speed. So by playing our sails in and out, by hauling on and slackening the sheets, we can vary the amount of drive being transmitted to the boat, and therefore the speed at which it will

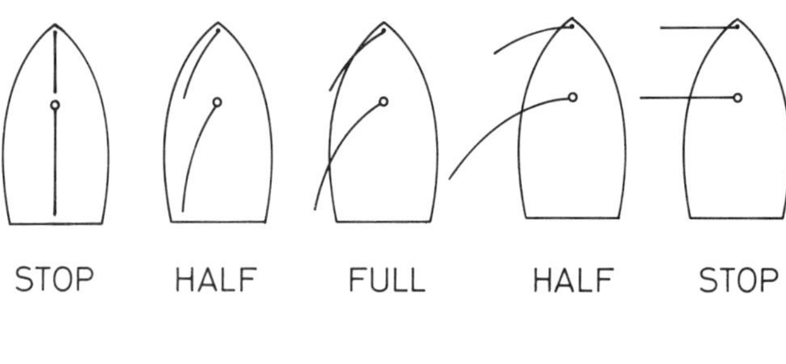

Fig. 71a THE THROTTLE

ig. 71b *Sailing closehauled.*

Fig. 71c *Sheets eased off to slow down.*

travel. See figs 71a, b and c. This technique is particularly useful for a slow and controlled approach to a mooring or anchorage, as we can slow down well clear by slackening off the sheets, then creep up by hauling them in just enough to drive us at the speed we want to go. We can use it for a slow approach to a hidden entrance, or we can slow down to allow a fleet of racing dinghies to get clear of a buoy we want to go round. There are a million and one ways in which this can be useful, its great attraction being that we can maintain the course we are steering, and by slowing down give ourselves more time to think. It is far more efficient and seamanlike than tacking and gybing off in various directions, all at full speed, while we try to decide how to approach something, or kill time to allow someone else to get out of our way in a crowded channel or entrance. The only thing we must be careful of is not to stop entirely, as we are then very likely to lose control, the wind blowing us off perhaps in the very direction we don't want to go.

So always keep her moving if you want to retain control. Remember that the boat will carry her way for quite a while, even if we let the sails flap completely, so we can afford to start slowing down well in advance of the time we need to. If we then want to pick up speed we can do so simply by hauling in a little on the sheets. Remember also that it is movement through the water that gives us control over the rudder, not movement in relation to the land, so look down at the water to check your speed, not at the land or the rate at which we are passing moored boats. The tide could be carrying us up the harbour at three knots so that we appear to be whizzing past the land even if we are stopped in the water. And if we are stopped in the water, we will lose control.

So, if we do want to slow down for any reason, we must be aware of what the tide is doing. In fact, we should be constantly aware of what the tide is doing, all the time we are sailing. And if the tide is running, it can be very useful to us when we want to slow down or stop for a few moments. All we have to do is turn into the tide and adjust our speed by playing the sails until we cease to make any headway in relation to the ground (past the shore, moored boats and so on). We will still be sailing through the water and so retaining control and steerage way (sufficient speed for steering), but we will be stopped relative to the harbour. And we can stay like that all day if we want to and don't get bored with the same scenery. We can certainly stay long enough to allow other boats to get clear of somewhere we want to go, or to enable us to take a good look at a tricky entrance or berth before charging into it.

It is all part and parcel of this business of balancing the forces acting on the boat so that they will take you where you want to go, or keep you where you want to stay. When you can learn to balance the drive from your sails, the leeway and the tidal drift so that your boat goes precisely where you want her to go, at precisely the speed you want her to go, you will be well on the way to becoming a fine and competent seaman. And it is not that difficult. It is mainly a question of awareness and observation. If you can be constantly aware of which way and how fast the tide is carrying you, constantly aware of where the wind is blowing from and how fast it is driving you, and constantly aware of how these factors are causing your boat to behave, you are more than halfway there. A slackening of the sails to slow down will increase the influence of the tide. Altering course to bring the tide more ahead or astern will reduce your sideways drift; altering to bring it more on the beam will increase the sideways drift. Head into the tide and slow right down, and if the tide is strong enough you can even go backwards (astern)! The tide can be a thorough nuisance to the sailor who doesn't know how to use it, and a friend indeed to the one who does. So observe it, feel it, and learn to use it.

8 On Handling Boats

When I was instructing sailing, a hard day's learning was invariably followed by a convivial and relaxing evening in the bar. This, in my opinion and that of my old maths master who used to recommend a two-week holiday in your local pub before an important exam, is an excellent way of allowing all that hard-earned knowledge to be quietly and efficiently assimilated into the brain. Now, much as I would like, gentle reader, to imbibe a jar or two with you, I think it might be a little difficult to organise, so I'll tell you a story instead. That, I hope, will give you a little break after all that manoeuvring.

But, just in case you might think you're not getting your instructional money's worth, I'll make it an instructional one—about handling and manoeuvring sailing boats.

Once upon a time, a long time ago, long even before I fell out of the little dinghy in Chapter 4, sailing boats did not have engines. Sailors in those days, particularly the professional seamen, fishermen and so on, whose livelihoods depended on it, were very proficient indeed at handling their boats under sail and making best use of tide and wind. Many of them would quite happily manoeuvre large unwieldy trading vessels into places, using only the wind and the tide, that you or I would jib at taking a motorboat into.

Just such sailors were the masters of the old trading and fishing boats of the Morbihan, a huge stretch of inland water just opposite Belle Isle in the Bay of Biscay. There is a very long and narrow entrance to the Morbihan from the sea, and the tide rushes through this at up to about eight knots. Now, as you can probably imagine, getting out of

One man and a boy used to sail Thames Barges like this round the south-east coast of England, carrying 100 tons of cargo in all weathers. So you should have no trouble handling a little boat like the one crossing her stern.

there in a slow old fishing boat against the flood tide (coming in) was well-nigh impossible unless the fishermen had a very strong wind behind them. So they simply waited until the tide slackened. Equally difficult, however, was getting out against a headwind, but they had a very clever trick for this. They would wait until the tide was ebbing strongly (half-ebb being the strongest), then sail out into the tide and aim back into the Morbihan with their sails squared away for running. They would then reduce sail, or let them flap, until they were going just fast enough for steerage way through the water, but travelling slower than the tide. The tide would then carry them backwards out of the entrance, under complete control sailing slowly forwards against the tide. Remember the suggestion I made at the end of the last chapter?

Nearer home, those lovely old Thames Barges used to work in and out of the rivers and creeks quite happily with a man, a boy and a haystack aboard. So shallow, it was said, that they could sail over a heavy dew, and they would sail up the tiniest Essex creeks and pull up alongside a farmer's field in order to load his produce. The stories of Thames Barges not only would fill a book, but have filled a good number already, so I will confine myself to telling you of one of their especially useful dodges for working up and down rivers when there was no wind. It is a technique known as dredging (pronounced drudging) and consisted simply of lying at anchor until the tide began to run in the direction they wanted to go. They would then haul up the anchor chain until the anchor began to drag, and let the tide carry them down (or up) the river, the anchor dragging along the bottom ensuring that they travelled slower than the tide. This meant that they had steerage way, as the tide, although taking them along, was still flowing past them and over their rudders, so they could use their rudders to swing the sterns and enable them to track sideways across the river in order to avoid obstacles such as moored boats. I would not, however, advise you to try it these days as so many moorings are laid in rivers now that your anchor would probably pick one up, and then you would be in a spot of bother. But the story does serve to illustrate how the elements can be used when once you understand their effects on your boat.

One of the finest ways I know of learning to feel and judge the influence of the elements is to take part in obstacle races. We used to stage them quite frequently when I was a young lad sailing dinghies, and I learnt a tremendous amount from them. A typical course to sail might be:

1) from the start to the first buoy under jib only;
2) heave to at the first buoy (see Chapter 12) and set the mainsail;

A crewman holds the foresail of a Thames Barge aback to help her tack. It should give you an idea of the size of her gear. Life will be much easier than this in your little cruiser.

3) sail to next buoy without using rudder (by adjusting jib and main to cancel out weather helm);
4) sail to next buoy backwards (by holding main out against headwind)—quite difficult;
5) go alongside sea wall, crew to buy and eat ice-cream.

And so on. They were great fun and amazingly instructive in the basic art of handling a boat under sail and really getting to know instinctively the feel of the elements and their influence on the boat. There are few things more satisfying than simply letting the wind and tide take your boat where you want to go.

9 Seamanship

What is Seamanship? Well, it is the art of doing all those nautical little jobs around a boat, such as tying knots, securing the boat to the jetty, coiling ropes, stowing gear and so on. Given the time and the knowledge, one could write a thousand books on the subject, never mind one chapter. However, to begin with we need only a fairly small amount of information, just sufficient to enable us to sail safely about the harbour, with the occasional short coastal trip. So let us take a look at what we do need to know for that.

Probably the first bit of seamanship we need to know is what to do with the ends of the halliards after we have hoisted the sails, as described in Chapter 3. We will find that, after turning up the halliard on the cleat, there will be a considerable length of rope lying on the deck. Clearly we cannot sail off with it lying about as it will all fall over the side as soon as we heel over—as will anything else on board that is not securely stowed or wedged, but we will come to the question of general stowage later in this chapter. In the meantime, have a look at the photo in fig 72. We see a very simple and efficient way of stowing the loose ends of our halliards. After turning the halliard up on the cleat we coil the loose end by holding the part nearest the cleat in the left hand and coiling it with the right hand, clockwise, into the left hand as the chap is doing in fig 73. When it is all coiled (and keep the coil about 18 inches to 2 feet in diameter—any smaller and it will be awkward and bulky; any larger, it will be unwieldy), simply wedge the coil behind the halliard so that the latter holds it against the mast. Slide it down to wedge firmly on top of the cleat, as in figure 74.

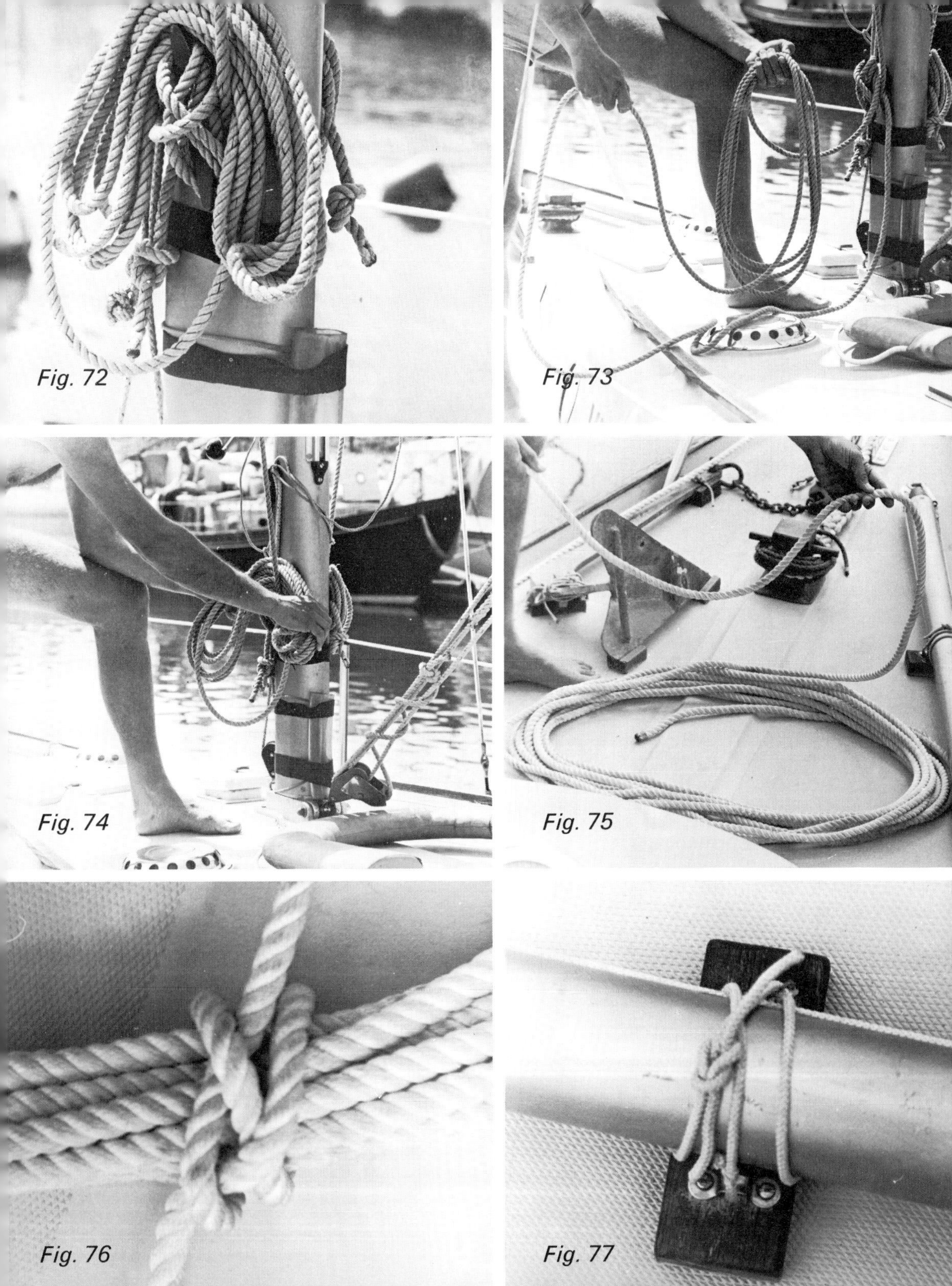

Fig. 72

Fig. 73

Fig. 74

Fig. 75

Fig. 76

Fig. 77

All our halliards are now neatly stowed away and they will not come adrift when the boat starts jumping about and heeling over. What else must we stow away before we go sailing? Mooring lines should be coiled in a similar manner to the halliards, unless they are very long, in which case it will be easier to coil them on the deck instead of in the hand. See fig 75. Once again, coil clockwise and make the diameter of the coil a comfortable size to handle: not so large that the coil is unwieldy and not so small that it becomes excessively bulky. Having coiled our ropes we cannot wedge them all between halliard and mast, of course, so what we do is tie them so they stay coiled and stow them in a handy cockpit locker or in the fo'c'sle (the very front of the boat down below). Sails are probably best stowed in the fo'c'sle as, being in bags, they can be put on deck in harbour to make extra space: so we usually stow our ropes in a cockpit locker, where they will be handy when we want them.

How do we tie the coils up so that they won't fall apart? A simple and very efficient way is by using the knot shown in figs 78 and 79, the Sailor's Coil Hitch. When you have made up the coil, take the free end and half hitch it around the body of the coil as in fig 78. (This turn, forming the beginning of many knots, is called a *half hitch*). Then pass the end round the back of the coil and tuck it over and under as shown by the arrow, so that the knot looks like fig 79. Work the knot tight carefully, starting at the beginning and working through, or it will come loose and fall off. (We term this 'coming adrift'). The finished knot is in fig 76.

One exception to this way of securing and stowing rope is the anchor warp, if you have a nylon one. As this will be very long, we can save locker space, and at the same time keep it handy, by stowing it on deck. Make it up into a fairly large diameter coil, starting from the anchor as we started from the cleat with the halliards. The reason for this is that any kinks will work themselves out if we coil towards the loose end. Then with four short lengths of small line, lash the coil to the guardrails for'ard, pulling the corners out so that the coil lies taut

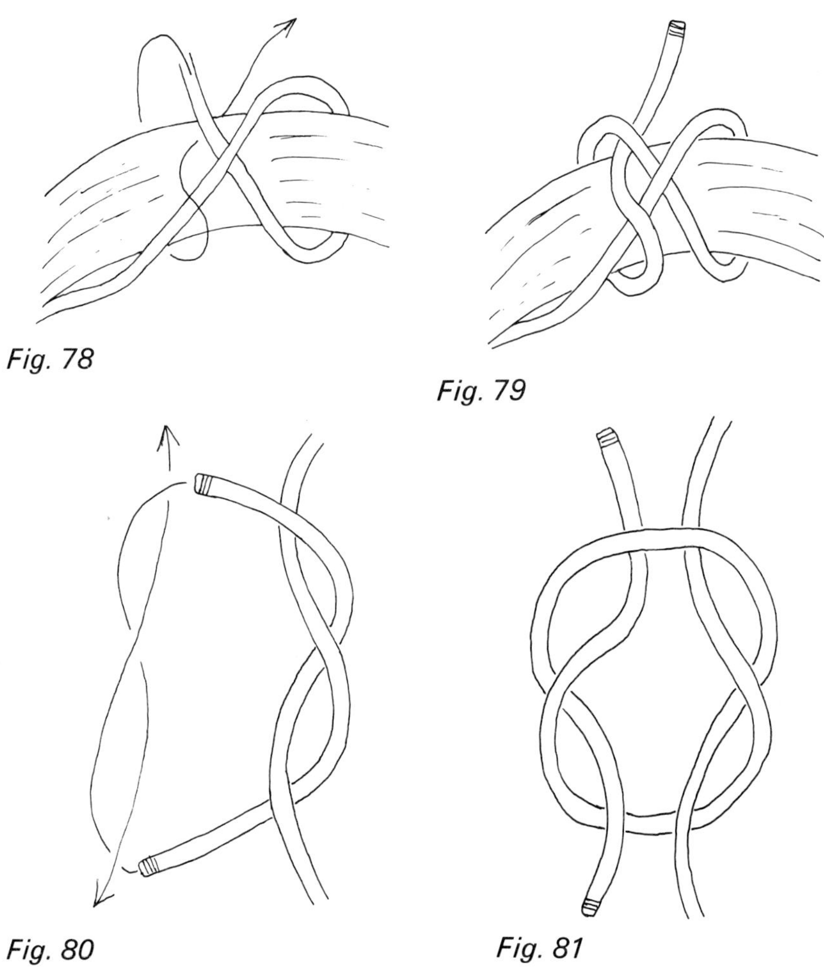
Fig. 78

Fig. 79

Fig. 80

Fig. 81

and secure against the rails. The knot we use for the lashings is the reef knot, shown in figs 80 and 81. Take an end of the line in each hand and lay the left one over the right, then carry it round the back of the right hand end and back up the front, as fig 80 shows. Then do the same with the right-hand end (that is, the original left-hand end, which is now on the right) as shown in fig 81. Fig 77 shows the finished knot, which should be drawn tight to grip all the parts of the coil firmly together and hold them against the guardrail wire. It can easily be wriggled loose when required.

All other gear we can classify as general stowage, and there are two golden rules for stowing it. Keep it wedged and keep it handy. Everything must be firmly wedged on a boat or it will rattle and crash about, getting on your nerves and possibly causing damage. And stow it near where it is likely to be used, if you possibly can. Deck scrubbers, boat hooks, oars for the dinghy, and so on, are best stowed on deck, lashed to the grabrails on the coachroof with short lengths of small line reef-knotted round the parts, or with bits of strong elastic with hooks on the ends (known as shock cord, available from yacht chandlers). Buckets, fishing lines and so on can all go in the cockpit lockers, along with the warps and fenders. Figs 82 (a to g) show various examples of stowage on deck.

Well, now everything is stowed we can think about getting the sails up, but first let us take a look at that ubiquitous nautical object—the shackle. A shackle is simply a U-shaped piece of metal (brass, galvanised steel or stainless steel) with a threaded eyebolt that screws across the open end. See fig 83. Shackles are used on boats for joining just about everything to everything else: shrouds to bottlescrews, bottlescrews to chainplates, sheets to sails, sails to halliards and so on. Consequently they are very important little things and bear looking after. Always keep the threads well greased (lanolin is excellent). Open and close them with a shackle key or marlin spike (see fig 84), and tighten them fairly well so they cannot undo if they flog about (particularly important with shackles joining sheets to sails). If they are permanently in position (shrouds to bottlescrews, for example), tie the eye of the pin to the body of the shackle with a bit of thin wire to stop it undoing. See fig 85. Use galvanised wire so that it won't rust (stainless steel is too springy), and copper wire with brass shackles to reduce the danger of electrolytic corrosion. And always carry a marlinspike with you so you can undo a shackle in a hurry if you need

Fig. 82a

Fig. 82b

Neat pockets at the foot of the mast hold winch handles.

Lockers either side of the cockpit and on the after deck will take a vast amount of gear.

Anchors are normally lashed into chocks with the cable attached.

A very neat way of stowing oars and deck scrubber.

Fig. 82c

Fig. 82d

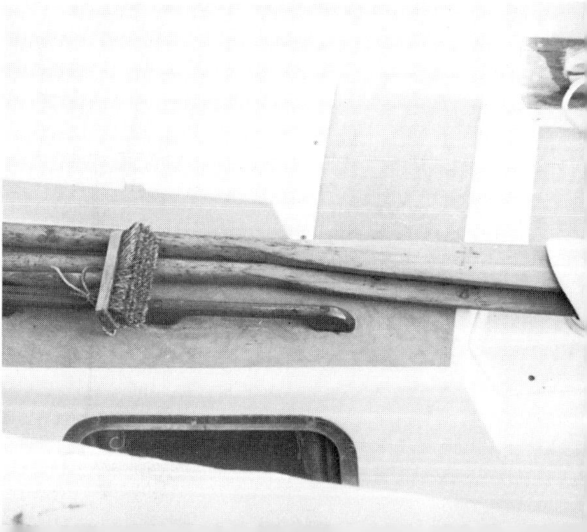

Fig. 82f

Fig. 83e

A general view showing stowage of spinnaker booms, oars, liferaft and rubber dinghy.

An excellent place to keep the dinghy outboard is clamped to a bracket on the pushpit.

A rubber dinghy stowed half inflated on the coachroof.

Fig. 82g

Fig. 83
Fig. 84
Fig. 85
Fig. 88
Fig. 89
Fig. 92

to. A pocket knife with a built-in folding spike is fine, or you can use one of the neat little sheath kits containing knife, spike and pliers—very useful.

Now let us take a look at that most nautical of nautical occupations—tying knots. It can be a fascinating business tying knots, a full-time hobby pursued by many a sailor in the old days and not a few today. When you consider that the Ashley Book of Knots (the bible on the subject) lists some 3854 varieties, you can begin to realise the incredible scope of the subject. Here, however, we are going to consider a mere four (for which I imagine you will be grateful, dear reader) on top of the two we have already discussed. The first is that old Boy Scout standby—the *bowline,* of folk song fame. This knot provides a loop, of any length you wish, at the end of a rope, and has many uses. But before we discuss them, let us tie the knot.

First we decide how long we want the eye to be (you'll see why when we look at the uses of the knot), then we make a small eye in the rope about double this length from the end (so the end can double back and tie into this small eye, leaving the main eye the length we require). See fig 86. The standing part of the rope (the main length leading away from the knot) must lie at the back of this small eye as it will be drawn in against the eye when the knot is tied. We then take the working end, bring it up through the small eye, round the back of the standing part, and back down through the eye. We work the knot tightly and neatly together and draw it taut by pulling on the standing part and the side of the eye that we have just led through the knot. See figs 87 and 88. An excellent way of remembering how to tie the bowline is to image the working end is a rabbit, the small eye its burrow and the standing part a nearby tree. The rabbit then comes up out of its hole, goes round the back of the tree and back down its hole again! Why the rabbit should do this is lost in antiquity but it is a good way of remembering the knot.

What do we use the bowline for? Probably its most useful application is putting an eye in the end of a mooring rope to slip over a

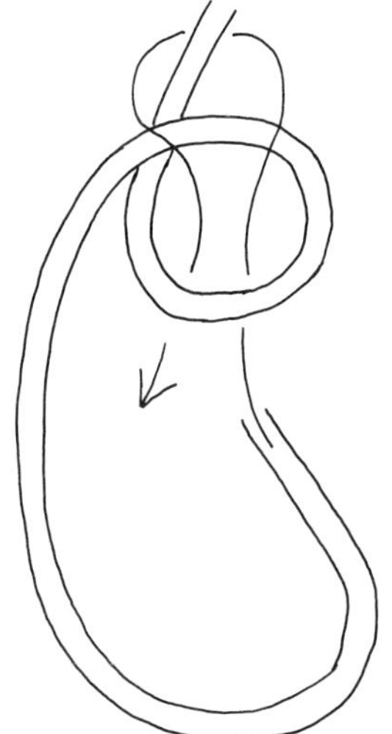

Fig. 86

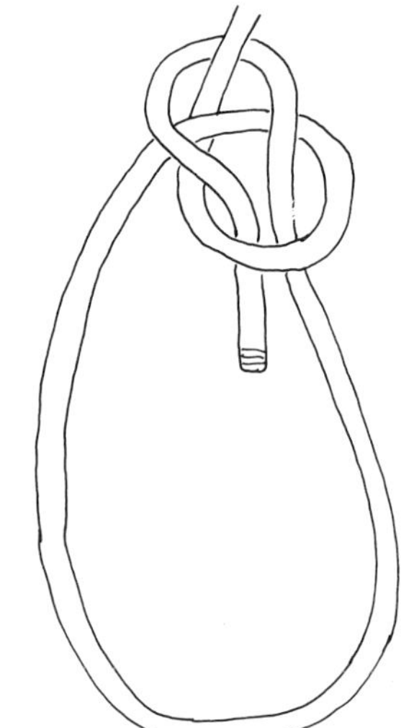

Fig. 87

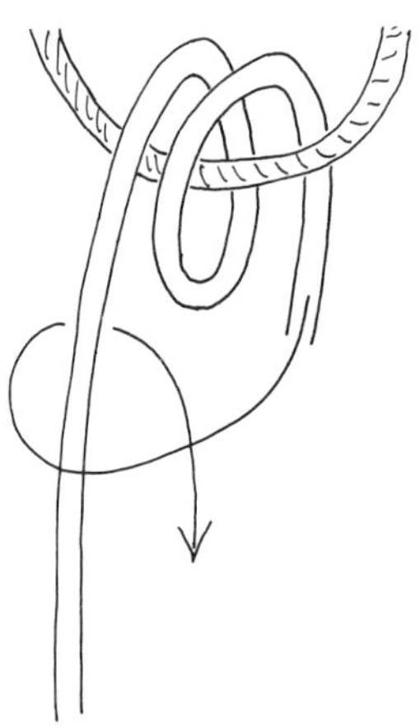

Fig. 90

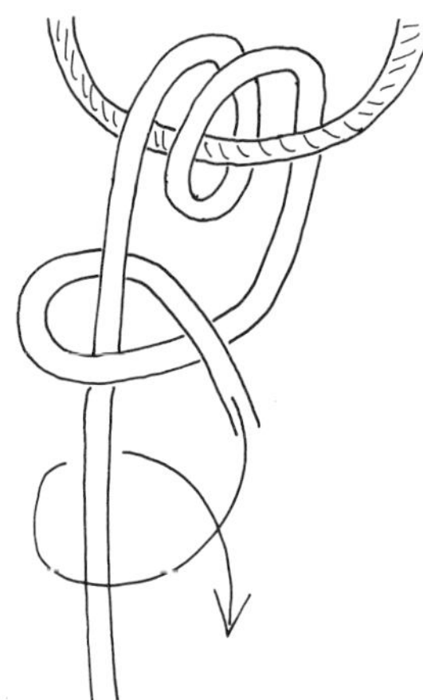

Fig. 91

bollard on the jetty-a bollard being a vertical lump of metal or concrete specially for mooring boats to. And we might mention here that if another mooring eye is already on the bollard when we arrive we don't just drop ours over the top, as the other fellow will have to remove it before he can get to his own. This isn't just a question of courtesy (although that is important) but if there is a lot of strain on our rope when he wants to move his, he might not be able to lift ours off and get it back on again. If it is two o'clock in the morning and pouring with rain he might be tempted just to let go of it, which is likely to be greatly to our detriment. So we dip our eye underneath his before putting it on the bollard. See fig 89.

There are a number of other uses for a bowline, some good, many bad, but the one above is the only one likely to concern us to begin with, so we will stick with that. The point to appreciate about a bowline is that it is not tied tightly around an object, but just dropped over. This means that any movement in the rope, such as the boat drifting back and forth along the jetty, will cause the eye to chafe against the object round which it is tied, and many modern synthetic ropes are particularly susceptible to chafe. A bollard, with its relatively large diameter, is no problem, but when we come to eyes in the tops of buoys or ringbolts (metal rings for mooring to) set in walls, the bowline is totally unsuitable. We need a knot that will grip the ring firmly and not slide about. The answer is the *round turn and two half hitches*.

In fig 90 we take a half turn through the ring, then go round again to complete the *round turn*. The *two half hitches* are then taken with the working end round the standing part as shown by the arrow and fig 91. The knot, if it is to fulfill its function of preventing chafe, must be drawn up good and taut. It will always be found easy to undo. This really is a useful knot as it can be used for almost any job: tying up to railings, ringbolts, buoys etc; tying fenders to the bottoms of stanchions (better than the common practice of tying to the guardrail as the latter can be unduly strained), securing lines to buckets and so

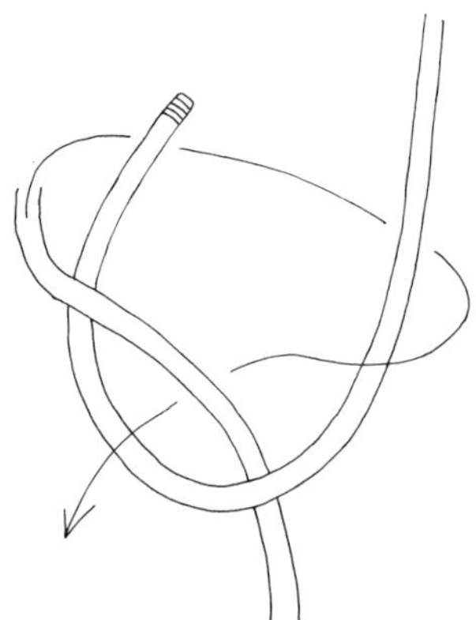

Fig. 93

on—in fact, more or less any time you want to tie a piece of rope to anything. Fig 92 shows a typical use.

The one exception to the above is when we want to tie a piece of rope to another piece of rope (to make a longer mooring line perhaps). For this purpose we use a *sheet bend*, or, if it is to remain in the rope for any length of time, a *double sheet bend*, which is less likely to come adrift with a lot of banging about.

Put an open loop in the end of one rope and pass the end of the other up through this loop, round the back of the loop, from the short end to the long end (standing part), and back across the front of the knot, passing under itself, as in fig 93. Draw up taut. See fig 94 (p. 145). It is important that we pass the end round the back of the loop from the short end first, so that the two short ends of the completed knot are on the same side. If they come out on opposite sides we have a left-handed sheet bend which is not so secure. To make a double sheet bend we simply pass the working end round the back of the loop a second time, across the front beneath itself again, and draw taut. See fig 95. The double sheet bend should be used for extra security, and also for joining two ropes of greatly differing sizes. The reef knot is NOT, repeat NOT suitable for joining two ropes, as it can easily capsize and fall apart. Use it for small lashings, as mentioned earlier, tying up parcels, and, as we shall see in the chapter on Strong Winds, for reducing sail area.

Well, we can now tie ropes together, tie boats to buoys and attach lines to walls and jetties, and that is more or less all we need. There is, however, one other knot I would like to show you, one that is not often seen in sailing books, but very often seen on lorries. That is the *waggoner's hitch*, and it is a very useful knot indeed on board ship. Lorry drivers use it for lashing down loads as it is quick to tie, simple to remember, and most effective. On board ship we find it the ideal knot for lashing down large objects such as wooden or fibreglass dinghies, large cans of spare fuel, and so on. Its great advantage over any other knot for this purpose is that it provides an added purchase

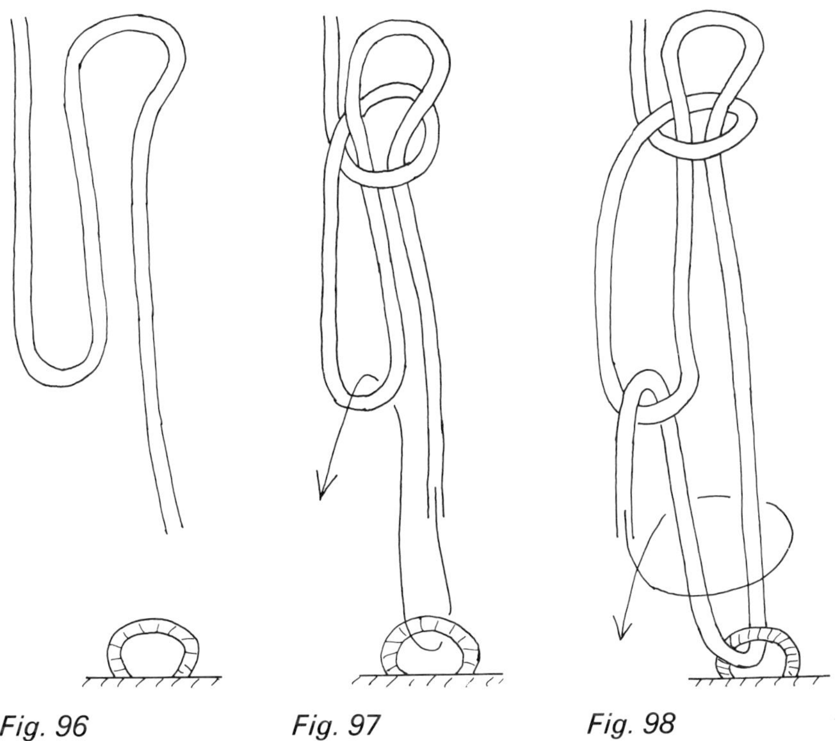

Fig. 96 *Fig. 97* *Fig. 98*

which enables you to pull down really hard on the standing part. As we said earlier, there is a lot of movement on a boat at sea and things must be lashed down very securely indeed if they are not to come adrift. Let's see how we tie it.

Pick up a bight (loop) fairly close to the final lashing point (eyebolt on deck etc) and lay it up alongside the standing part as in fig 96. The rope will have been secured at one end (round turn and two half hitches) and laid over the object to be lashed down, so will be hanging down the opposite side. We then form a loop in the standing part (as we did for the bowline) and slip it over the top of the bight, as in fig 97. The working end is then passed down through the fastening point and back up through the loop of the bight, as indicated by the arrow, to form fig 98. Haul down on the working end as tightly as possible (you can see that the knot forms a simple purchase) and secure the working end with a couple of half hitches, as indicated by the arrow, just as we did with the round turn and two half hitches. Two simple lashings like this will hold a dinghy or whatever secure against anything, and we see a dinghy so lashed in fig 99.

Another excellent way of tightening lashings is by frapping them. This means pulling them sideways with another small lashing as shown in fig 100. If we need a particularly tight and secure lashing on the dinghy for instance, we can lash it down with a couple of waggoner's hitches, then frap the two lashings together on top of the

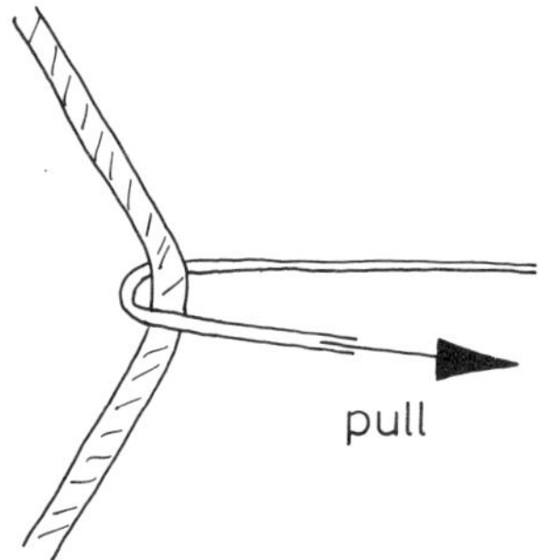

Fig. 100

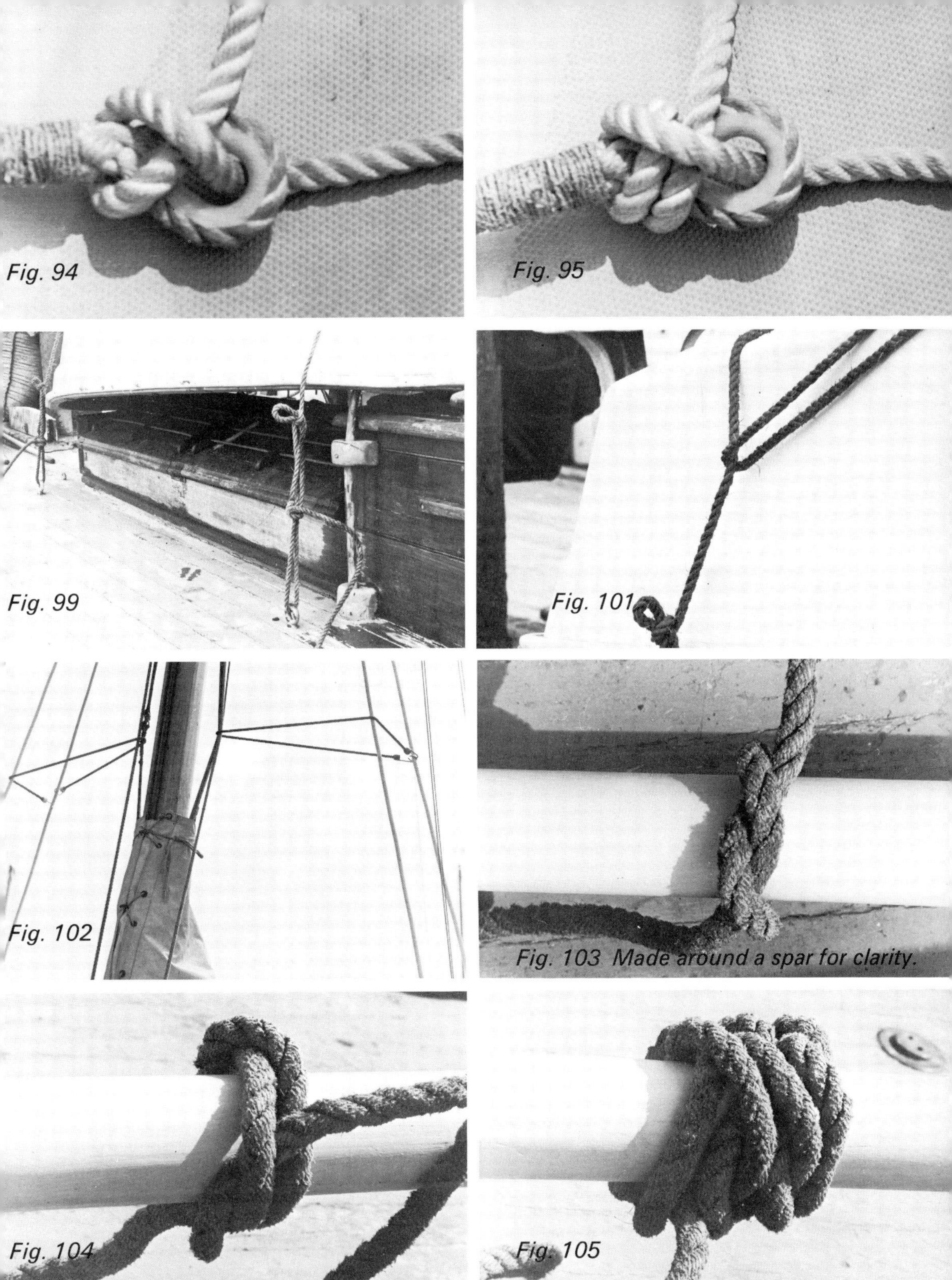

Fig. 94

Fig. 95

Fig. 99

Fig. 101

Fig. 102

Fig. 103 Made around a spar for clarity.

Fig. 104

Fig. 105

dinghy. See fig 101. But the most useful application of frapping lines (as they are called) is for pulling halliards away from the mast when the boat is on the mooring. This prevents them banging against the mast and keeping you awake all night. The noise made by halliards flapping against a metal mast has to be heard to be believed. With a wooden mast they will knock all the varnish off and turn the wood black, and eventually rotten. So do frap your halliards when moored up: your neighbours will certainly appreciate it even if you can sleep through the racket. Haul them out towards the shrouds with short frapping lines of small rope, or use lengths of shock cord with hooks on the end. These are obtainable made up from chandlers. And fix them as high up as you can reach so that they have the maximum effect, one on either side of the mast and both the same height, for neatness. See fig 102.

One more thing we must mention before leaving ropework is the prevention of ropes' ends from unravelling. We do this by means of whippings, which are simply small lashings with very small twine round the end of the rope. The simplest, and one of the best, is the *west country whipping*, so we will stick to that. It consists simply of a series of overhand knots made on opposite sides of the rope, an overhand knot being the first half of a reef knot. Take about two feet of whipping twine and middle it around the end of the rope. Taking the left over the right and tucking it through, we make the first half of a reef knot, as in fig 103. Then, instead of finishing the reef knot, we haul this as tight as possible and take the ends round the back of the rope and do another overhand knot as in fig 104. Then another at the front, another at the back and so on, until the whipping is about half an inch long, hauling each knot as tight as we can. We then finish off by completing a reef knot. See fig 105.

As added security with synthetic rope such as nylon, terylene, polypropylene and so on, we can melt the end of the rope into a fused mass using a lighter or matches. We can do the same with the ends of the reef knot that finishes the whipping. Cut the ends off leaving about a millimetre, then apply a light until they begin to melt, and squash the melting twine into the reef knot. Do it quickly and firmly with your thumb or it might be rather painful. The best way of doing this melting, if you are working in the garage at home, is with a large-tipped soldering iron. The molten rope left on the iron can be cleaned off with a file or sandpaper when cold.

A very useful temporary whipping can be made simply by wrapping plastic electrical insulation tape round the end of the rope. Tuck the end under a strand to begin with, then wind it down good and tight for three or four layers. It will last a surprisingly long time but is not very attractive.

Well, I think that's about as much as we need to know about ropework for the time being. Learn these few knots well; they can be most important, and knowing a few knots well, being able to tie them quickly and instinctively, is far more use than being able to name a couple of dozen but needing the book to tie them.

10 Safety and Weather

Safety is a very emotive word these days, when those who rule us seem sometimes to be so intent on keeping us alive that little is left for actually living. The danger, of course, is that the whole subject of safety can easily become so boring that it is ignored.

But safety is an important subject, and as with ropework, there is quite a lot to it, so I'm going to talk about it for a while. But I'm not going to subject you to a diatribe on how you mustn't go to sea when Grannie's corn twinges, or the importance of wearing a lifejacket in the pub. I'm going to talk about the simple, elementary precautions all real seamen take when they go to sea. For there is little point in having an exciting adventure on the way over to Calais if you don't get home to tell the tale.

To go to sea or not to go to sea—that is without doubt one of the most difficult decisions the small boat sailor ever has to make. And one of the most important. For it is the failure to make this decision correctly that causes a very large proportion of the sailing accidents that we read about. So often a sailor gets into trouble not because he has insufficient experience to cope with the conditions he meets, but because he has insufficient experience to *realise before sailing* that he will not be able to cope with them. And this is the crux of the problem—only experience can tell you whether it is safe for you to go to sea or not. There are so many variable factors involved that it is totally impossible to lay down any hard and fast rules. Identical weather conditions in one place may be dangerous, in another perfectly safe. It may be safe for one boat, but not for a different type;

safe for people with a certain degree of experience, but not for others with only slightly less. It may be safe while the tide is flooding, but not when it turns and ebbs; or vice versa. And so on.

The obvious, glib answer is to ask an experienced local sailor for his opinion. But that is not always a good move. For one thing you are placing a certain responsibility on him, and for another, he probably won't know your experience or your boat. We can certainly ask him what he thinks of the conditions and whether they are likely to change, but we cannot expect him (except in obvious, extreme cases) to tell us whether we should set sail or not. That final responsibility must rest with us. So let us have a look at the factors involved and see if we can sort out some ideas on how best we can make this decision—to sail or not.

The basic problem is the weather, and we can divide weather that is likely to cause us trouble into two categories—bad visibility and strong winds. Let us consider bad visibility first, as it is generally easier to make a decision on visibility than on wind. There are two types of bad visibility—driving rain and spray, and mist and fog. The former, of course, is always associated with and caused by strong winds, and we can dispose of it simply by saying that if the wind is strong enough to cause poor visibility through rain and spray, it is far too strong for all but the most experienced of sailors to be out in. It is also jolly uncomfortable, and quite likely to put you off sailing for life!

Mist and fog is not so easy. If we look out towards the nearby moored boats and cannot see them, then we do not put to sea. Fog is without a doubt the most frightening and dangerous of conditions for the small boat sailor, creating the two-fold dangers of getting lost and possibly wrecked on the coast, and of being run down by a ship. If we arrive at the harbour for a sail and it is foggy, we go home. It is as simple as that. But it is not always thick and obviously foggy. We can have early morning mists that are generally certain to clear by midday. We can have bright, sparkling, sunny harbours, and fog as thick as a bucket half a mile offshore. And we can have calm, peaceful mornings that tempt us out to sea with the mackerel lines over the stern, with a fog that comes down like a blanket the moment we stop bothering to check our position. So it is not always easy to decide what we can safely do.

Fortunately we have someone who can help us considerably with this—the Meteorological Office. Whatever you may think of their forecasts when you head for the beach on a Bank Holiday, their special forecasts for shipping are pretty good, and listening to, and understanding them is a must for the sailor. Broadcast regularly

---

BBC Shipping Forecast Times
Radio 2—1500 metres (200 Khz) only
0633
1355 (1155 on Sundays)
1755
0033

Radio 4—285 m (1052 KHz), 330 m (908 KHz), 434 m (692 KHz) and on V.H.F. (92–95 MHz)
Special inshore forecast broadcast at closedown of programmes (approx 2350) each night. On the Scottish wavelength (809 KHz) the times are 2307 on weekdays, 2321 on Saturdays and 2315 on Sundays.

Radio 3—464 metres (647 KHz) and V.H.F. (90–92.5 MHz)
Inshore forecast daily at 0655.

Coastal Radio Stations give forecasts over the air at certain times for the area they cover. See *Reed's Nautical Almanac* for details (Appendix B).

Certain Meteorological Offices will give forecasts by telephone, and coastguards will give present weather conditions by phone. Full details are in *Reed's Nautical Almanac* (see Appendix B).

Fig. 106

throughout the day (in Britain on Radio 2 at the times shown in figure 106) these Shipping Forecasts give us three very useful types of information. The first thing we get is what is know as the General Synopsis. This is a rather technical description of the prevailing weather pattern over the area covered by the forecast. It enables those with sufficient experience and knowledge of Meteorology to assess how the weather is likely to behave in specific areas of interest to them that are not covered by the forecast. It also enables one, if one listens to and studies it over a period of days, to deduce how the weather will develop over a period of days or even weeks, where the Shipping Forecast commits itself only to predicting the weather twelve hours ahead. An understanding of the General Synopsis is not really essential to us at this stage, and would serve only to confuse, so we will leave it for more experienced days.

What is essential, however, is the main meat of the Shipping Forecast. This comes in two parts: first, the forecast of wind, visibility and general weather conditions for various areas around the country and second, present weather conditions at various observation stations around the country, as shown in fig 107. With a knowledge of both the present weather conditions off the coast and the forecast conditions for the following twelve hours, we are in a good position to be able to judge whether to sail or not. But let us take a look at a typical forecast, as it can sound rather like Chinese unless one knows how to interpret the terminology. It is not difficult, as with many things, if you know how.

The following is a fairly typical example of what you will hear when that cheerful fellow announces: 'Good evening, gentlemen; here is the Shipping Forecast issued by the Meteorological Office at 1710 hours', as the rain hammers down on your coachroof in torrents and the wind screams through your rigging like a banshee, and you thank God you're tucked up in a cosy little Marina just down the road from an equally cosy little pub. But before you sell the boat and take up golf, remember it might be a good forecast for the morrow. This example is

SOUTH-EAST ICELAND
FAEROES
BAILEY
FAIR ISLE
VIKING
HEBRIDES
CROMARTY
FORTIES
FISHER
ROCKALL
MALIN
FORTH
DOGGER
GERMAN BIGHT
TYNE
IRISH SEA
HUMBER
SHANNON
THAMES
FASTNET
LUNDY
DOVER
WIGHT
PORTLAND
PLYMOUTH
SOLE
FINISTERRE
BISCAY
SS Sule Skerry
B Bell Rock
D Dowsing
G Galloper
V Varne
RS Royal Sovereign
PB Portland Bill
S Scilly Isles
Va Valentia
R Ronaldsway
M Malin Head
T Tiree
J Jersey

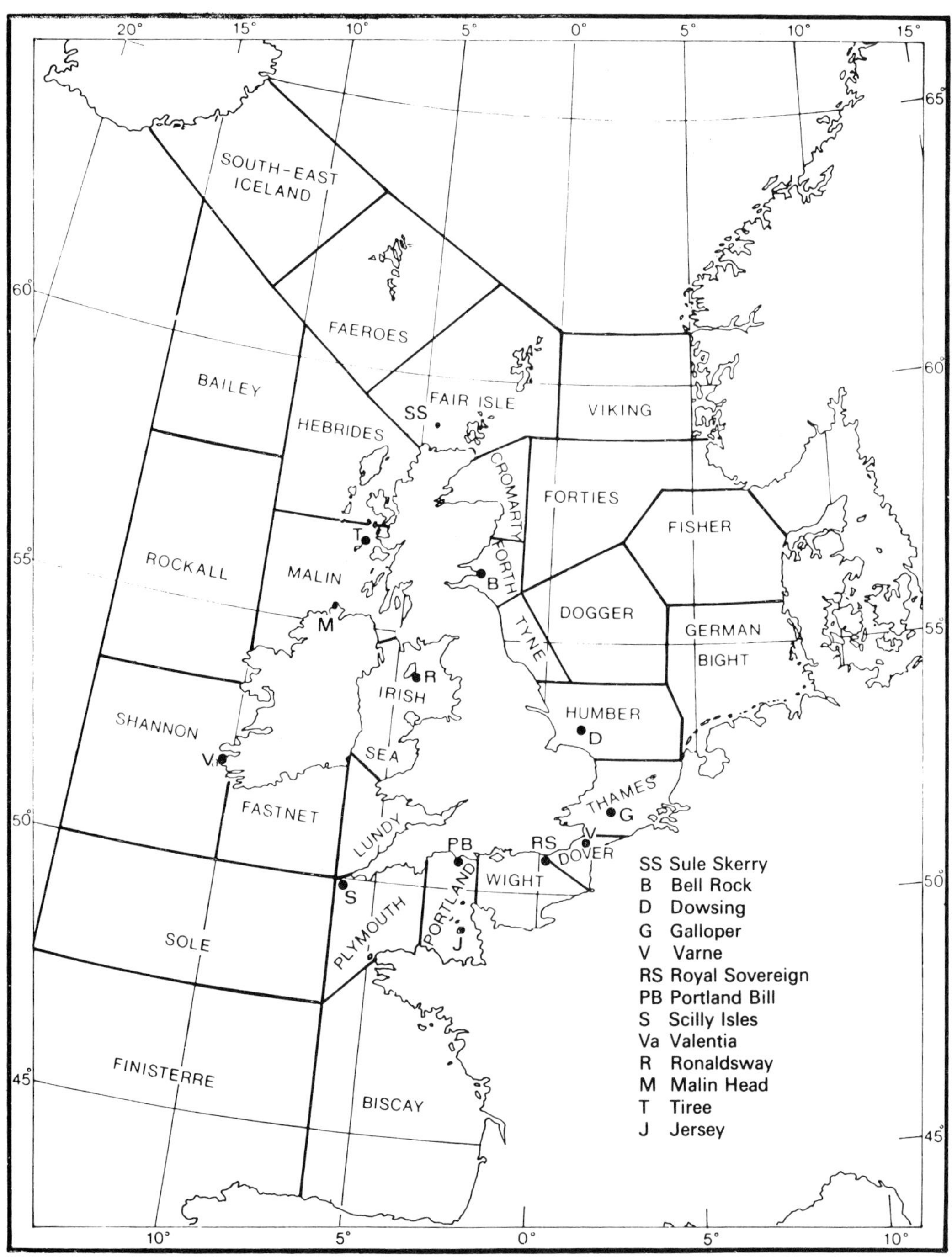

Fig. 107

quoted from a British Shipping Forecast, but the type of information given will be the same wherever you are, except that in the Southern Hemisphere winds blow clockwise round a Low and anti-clockwise round a High. In the Northern Hemisphere these directions are reversed.

'The General Synopsis at 1300 hours. High, North Germany, 1022, slow-moving. High, Jan Mayen Island, 1019, moving slowly south-east to arrive Norwegian Sea by 1300 tomorrow. Shallow Low, north-west Finisterre, 1005, moving north-east, expected north-west Poland, 1002 by 1300 tomorrow.'

Briefly and basically, this gives us the whereabouts, intensities and movements of the areas of high and low pressure that make up the prevailing weather pattern. Put very simply, it is the interaction between these areas of high and low pressure that creates the weather—the air, loosely speaking, flowing from areas of high pressure to areas of low pressure to produce wind. The figures—1022, 1002 etc—denote the heights and depths of the highs and lows in units known as millibars. The importance of these figures, to the experienced, lies in the fact that, just as water will flow faster down a steep mountainside than a shallow one, so air, and therefore wind, will flow faster the steeper the gradient between neighbouring high and low pressure areas. And now let us stop before we get too deep.

After the General Synopsis the announcer will read out the Area Forecasts, those areas having the same weather being lumped together. What we are given is the name of the area (or areas), followed by the wind direction and strength, followed by the general weather conditions (rain, snow, fair etc), followed by the visibility. For example: 'Viking, Forties, Cromarty, Forth—variable 2 becoming south-east 3 to 4; rain at times; good becoming moderate. Tyne, Dogger—variable 2 becoming southerly 3 to 4; fair; moderate, locally poor'. And so on, clockwise around the coast until he reaches South-East Iceland, the order being—Fisher, German Bight, Humber, Thames, Dover, Wight, Portland, Plymouth, Biscay, Finisterre, Sole,

BEAUFORT SCALE OF WIND FORCE

Beaufort Wind Force	Mean Wind Speed Knots	Descriptive Term	Sea Criterion	Probable Height of Waves in Feet
0	0	Calm	Sea like a mirror	-
1	02	Light air	Ripples with the appearance of scales are formed but without foam crests.	$\frac{1}{4}$
2	05	Light breeze	Small wavelets, still short but more pronounced, crests have a glassy appearance and do not break.	$\frac{1}{2}$
3	09	Gentle breeze	Large wavelets. Crests begin to break. Foam of glassy appearance. Perhaps scattered white horses.	2
4	13	Moderate breeze	Small waves, becoming longer; fairly frequent white horses.	$3\frac{1}{2}$
5	18	Fresh breeze	Moderate waves, taking a more pronounced long form; many white horses are formed. (Chance of some spray)	6
6	24	Strong breeze	Large waves begin to form; the white foam crests are more extensive everywhere. (Probably some spray)	$13\frac{1}{2}$
7	30	Near gale	Sea heaps up and white foam from breaking waves begins to be blown in streaks along the direction of the wind.	18
8	37	Gale	Moderately high waves of greater length; edges of crests begin to break into spindrift. The foam is blown in well-marked streaks along the direction of the wind.	23

Fig. 108

Beaufort Wind Force	Mean Wind Speed Knots	Descriptive Term	Sea Criterion	Probable Height of Waves in Feet
9	44	Strong gale	High waves. Dense streaks of foam along the direction of the wind. Crests of waves begin to topple, tumble and roll over. Spray may affect visibility.	23
10	52	Storm	Very high waves with long overhanging crests. The resulting foam in great patches is blown in dense white streaks along the direction of the wind. On the whole the surface of the sea takes a white appearance. Tumbling of the sea becomes heavy and shock-like. Visibility affected.	29
11	60	Violent storm	Exceptionally high waves. (Small and medium-sized ships might be lost to view for a time behind the waves.) The sea is completely covered with long white patches of foam lying along the direction of the wind. Everywhere the edges of the wave crests are blown into froth. Visibility affected.	37
12	68	Hurricane	The air is filled with foam and spray. Sea completely white with driving spray; visibility very seriously affected.	45

The column showing the probable height of the waves in feet has been added to show what may be expected in the open sea remote from land. In enclosed waters, or when near land with an off-shore wind, wave heights will be smaller, and the waves steeper.

It must be realised that it may be difficult to estimate the wind force by the sea criterion, especially at night.

The lag effect between the wind getting up and the sea increasing should be borne in mind.

Fetch, depth, swell, heavy rain and tide effects should be considered when estimating the wind force from the appearance of the sea.

Lundy, Fastnet, Irish Sea, Shannon, Rockall, Malin, Hebrides, Bailey, Fair Isle, Faeroes, South-East Iceland.

Winds are always named with the direction they blow FROM, so a southerly 4 will blow from the south at a strength of force 4. In figure 108 we see the forces by which the strength of the wind is described, and the actual speeds in miles per hour that they represent. This isn't just a bit of nautical mumbo-jumbo, but a very convenient and concise shorthand, and you will very soon find yourself thinking of wind strengths purely in terms of forces rather than miles per hour.

The weather and visibility, once we know where they come in the description, are fairly obviously described, so it will be helpful to run completely through the rest of this forecast so that we can see a fairly wide selection of the sort of information that is given.

'Fisher, German Bight—variable 2 to 3; fair; moderate, locally poor. Humber, Thames—variable 2 becoming southerly 3 to 4; fair; moderate, locally poor with fog patches. Dover, Wight, Portland, Plymouth—south-easterly 2 to 3, occasionally 4 later; fair; moderate to poor with fog banks. Biscay—south-easterly 3 to 4; fair at first, showers later; moderate. Finisterre, Sole—south by west 4 to 5; showers; moderate becoming good. Lundy, Fastnet, Irish Sea—south to south-east 4 to 5, occasionally 6 to 7 in Fastnet at first; fair at first, showers later; moderate, locally poor with fog banks. Shannon, Rockall, Malin—southerly 5 to 7 becoming 3 to 4; showers; moderate, locally poor. Hebrides, Bailey—south-east 4 to 5, increasing 6 to 7; rain at times; good becoming moderate. Fair Isle, Faeroes—variable 2, becoming easterly 5 to 6, perhaps 7 later; rain at times; good becoming moderate to poor. South-East Iceland—variable 2, becoming easterly 5 to 6; fair at first, rain later; good; no icing.'

By this time, unless we have developed a form of shorthand in order to get all the information down, we will still be laboriously writing down the word Biscay! Have a look at fig 109. Maps like this (without the forecast information) are easily obtainable from chandlers or chart agents, and generally come either as a pad containing a number of them, or as one of those magic-write jobs that rub out by sliding something along behind the plastic front. Personally I like the latter as they are small and simple, but the pads have the advantage that past forecasts can be kept and compared with the present one in order to see the trend of the weather changes. Whichever you use, it can be annotated as in the figure just as quickly as even the fastest-speaking BBC announcer can rattle off the forecast. And if the programmes are running a little late, they can sure rattle them off fast! Compare the information on the figure with the forecast that we have just related, and you will see how the shorthand works. You can work out your own of course (you may even be a qualified shorthand typist!), but the advantage of plotting it directly on to the map is that it thus gives a very clear picture of the conditions all round the coast, and, as we shall see shortly, the forecasts for areas adjacent to your own can very often be more important than that for your own.

Before we go on to the present weather reports, let us take a quick look at these wind directions as many of you will probably have been baffled by such esoteric terms as south by west and so on. The direction North is towards the North Pole, South towards the South Pole. If we drive from Southampton to Newcastle we are going roughly North; South will be behind us, West on our left hand and East on our right. (These last two are easily remembered as their initial letters spell WE). If the wind blows against us on this journey, it is a North wind; behind us a Southerly and so on. The various directions in between these four main ones are shown in the diagram in fig 110, and they have a certain logic to them. Midway between North and East is North-East, between North and North-East is North-North-East, and just to the East of North is North by East. The same follows for all the other sections. Some compasses (gadgets that tell us which way the boat is pointing) are marked like this, but not all. We shall look at them in the chapter on Navigation. These directions are, however, invariably used for denoting wind direction. Now let us finish off the forecast.

H1019
S Nor. Sea 1300
SOUTH-EAST ICELAND
FAEROES
BAILEY
HEBRIDES
SS
FAIR ISLE
VIKING
CROMARTY
FORTIES
FISHER
ROCKALL
MALIN
T
B
FORTH
DOGGER
M
TYNE
GERMAN BIGHT
R
IRISH SEA
SHANNON
Va
HUMBER
D
H1022 slow
THAMES
G
FASTNET
LUNDY
PB
RS
V
DOVER
WIGHT
PORTLAND
S
NW Poland 1300
L1005
SOLE
PLYMOUTH
J
FINISTERRE
BISCAY
SS Sule Skerry
B Bell Rock
D Dowsing
G Galloper
V Varne
RS Royal Sovereign
PB Portland Bill
S Scilly Isles
Va Valentia
R Ronaldsway
M Malin Head
T Tiree
J Jersey

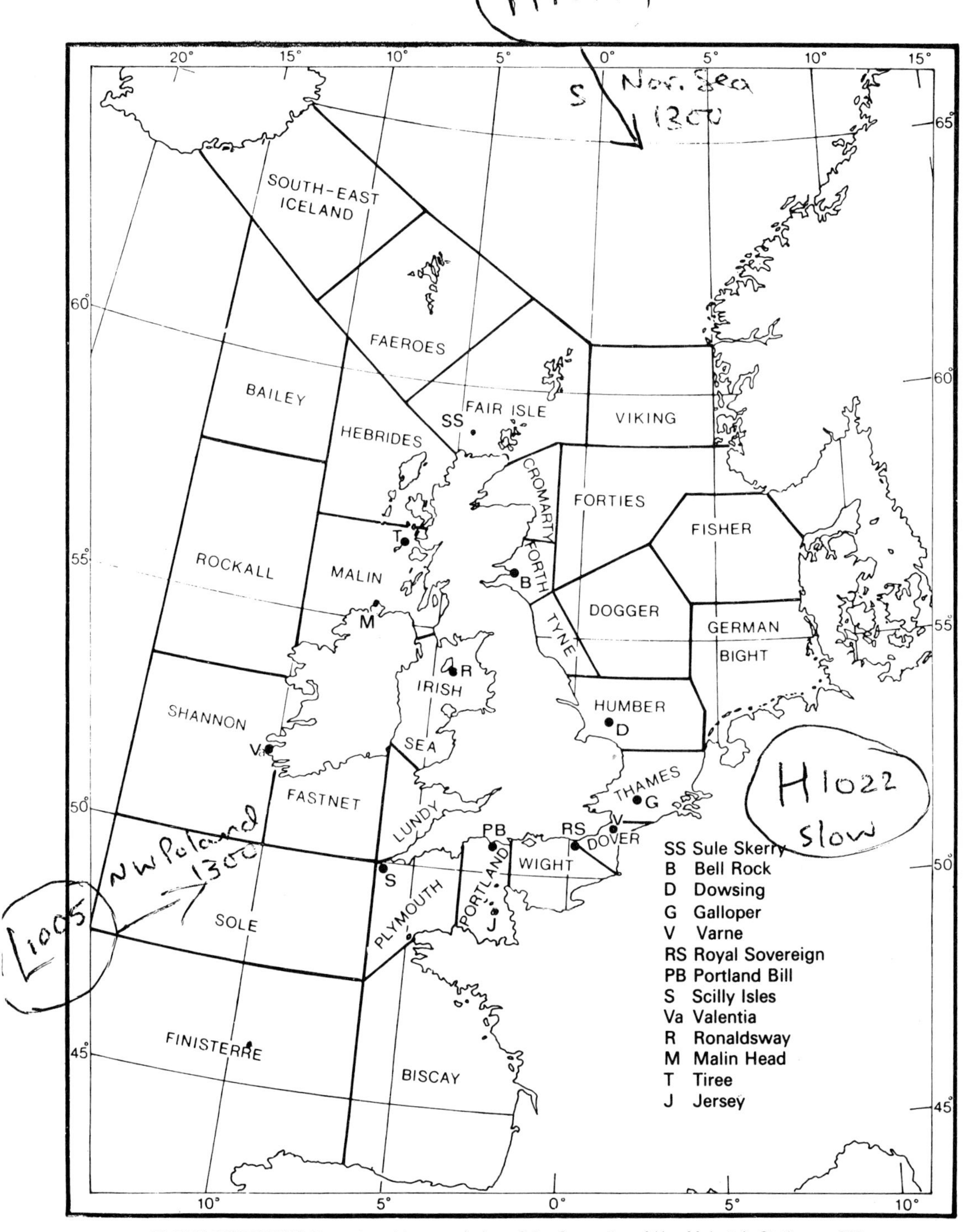

Fig. 109

Date 10th June 1976
Time 1710

Sea Areas

Sea Area	Forecast	Sea Area	Forecast
VIKING	V2 bec SE 3/4	BISCAY	SE 3/4 - F lsr Sh lat - M
FORTIES	R G bec M	FINISTERRE	S x W 4/5
CROMARTY		SOLE	Sh M bec G
FORTH		LUNDY	S/SE 4/5 occ 6/7 F lsr
TYNE	V2 bec S 3/4	FASTNET	F lsr, Sh lat,
DOGGER	F M loc P	IRISH SEA	M loc P FBs
FISHER	V 2/3	SHANNON	S 5/7 bec 3/4
GERMAN BIGHT	F M loc P	ROCKALL	Sh M loc P
HUMBER	V2 bec S 3/4	MALIN	
THAMES	F M loc P FPs	HEBRIDES	SE 4/5 mic 6/7
DOVER	SE 2/3 occ 4 later	BAILEY	R at times G bec M
WIGHT	F M/P FBs	FAIR ISLE	V2 bec E5/6 perhaps 7 later
PORTLAND		FAEROES	R G bec M/P
PLYMOUTH		SOUTH EAST ICELAND	V2 bec E5/6 F lsr - R lat - G

no icing

Coastal Stations

Station	Report	Station	Report
TIREE		PORTLAND BILL	E4 - 6' - 1018↓s
SULE SKERRY	Calm - 27' - 1019↑s	SCILLY ISLES	ExS 4 - 6' - 1015↓
BELL ROCK	SSE 3 - 12' - 1018—	VALENTIA	SExS 5 - haze 13' - 1010↓
DOWSING	SE4 - 11' - 1019	RONALDSWAY	SE2 - 5' - 1017↓s
GALLOPER	NNE3 - 11' - 1019↓s	MALIN HEAD	ExN 4 - 22' - 1015↓s
VARNE	N3 - 5' - 1019	JERSEY	
ROYAL SOVEREIGN	NExE3 - 11' - 1018↓		

Remarks

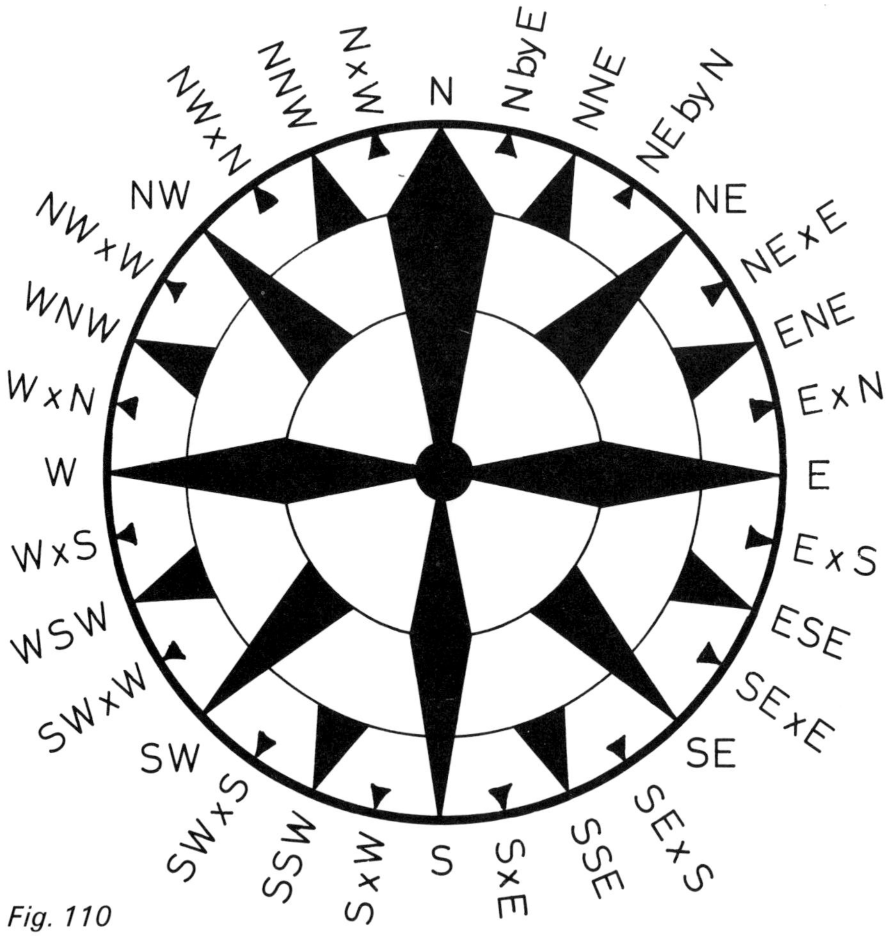

Fig. 110

'Here are the reports from Coastal Stations at 1600 hours. Tiree—south-south-east 2; rain in past hour; 8 miles; 1016 falling slowly.' We have the name of the station (see fig 107), followed by the wind direction and strength; the general weather; the visibility; the barometer reading and its movement. A barometer is a gadget that measures air pressure in millibars, and is an extremely important instrument on board a boat, being one of the best methods of foretelling the onset of bad weather. We will look at its uses in more detail towards the end of this chapter. For now, let us finish the reports from coastal stations. 'Sule Skerry—calm; 27 miles; 1019 rising slowly—(if there is nothing special to report on the weather—rain etc—nothing is said). Bell Rock—south-south-east 3; 12 miles 1018 steady. Dowsing—south-east 4; 11 miles; 1019. Galloper—north-north-east 3; 11 miles; 1019 falling slowly. Varne—north 3; 5 miles; 1019. Royal Sovereign—north-east by east 3; 11 miles; 1018 falling. Portland Bill—east 4; 6 miles; 1018 falling slowly. Scilly—east by south 4; 6 miles; 1015 falling. Valentia—south-east by south 5; haze; 13 miles 1010 falling. Ronaldsway—south-east 2; 5 miles; 1017 falling slowly. Malin Head—east by north 4; 22 miles 1015 falling slowly. And that is the end of the shipping forecast. Good sailing.'

All that takes less than five minutes for the announcer to read out, so you can see it comes out quite quickly. However, now that we have it all plotted on our little map, what does it all mean?

Well, let us take the area forecasts as they are basically the most important. Let us imagine we are sailing from Plymouth Harbour. We listen to the forecast and it says: 'Dover, Wight, Portland, Plymouth: south-easterly 2 to 3, occasionally 4 later; fair; moderate to poor with fog banks.' Well, the wind is fine. Force 2 to 3 is a lovely peaceful sailing breeze, force 4 a bit stronger—enough to give us a good thrash to windward, with a bit of invigorating spray in our faces. The weather is given as fair, which is pretty meaningless but probably means it won't rain. But the visibility is a different matter. Unless you are very experienced it would be extremely foolish to go out to sea with visibility forecast as 'poor with fog banks'. You might not run into a fog bank, but then again you might; and it is a pretty unnerving, as well as dangerous experience. You would probably be all right to sail in the harbour, as fog banks tend to lie offshore, but keep a weather eye skinned for any sign of it rolling in from seaward, and keep a constant check on your position. If you see the fog begin to roll in from seaward, get back to your mooring immediately.

If the visibility had been given as good, then off you go. You have a lovely day's sailing ahead. If it is moderate, then be careful. Don't stray too far from the harbour, and check the adjacent area forecasts. If they give fog, or poor visibility, then be prepared for it to drift into your area. As a general rule the weather comes into the British Isles from the west, so it is the areas to the west of you that need checking. The prevailing weather pattern is a continuous series of depressions (low pressure areas) coming in from the Atlantic. These invariably produce the strong winds and rain, and the rapidly changing conditions that can be so dangerous to the unwary sailor. So listen in the General Synopsis for news of depressions and check the area to the west of you. In this forecast, for instance, we have a shallow low (shallow meaning not very intense, and therefore unlikely to produce very strong winds or gales) to the north-west of Finisterre moving north-east. And if we check the area to the west of us (Sole) we find that the winds are indeed stronger than those forecast for us in Plymouth. It has also shifted to west of south (a sign of an approaching depression), and rain is forecast. So we must be aware of the possibility that that weather will reach us a bit sooner than forecast. If the depression suddenly decides to speed up, then it will. And force 4 to 5 can be quite a strong wind for an inexperienced sailor.

To elaborate a little on this prevailing weather pattern, we can say that depressions (low pressure areas) generally come in from the west, bringing wind and rain, at speeds of anything up to 30 miles per hour. The steeper the fall in pressure from edge to centre, the stronger will be the winds. See fig 111. This shows how they are drawn on weather maps, the lines simply joining places of equal pressure, much like the contour lines on a map. The closer together the lines, the stronger will be the wind. Gales (force 8 and over) are generally caused by deep depressions and are to be avoided. Anything over force 6 in fact is a lot of wind for a small boat in anyone's hands, force 6 itself often being referred to as a yachtsman's gale.

Anticyclones (high pressure areas) can come from anywhere, are

HIGH
1025
1024
1020
1016
1012
LOW
995
996
1000
1004
1008
1012
1016

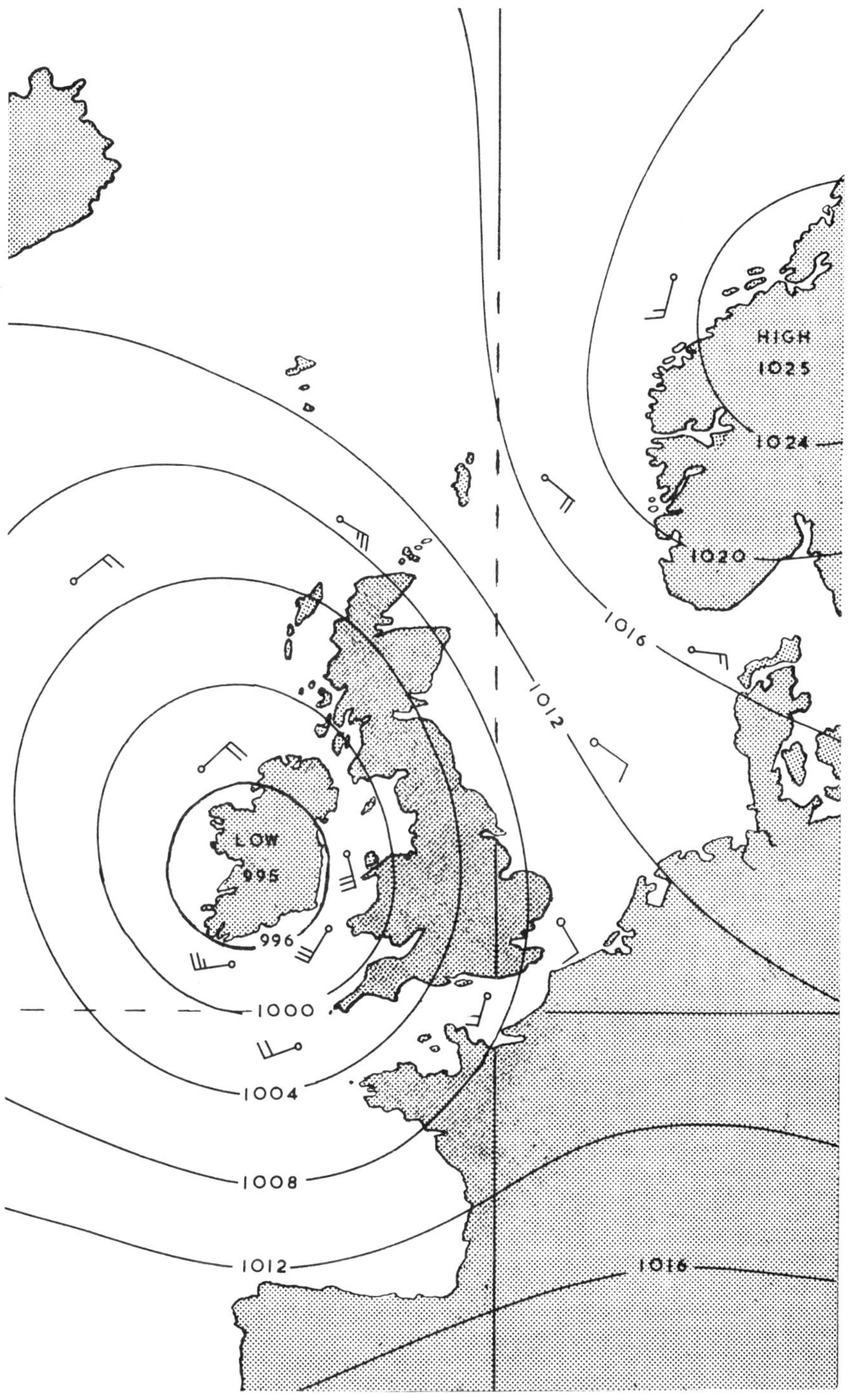

Fig. 111

generally much slower moving, and tend to bring fine weather, light winds and frequently fog. They also divert the courses of depressions, just like opposite poles of a magnet, so an anticyclone over France, for instance, will tend to push the arriving depressions to the north, very often out of harm's way for those of us who sail in the English Channel.

And that is as far as we are going to go into the weather. There is enough here for us to make some useful sense out of the shipping forecast, and assess the weather well enough to help us make the decision to sail or not. Remember that, particularly with approaching depressions, the weather can change very quickly indeed; not even the Met. Office can guarantee that the depression will continue on the same course and speed. As we saw before, a slight increase in the speed of approach of a depression can bring the weather forecast for Sole into Plymouth long before the Met. boys say it will. So think ahead, and watch your barometer. The barometer tells us the air pressure, and in this instance, in Plymouth, would be falling steadily and slowly due to the approach of the depression. If the rate of fall stays constant, then the Met. forecast is probably right. If it begins to fall quicker, then it probably means the depression has increased its speed. The wind will begin to pipe up, and suddenly we will not be enjoying the force 2 to 3 that was forecast for Plymouth, but the 4 to 5 given for Sole. We might even pick up the 6 to 7 given for Fastnet. And that is a lot of wind. So watch that barometer—it is one of the sailor's best friends.

Finally, let us not forget the present weather reports from coastal stations. They give us the priceless information of how far the weather has progressed in accordance with the forecast. This is particularly helpful for seeing how a depression is moving in. Sailing off Plymouth, for example, with the forecast we have discussed, we know that the weather at the Scillies is the weather we will experience in a few hours' time.

So listen to all the forecasts religiously, if possible a few days before sailing so that you can see how the weather is progressing and whether it seems to be building up to anything. If you cannot fathom it out, ring your local Met. Office (listed in *Reed's Nautical Almanac*—the yachtsman's bible) and ask for a local forecast. Tell them what you intend doing; they are invariably very helpful and friendly. Then decide whether the conditions are suitable for you to sail. If in doubt—don't. Stay on the mooring and watch how the weather shapes, compared with your assessment of it. There is no better way to learn.

11 Safety and Equipment

If we study the weather properly, as we discussed in the last chapter, and stay on the mooring when conditions are likely to be bad, we are more than halfway to living to a ripe old age. There are a few other considerations, however, and we shall take a look at them now.

The first is the business of falling overboard, which is not to be recommended for various reasons. There are two ways of approaching this problem: you can prevent it or you can cure it. We prevent it by means of harnesses such as the one shown in fig 112. Made of webbing, they simply strap around the shoulders and a line is attached with a spring clip for fixing to a strong point on the boat, such as a stanchion or shroud. NEVER clip them to the guardrails as this imposes an unfair strain on them. Then when you do fall against them, they may be weakened to the extent that they will not hold you. Ideally these should prevent you from going over the side at all, but on a very small boat a line long enough to give you manoeuvrability (very important) will probably be too long to prevent this. They will, however, keep you attached to the boat, which is half the battle. Whoever is left on board can then round up into the wind or heave to (see next chapter) and haul you back aboard.

A lifejacket, shown in fig 113, will not, of course, stop you going over the side, but it will keep you afloat when you get there. And it can be surprisingly difficult even for a strong swimmer to stay afloat when he is loaded down with jeans and sweaters and so on. There are two basic types of lifejacket, the buoyancy aid (fig 114) and the true lifejacket (fig 113). The difference is that whereas a lifejacket will keep

Fig. 112

Fig. 113

Fig. 114

you afloat indefinitely and your head above water, the buoyancy aid (as its name implies) will simply help you stay afloat, and it will not hold your head above water. The buoyancy aid, however, as you can see from the photos, is a good deal less cumbersome. It is also cheaper. And therein lie its virtues.

The whole question of safety, and particularly lifejackets, is a very emotional one, but I shall stick my neck out against the pundits and try to make it as simple as, in reality, it is. The fact of the matter is that for pottering about in the harbour or sheltered waters a buoyancy aid is perfectly adequate. The chances of being in the water more than a few minutes are very small indeed, and only a gentle treading of water is necessary to stay afloat with a buoyancy aid. Children should wear them at all times, and adults in rough weather or if they cannot swim well. If you are unsure of your footing at first, then wear one until you have more confidence, and have developed sea legs. In the final analysis, carefulness and commonsense are probably the greatest of all guarantees of safety. The old adage of one hand for the ship and one for yourself still basically holds good, and in sheltered waters will keep you on board as well as anything. It is too easy to get so obsessed with the questions of safety harnesses and lifejackets that you forget simply to hang on tightly to something, just as you would on a swaying tube train!

At sea, however, things are different. The waves are bigger, and the motion of a small sailing boat can be very sudden and violent at times. It is easy to be caught unawares as the boat lurches, and be thrown over the guardrail (or under it), and the force of a sudden lurch can pull your hand free from a grip without even trying. In all but the quietest of weather at sea, the most experienced sailors invariably wear a harness at all times, even when sat in the cockpit.

Wearing a harness obviates the need to wear a lifejacket, but not the necessity for carrying them on board. And they should be true lifejackets, not buoyancy aids. If you do go over the side at sea, you may well be in the water for quite a long time. But when do we wear lifejackets? Well, if the probability is that you will be going over the side of a boat that remains afloat, then wear a harness. The boat is the best lifejacket you have, so keep yourself attached to it. If the probability is that the boat will sink (in fog, when the main danger is collision or stranding, for instance), then wear a lifejacket, but NOT a harness: with a sudden sinking, such as might happen in fog, you may get tangled up in it, and a boat can sink pretty quickly if it gets run down by a big ship.

But above all, enjoy yourself. That is what we all go to sea for, not to get tangled up in a lot of lines, jackets, red tape and amateur dramatics. There is quite enough of that ashore. Safety is simply a matter of commonsense and a few elementary, logical, seamanlike precautions: such as always having the auxiliary motor running and ticking over when entering harbour or negotiating narrow and restricted waters—just in case we should need to manoeuvre more quickly than the sails will allow us; giving the engine an occasional run for a few minutes when sailing in fog, so that we can be sure it will start instantly and give us power immediately should we need it, when a super-tanker looms out of the mist on a collision course; or having the anchor ready for letting go in restricted waters. It is a question of thinking ahead, and being prepared for anything that might happen.

But aside from commonsense there are certain items of equipment we should carry on board in case of emergency. The two most important are probably a box of flares, and a liferaft. Neither are really necessary for pottering in the harbour, but I am sure you won't be content to stay there very long when you see the blue horizon beckoning. Firing a red flare will alert anyone who sees it, and someone, probably the lifeboat, will come rushing out to help you. These are for real emergencies only, and the lifeboat cox'n will not be very pleased if he is called out simply because you want a tow in to make the pub before closing time! It happens. Neither will he be pleased if he is called out for a simple problem that could easily have been prevented by a little forethought. The lifeboat is not like the A.A.

or R.A.C., and one of its jobs is not to fill up your petrol tank if you run out twenty miles off shore. It is, quite simply, to save your life if it is in danger, and a red flare will call it out. So have a box on board, just in case, and read the instructions, so you will know what to do if you have to fire one in a hurry.

Liferafts are a mixed blessing on a small boat. They are expensive, need regular servicing and proper stowage on board—handy but clear of the water, where they invariably take up a lot of space just where you want to sunbathe or stow the dinghy. As with lifejackets, this can be a very emotional, and often overdramatised, question. My advice is that if your sailing consists of harbour work and short coastal hops, a perfectly adequate compromise is to have a rubber dinghy (a good one) as your tender, and keep it stowed, fully inflated if possible, half inflated if there just is no room, on the coachroof, and let that serve as a liferaft also. Lash it down with small line that can easily be cut in a hurry, and keep the pump in it, tied on to something. If you're going any distance offshore, then a proper little liferaft should be stowed on the coachroof and the inconvenience tolerated.

Even half a mile off the coast you are a long way from the shops if something breaks, so carry a good stock of spares such as shackles, small cordage for lashing things, spare plugs for outboards and petrol auxiliaries, fan belts, light bulbs and so on. There is no need to carry the vast stocks of spares that long-distance sailors take with them, as a bit of string and a few lengths of wood will enable you to lash up most things sufficiently to get you home; but do carry a set of tools, particularly for dealing with engine problems. We will look at this again in the chapter on handling under power.

What else must we carry on board? Well, one of the greatest hazards on board a boat is fire, in spite of all that water around us. If we get a fire on board a boat, it will almost certainly be involved with fuel, or fat in the galley, so water is not simply useless but positively dangerous, as it will simply spread the fire around with the burning fuel floating on top of it. Fire, therefore, is an absolute menace on board and we must be equipped to deal with it promptly and efficiently. Far and away the best equipment for dealing with galley fires is an asbestos fire blanket. Keep one hanging up near the galley—not in it or you might not be able to reach it. For engine and fuel fires the best answer is a decent-sized foam or dry powder extinguisher, handy to but not in the engine compartment. Another one right for'ard is an excellent idea as a back-up, and if you can afford them, a couple of tiny aerosol dry powder jobs could be useful for small flare-ups. There is a type available that can be shut off at any time, so it avoids too much mess if you put the fire out quickly. But do remember afterwards that it is part-used.

The prevention of fire, as with most things, is largely commonsense, but there are a few useful points I would like to make. If you are planning an inboard auxiliary engine, make it a diesel, which is far safer than petrol. Small diesels are available these days that do not have the problems of weight and vibration that have always constituted the argument against them. Personally I would never have an inboard petrol auxiliary. It is too easy for something to go wrong without you noticing immediately, and a petrol leak will not drip harmlessly onto the road as it will from your car, it will pour into the bilge and mix with the air just as it does in the cylinder of an engine, until you light the stove to make a cup of tea and it explodes just as it does in an engine cylinder. And it will blow your boat to bits!

If you have a petrol outboard, stow the fuel in cans on deck, then any leakage of fumes or spillage of fuel will go overboard. But be very careful where you smoke, and make sure the cans seal properly and are lashed securely as far from the cockpit (where people are likely to smoke) as possible. You cannot be too careful.

Gas for cooking stoves poses a similar problem, except that the system is simpler and therefore much easier to make safe. The gas bottles should be in a cockpit locker that is sealed off from the bilge with a drain hole over the side, so that any leakage will drain harmlessly away. Make sure all the piping is solid, secure and of a proper material recommended for use with low-pressure gas systems. Any old bit of rubber tubing is not good enough, it should be either copper piping or a special reinforced plastic material, and the latter should really only be used where it needs to be flexible. If you then make sure the stove is not in a draught that could blow it out, and always make a point of turning off the gas at the bottle when you have finished cooking, you will be all right.

You can buy special gas and petrol detection devices which sound an alarm if the concentration of vapours in the bilge begins to get towards the dangerous mark. They are rather sensitive, however, and need to be set up carefully if they are not to be totally useless; either not reacting when petrol is thrown over them, or regaling you with a symphony of buzzers and red lights whenever you sail past a sewage outfall. A much simpler and cheaper way of keeping the bilge clear of dangerous vapours (for a certain amount, especially gas, always gets about the place) is just to give the bilge pump a dozen dry strokes every morning. If you have a drop of water in, pump that out first, then give an extra dozen strokes. That will pump out any vapours lying in the bilge, and done regularly will keep the boat free and prevent a dangerous build-up

Another useful safety dodge for gas is to smear a little soapy water round the connection when you change a bottle. The slightest leak will show up as a succession of bubbles coming though the foam. If this happens, check the washer is not worn, and replace it if it is. Always carry a few spares of these gas bottle washers, and use the proper spanner supplied for doing up this joint. Keep it in the locker next to the bottles.

Although fibreglass boats should not leak like wooden ones (which generally work a bit here and there and produce seepages, especially if old), there are various places water can get in, such as through the stern tube, which is a tube through which the propellor shaft passes. This should have a grease nipple on it which enables you to pump grease in every now and then (every few hours when motoring—once a week when not) to supplement the packing and prevent leakage; but dribbles can occur. Water also gets in through hatchways from rain and spray, and it wants removing. So make a point of pumping out the bilge pump once a day as a habit, finishing off with the dry strokes for gas. You will then be able to tell in good time whether she is making any more water than usual, and you can search for the reason immediately. It will probably be that the stern tube greaser has run out of grease!

Always carry some form of standby bailing system in case the pump packs up, even if only a bailer and bucket (which at least have the

Fig. 115 This is the large version operating two diaphragms, one either side of the body.

Fig. 116 One side is open, showing the diaphragm (centre) and the rubber flap valves in the bottom corners. All are removed simply by unscrewing the plates holding them in, and the central nut attaching the diaphragm to the handle. The other side of this pump is identical.

merits of being unlikely to break down!). A spare bilge pump is ideal, and spare diaphrams and valves should also be carried. Whale-type pumps are simple, easy to operate and very effective. See figs 115 and 116. If you have one, take it to bits and see how it works so that if it breaks down (usually through foreign matter jamming the valves) you can mend it quickly and easily. All you have to do is unscrew the large clip holding the diaphragm to the body of the pump, and pull the two apart. Unscrewing a bolt through the handle enables you to replace the diaphram (if it gets torn), and the valves are simply rubber flaps screwed to the body which can be cleared or replaced in seconds.

If you are going any distance off shore, carry a radio with the long wave so that you can listen to the shipping forecasts, and always have hot drinks and plenty of warm clothes on board. It is surprising how cold it can suddenly turn at sea. Oilskins and rubber boots (short, lightweight ones are best) are also a must for keeping dry. Nothing makes you more miserable (and consequently inefficient) than being cold and wet, and even if you set sail in a swimsuit in blazing sunshine, the weather can turn cold and wet very quickly.

A compass, of course (as we shall see in the chapter on Navigation), is a must for coastal sailing, but it is also wise to have one on board at all times, just in case. You might get caught out by sudden fog or mist, and if you have a compass on board, a quick check of the direction of the harbour before the mist closes in will tell you which way to steer. If you haven't got one you will very soon find out how easy it is to sail in circles when you don't know your heading!

There may seem to be a lot to remember in all this safety business, but remember that very little of it is essential for your exploratory potter around the harbour. Lifejackets for the children and a little care and commonsense will be quite sufficient. Make sure everything is working properly and you have a grasp of the basic techniques of sailing as discussed at the beginning of the book, and you won't go far wrong. A few trips round the harbour or bay to get to know the boat and her equipment, and all this will become very much clearer. You can then gradually progress to more ambitious things as you become experienced and more knowledgeable.

One last thing we must mention before we leave this chapter, is the business of avoiding other boats. There are very clear-cut International Rules for this and they state quite simply that:

1) All boats under power (be they motor boats or sailing boats under auxiliary engines) must keep clear of boats under sail;

2) When two boats approach under sail, the one on port tack (with the wind coming from the port side) must keep clear of the one on starboard tack, whether close-hauled, reaching or running;

3) If two boats are on the same tack, the one that is to windward of the other must keep clear. This can have quite subtle interpretations when racing, but as far as we are concerned it means boats running keep clear of those reaching, and they both keep clear of boats that are closehauled.

If you see another boat on a steady bearing and you are obliged to keep clear, then alter course decisively and in good time so that you pass well clear and the other fellow can see exactly what you are doing. If you are not obliged to keep clear, then hold your course so that the other fellow can be certain of which way to turn to avoid you. If he doesn't, you must be prepared for a last-minute panic alteration of course. So keep your eyes open, if it is your right of way.

The one big overriding factor in all these rules is that a boat overtaking another (be they power or sail) must always keep clear. And a commonsense factor is that big ships (power or sail) operating in confined waters have right of way over everything. And finally, if in doubt—get out, in good time. You'll be amazed how many tiddley little coasters offshore seem to think they are large ships in confined waters!

As I said before, safety is largely a matter of seamanlike commonsense. Think ahead, plan ahead and act in good time. Considered like this, the rules are not a lot of bureaucratic nonsense designed to spoil our sailing—they actually increase our enjoyment, not only by ensuring that we get home to tell the tale, but also by the satisfaction we gain from being in control of what we are doing. A short coastal cruise (or any cruise, for that matter) properly planned and executed is a joy. Improperly planned and poorly executed it can be a nightmare, however warm and sunny the weather.

12 Strong Winds

There comes a time in every sailor's life when the wind pipes up and up and up, and the boat heels over more and more until the sea is washing over the side on to the decks. This can be very exciting to look at in a photograph or watch on film, but it can be very frightening to experience until you are used to it.

It is rarely as dangerous as it feels, but it is uncomfortable, it is inefficient, and it puts a lot of strain on the boat and her gear, so we like to avoid it. As we mentioned in the initial chapters on sailing, this heeling over is caused by the sideways component of the wind blowing flat on to the sails, so it follows that we can reduce the heeling by reducing the amount of sail we have set. At the same time, however, we must keep the sails balanced. Too much aft and the boat will tend to screw up into the wind. Too much for'ard and she will tend to bear away. So we must reduce sail evenly in order to keep the boat balanced, and this means a bit off the mainsail and a bit off the jib. How do we do it?

Let us take the mainsail first. There are two basic ways of reducing the area of the mainsail, known as slab reefing and roller reefing, the latter being more common these days. With roller reefing the boom can be rotated about the gooseneck by means of a handle that fits into the reefing gear by the gooseneck. See fig 117. All we do, basically, is slacken off the halliard and wind on this handle. The boom rotates and winds the mainsail about itself until you are left with just the amount of sail you want, when the halliard is hauled taut again to set up the sail. See figs 118 and 119. And that, in essence, is all there is to it, apart from one or two little points of which we must be careful.

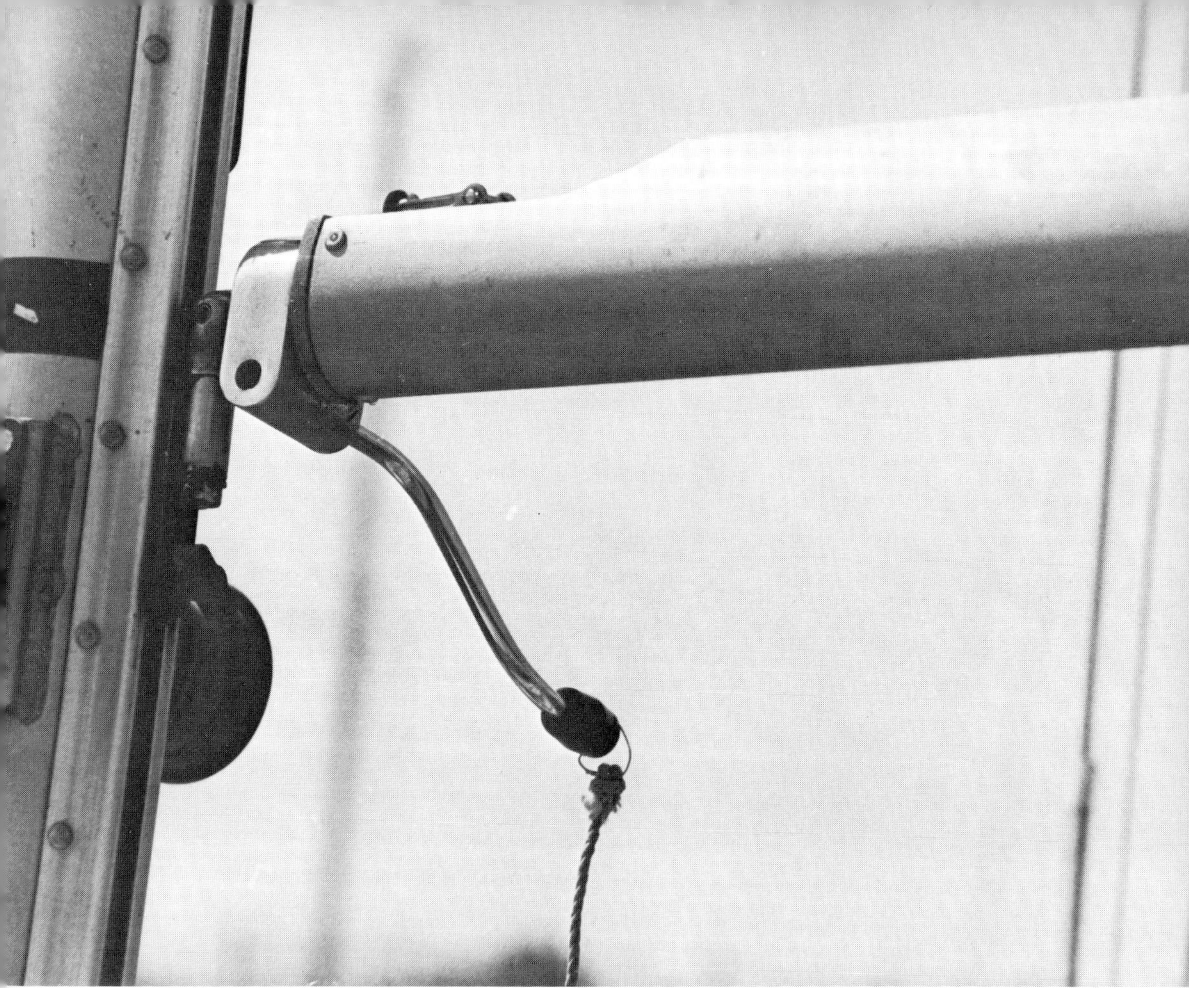

Fig. 117

First, if we want to put in reefs before leaving the mooring, it is easiest to haul the mainsail right to the top of the mast before winding it down. One person should wind the reef down while another slacks away steadily on the halliard so that slight tension is kept on it. This ensures that the sail is wrapped tightly and securely round the boom. If you have sliders on the luff of the mainsail that run up the mast on a track, you will probably find a sort of gate or split pin at the bottom of the track to prevent the slides falling off when the sail is lowered. This must be removed as, of course, the slides must be allowed to come out of the bottom of the track while the sail is wound on to the boom.

Second, a neater stow around the boom and a better shaped sail will result if the end of the boom is lifted slightly with the topping lift. The weight of the boom needs to be taken on the lift anyway while reefing, as the sail will not hold it up during the process, so you may as well top it up a little more (about six inches) while you are at it. The final reefed sail will set very much better. And check the angle of your battens. If they are more or less parallel to the boom, they will roll in with the sail. If not, they must be removed.

If you have a kicking strap (boom vang) that secures to a claw round the boom, the sail will roll round inside this quite happily and the vang will remain operational. If yours fits into a hole in the boom it must be removed in order to reef, but can still be used if you attach it to a length of webbing and roll this in with the sail. It is well worth doing this as, in weather that necessitates reefing, a boom vang is especially useful to stop the boom skying into the air when you are sailing off the wind.

When you have the mainsail down as far as you want it, the handle can be removed from the reefing gear (which has a ratchet to hold it) and the sail reset by tightening the halliard, and the tack tackle if you have one. Then tighten the kicking strap and you are ready to go—unless you have taken in more than a couple of reefs (each reef being a full turn round the boom), in which case you will probably need to change to a smaller jib in order to keep the boat balanced. Changing jibs consists simply of taking one off and putting another on.

You'll probably have a selection of jibs on board, and they are generally numbered according to their size, number one being the largest. You may also have a genoa which is a very large jib that overlaps the mainsail when it is set. So you would change down from the genoa to the number one, to the number two, to the number three (if you have one) to the storm jib (which is a tiny little sail designed really for heaving to, which we shall discuss in a minute).

Fig. 118

Fig. 119

All this is very fine and simple, but if we have to reduce sail out at sea it is not quite so easy. The basic principles are exactly the same, but actually carrying them out requires a little more seamanlike thought.

The first thing we do when we want to reef is make the boat as stable and still as possible, and we do this by heaving to. This means quite simply hauling the jib aback, as we would to pay off from a mooring, slackening the mainsheet off so that the mainsail lies fluttering in the wind, and lashing the tiller down to leeward. See fig 120. The boat will then lie quietly with the minimum of motion, with the wind just for'ard of the beam—almost ideal conditions for reefing. She will be almost stopped in the water and will remain like that for as long as you need. The reefing can then be carried out as described. If you haven't already got a harness on because of the weather, then put it on for this job. Although the boat will lie fairly still, the odd wave will give her the occasional lurch, so secure your harness so that it holds you as close to the mast as possible. You can then safely use two hands for the job. The easiest way of heaving to is simply to go about, but do not change the jib over. As soon as she has gone round and the jib is backed, you can let the mainsail slack and lash the tiller to leeward.

Clearly heaving to would be no good for changing jibs, as we need the headsail to keep us hove to. So we adopt a different technique, that of running downwind. If we put the boat on a dead run it will produce relatively stable, dry and upright conditions on the foredeck, and the jib can be changed with little more trouble than would be experienced on the mooring. Keep the wind very slightly on the lee side of the mainsail and it will then be deflected from the jib, making it fairly easy for the man on the foredeck (who should always wear a harness) to let go the jib sheets, undo the halliard and take it for'ard to the pulpit, where he can sit in comfort and security while he gathers the sail in from the tack, pulling down on the luff and forward on the foot. He can control the halliard by letting it run out between his elbow and body.

Fig. 120

When the sail is safely gathered in, unshackle the sheets and halliard and clip them to the guardrail or pulpit to stop them blowing away. Then unshackle the tack and bundle the sail straight down the forehatch. It can be bagged later. Haul the new sail out of its bag down below and bring the tack out of the hatch and shackle it to the stem fitting before pulling the rest of the sail on deck. When the tack is safely secured, the rest of the sail can be hauled out slowly and hanked on to the forestay, working from the bottom up, then shackled to the halliard. Then shackle the sheets in place and haul up the sail. You can then resume your course and be on your way in a more comfortable and less strained boat.

These jobs can, of course, be done as you are sailing along, without heaving to or running downwind. Racing boats do this all the time. But it is more difficult, most uncomfortable, and for the inexperienced there is far more risk of making a mistake and losing a shackle or a crew member over the side. As a cruising technique there is nothing to recommend it whatsoever.

Shaking out a reef is simply the reverse process of putting one in. We simply heave to, take the weight on the topping lift, and haul the sail up on the halliard as far as we want it, while one man unwinds the sail from the boom. Then tighten up, let go the topping lift, and sail away into that greatest of all delights after a hard thrash—a dying wind. Changing up to a larger headsail is exactly the same process as changing down, as long as we have remembered to put it in the bag head first and tack last, so that the latter will come out first.

You may find your boat has a trysail. This is a very small, strong sail that is rigged in place of the mainsail, normally in conjunction with the storm jib, for heaving to in very strong winds (around gale force). Unless you have a very lightweight mainsail, or envisage the odd trip round Cape Horn, they are an absolute menace. Cumbersome, awkward and difficult to rig, useless for sailing to windward, the best place for a trysail is in the garden shed. With modern sailcloth there is no reason why you shouldn't be able to reef your mainsail right down to an area at least as small as the trysail, and it will be easier to do and will produce a more efficient sail.

Before we finish with the subject of shortening sail, let us take a look at the other reefing system I mentioned, the slab reefing arrangement. Although the majority of small cruising yachts are fitted with roller reefing these days, slab reefing (an old system in existence before roller reefing was invented) is making a bit of a comeback, especially among racing boats, as it has undeniable advantages over roller reefing. The main advantage of a suitably rigged slab reefing system is that taking a reef in is very much quicker than using roller reefing. It also generally leaves a better shaped sail.

At varying distances above the boom you will find two or three rows of eyes in the sail with short lengths of light line hanging from them, one either side of the sail. In line with each row, on the luff and the leach of the sail, are much larger eyes. The principle of the system is that the sail is lowered until one of the rows (depending on how much you want to reduce the sail area by) is just above the boom. The large eye on the luff of the sail is now where the tack normally is, and in fact becomes the tack by being hooked into a hook fixed to the gooseneck for the purpose. The eye on the leach of the sail becomes the clew, and normally has a line rove through it permanently, which passes through cheek blocks on the boom to a small tackle. This tackle is hauled taut to draw the eye down on to the boom where the clew normally lies. The loose belly of sail is then tied up by the short lines, which are known as reef pennants.

If it is desired to take more sail off, then the second row of reef points is drawn down in the same way and a second reef taken in in exactly the same manner. It should be obvious why it is called slab reefing. The greatest advantage of the system from a cruising yachtsman's view point is that a very deep reef can be taken in very much quicker than can the same amount by roller reefing. And if the reef points are positioned correctly in the first place, a perfect setting sail will result every time, however deep the reef. The disadvantage is that you are limited to two, perhaps three different sizes of reef, whereas roller reefing provides an infinitely variable size of reef. You pays your money and you takes your choice; although I have seen a roller reefing system with a single deep reef provided for emergencies, which would seem a good compromise.

Well, that, simply, is how we shorten sail. But there are times when we might be caught out in a sudden violent blow and find ourselves overpressed, even with all sail shortened down. Or after a long session beating to windward in a blow we might need a rest. Or we might just want to stop for lunch. The solution to all these problems, and many others (stopping just off a harbour for a good look round before entering, for instance) is the same. We heave to. The strain on the boat will ease, the motion will ease; we can get below for a dry out and a warm up; we can get a meal together; we can generally relax a little and wait for the wind to ease off. The only proviso is that we have a good bit of room to leeward to allow for our drift while hove to. It is no good heaving to for a rest or to ride out a storm, if by so doing we allow ourselves to drift down on to the rocks. Hove to we will probably sail forward very slowly ($\frac{1}{4}$ to $\frac{1}{2}$ a knot perhaps) and drift downwind at anything up to two knots or more if the wind is very strong. So a good bit of searoom is most important—twenty miles or so if possible.

The last thing I am going to say about strong winds is: avoid them, until you have a reasonable amount of experience and feel confident in yourself and your boat. And force five is a strong wind for an inexperienced yachtsman. Things happen very quickly in strong winds, and there is no time to mull over decisions or make mistakes. And mulling over decisions and making mistakes are an essential part of early experience. Make the most of them and leave the strong winds till later. A bad experience in heavy weather could easily put you off for life. And that would be a pity, as sailing, in both light and strong winds, is a wonderful pastime.

13 Handling Under Power

Let's have a bit of a rest from sailing for a chapter, and take a look at how we handle the small sailing cruiser under auxiliary power. Now, before we could learn how to handle the boat under sail we had to know roughly how the sails worked: not in any great scientific detail, but enough to know what would happen when we pulled the sails in or let them out, and so on. In like fashion, before we can learn how to handle her under power, we must know something of how the engine and propeller actually drive us through the water, which is rather different from the action of a car's engine on land.

Handling a boat under power, especially a sailing boat which has been specifically designed to be handled under sail, is just as much an art as handling under sail. In some ways it is easier, in others not so easy. But it is very important in the crowded harbours of today to be able to manoeuvre a boat efficiently under power. Entering harbour and picking up our mooring under sail is very nice and satisfying, but in a harbour crowded with boats sailing, rowing, motoring and often generally making a mess of things, it can easily be argued that not only is it easier to come in under power, but it is more seamanlike. At the very least we should always have the engine ticking over in neutral in case we should need it in a hurry.

So let us have a look at how the thing works. In a conventional rear-wheel-drive motorcar the engine whizzes round driving a shaft which in turn drives the back wheels. Substitute a propeller for the back wheels and we find a boat's engine does much the same thing. The only real difference, as far as we are concerned, is that a boat's engine does not need a selection of gears for going slowly or up hills. All we have is ahead, neutral and astern, and very often with outboards we don't even have astern. If we run the engine slowly the boat will go slowly; if we run it quickly the boat will go quickly (but only after a while—the acceleration of a small sailing boat under power is rather like that of a bicycle!). To go astern we put the gear lever into astern, which reverses the rotation of the shaft and propeller, and, again after a while, the boat will gradually stop, then slowly begin to move astern. And this slowness of reaction is very important to remember when we begin driving around: if we don't take it into account we are going to leave a lot of expensive dents around the place.

A propeller moves through the water in much the same way as a screw moves in wood: turn it one way and it goes forward; turn it the other way and it goes backwards. As it goes it takes the boat with it. Now there are two basic types of propeller—right-handed ones and left-handed ones. Right-handed ones turn clockwise to go ahead, and anticlockwise to go astern. Left-handed ones are the other way round. On the face of it, it wouldn't seem to matter which one you have, as it will be connected to the gearbox in such a way that when you put the gear lever ahead, the boat will go ahead regardless of which prop you have. It does matter, however, and the reason is that as the propeller goes round it not only climbs forward through the water, but it also climbs sideways. A propeller turning clockwise will climb to the right when viewed from astern, and to the left when turning anticlockwise. See fig 121.

As it climbs sideways, of course, it takes the stern of the boat with it, and this, clearly, is going to produce problems. This 'paddlewheel effect', as it is called, has a marked effect on the behaviour of the boat, so let us have a good look at it. Its influence is felt most strongly as the propeller begins to turn. Once it is turning steadily, the effect decreases considerably, to almost negligible proportions. This is most convenient, as it means that, far from being a nuisance, the paddlewheel effect can be put to good use, to swing our stern sideways

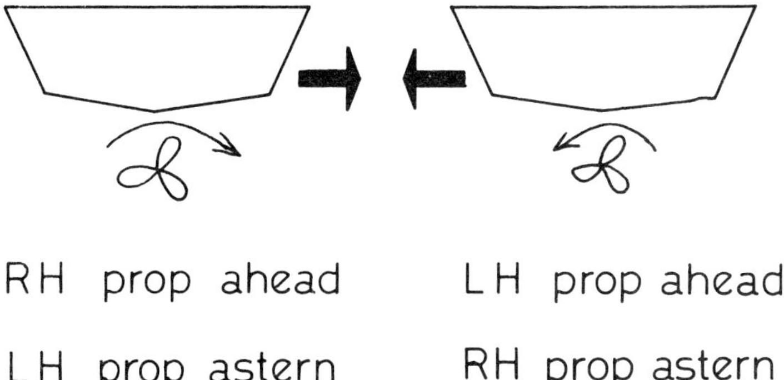

Fig. 121

when we want to snuggle into a tricky berth, for instance. We can utilise it to help us turn sharply in a confined space, or to swing our stern out from a wall when we want to leave, and so on. The paddlewheel effect is a great friend to the motoring sailor who knows how to use it. So let us learn.

If we have a right-handed prop it will turn clockwise when we go ahead, and therefore will swing our stern to starboard as we begin to move off. When we go astern the prop will turn anti-clockwise, so the stern will swing to port. How much it swings depends on the size of the prop, the amount of power applied to it, the shape of the boat, and so on. This is best determined by getting out into a wide open space and trying it! The left-handed prop works the other way round, but for the rest of the chapter I am going to stick to the right-handed prop in order to avoid confusion. If you have a left-handed prop, then just read left for right all through. If you don't know what your prop is, put the gear lever into ahead and watch which way round the prop shaft goes. If it turns clockwise viewed from astern, then you have a right-handed prop, and vice versa.

Now let us see how we can use this paddlewheel effect in our manoeuvrings, for manoeuvring is what we are going to talk about, simply motoring around under power being little more difficult than driving a car. As long as we remember how long it takes for a boat to pick up speed and to stop.

Let us imagine we want to go alongside a wall port side to (with our port side against the wall). This will have been dictated by the approach to the berth and the tidal stream direction, in just the same way as an approach under sail is. We don't have to worry about the wind direction in the same way, however, except insofar as it might cause us to drift a little if it is strong enough. We will look at that in a minute. For the time being let us imagine the wind is light and its effect on us negligible, in which case we simply motor in alongside the wall much as we would park a car at the kerb. The main difference is that we haven't got any brakes, so we have to go astern for a short while in order to stop, and we have to do it some way before we get to where we want to stop. And while we are doing it, the stern will swing to port (right-handed prop) and crash into the jetty. Which won't impress the neighbours.

Fortunately there is a very simple way of preventing this. We approach at a slight angle to the wall (something like thirty degrees) so that when we go astern our stern will be sufficiently far from the wall to swing in to lay us parallel by the time we have stopped. We can then step ashore and secure the lines. Sounds easy? It is. But remember how long it will take her to stop, and make the approach fairly slowly, go into neutral some way from the wall, then go into astern and give a sharp burst of power just before you want to stop. All being well, she will swing neatly and stop right where you want her. But make sure you get her close enough to the wall to step ashore with your lines, so don't be so preoccupied with your stern that you forget where the bow is going. The bow should be almost against the wall when you go astern (and put the tiller over towards the wall at the same time to help her in), as when the stern swings in the bow will swing out a little. Try it a few times in an open space first so that you are sure how much the stern will swing, and how far the bow will swing out. See fig 122.

And that, basically, is it. With a left-handed prop we get the same

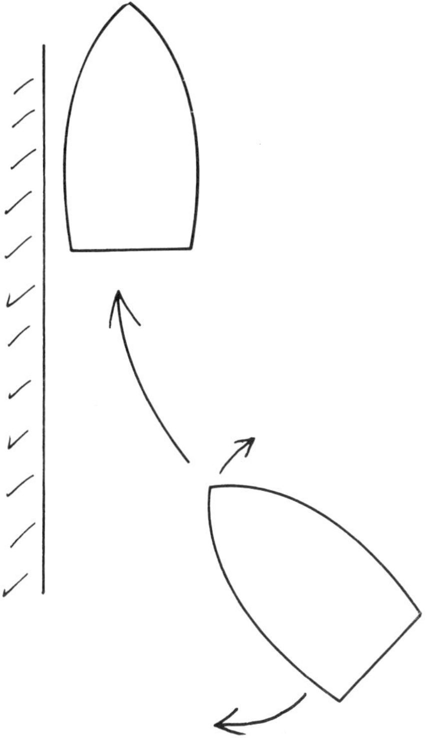

Fig. 122

effect when going alongside starboard side to. Which brings us straight to the next problem, which is: how do we go alongside starboard side to with a right-handed prop, or port side to with a left? In these cases the paddlewheel effect will tend to swing our stern away from the wall, and clearly we cannot approach from the shore side of the wall in order to utilise the swing. In these instances, then, instead of utilising the paddlewheel effect, we must counteract it. And we do it by utilising the paddlewheel effect when going ahead. When we go ahead with a right-handed prop, remember, the stern will swing to starboard, which is where we want it. So what we do is to make our approach much the same as for berthing port side to, only a bit slower. Then, just before we would normally go astern, we give her a quick burst ahead with the tiller hard over towards the wall. As soon as the stern begins to swing towards the wall we chip her into neutral, and immediately give her the burst astern that we would for berthing port side to. If we have judged it correctly, the initial inward swing imparted by the burst ahead will counteract the outward swing and put her neatly right into the berth. We can then step ashore calmly with the lines.

This manoeuvre is quite tricky to judge, so it is a question of getting out into open water and trying it. It won't take long to work out just how much kick ahead we should give her and when, then we can go and try it on a real wall. But have plenty of fenders hanging over the side for the first few attempts!

Another way of going alongside the wrong side for the prop, if we have a long clear wall with no other boats that we must slot in between, is simply to approach as slowly as possible in much the same way as we would under sail, and let her coast in in neutral, using the absolute minimum of stern power to stop. The paddlewheel effect will then be more or less negligible. But it is not as satisfying as doing it the proper way; neither is it as useful, as you cannot get into a short berth between other boats without a lot of palaver and pushing and shoving, and throwing ropes about. For really good berthing, that will have the locals nodding in approval, you must imagine your boat is a 50,000-ton tanker that cannot be pushed around if you don't quite get into the right place first time.

What about the wind and tide? Well, as a general rule we always berth heading into the tide, and in most berthing situations we will find the tide running alongside the wall. If we are not sure which way it is going, we simply do a dummy run a little way off the wall and see how it affects us. On the few occasions that we find the tide setting on to or off the wall (a jetty on piles for instance), we have to modify our approach. If it is setting us on to the jetty, we simply aim to berth a couple of yards clear so that the tide will set us on. If it is setting off the wall, we must approach a little faster at a slightly steeper angle; give her a good hard swing with the tiller over and a sharp burst ahead, virtually as we are about to hit the jetty; then get the lines ashore and secured as quickly as possible, before we get carried away.

The wind poses much the same problems, except that a very much stronger wind is needed to have the same effect on us. Up to about force three we can virtually ignore it. After that we simply realise that a wind blowing from ahead, with the tide, will cause us to stop more quickly, so less stern power will be needed. If it blows from behind us, it will tend to push us on so a little more stern power will be needed to stop. If it blows onto or off the wall, we handle it in the same way that we do the tide. If the wind is very strong, force six or so, it may be necessary, when it blows off the quay, to approach almost at right angles, and pass both head and stern ropes ashore from the bow, hauling the boat into position using the ropes. If it blows onto the quay, we must be very careful (as with a strong tide) not to land up too far off, or we might be drifting too fast for comfort when we get alongside. Have plenty of fenders over!

Well, we are safely alongside, now how do we get off? This is where motoring really scores over sail, and what we basically do is use the paddlewheel effect to swing our stern clear of the wall. We can then go astern till we are well clear of the wall, and motor off. All very simple if we are berthed port side to with a right-handed prop: we just let go all the lines bar the for'ard spring, put the tiller hard over away from the wall, and go slowly ahead. Have a fender over close to the bow and she will pivot on this fender (the forespring preventing her from going forward) until the stern is well clear of the wall. Let go the forespring and go gently astern till we are clear of the berth. We can do the same berthed starboard side to with a left-handed prop. As we go astern, of course, the stern will tend to kick back towards the wall, pulling us round in a curve so that we end up parallel to, but well clear of the wall. See fig 123.

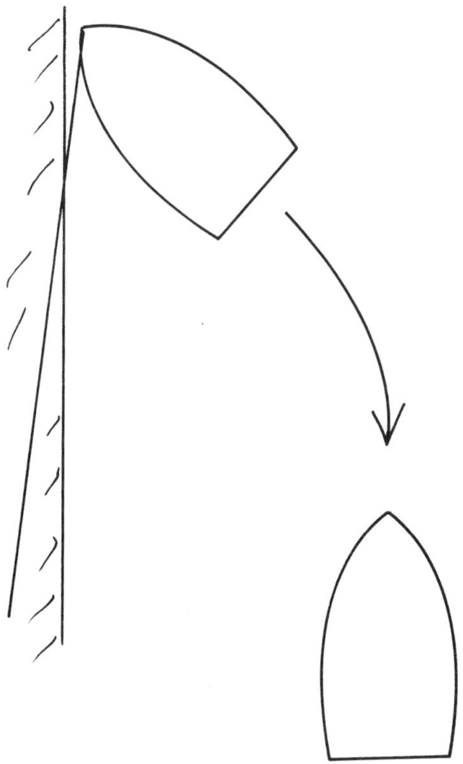

Fig. 123

Starboard side to with a right-handed prop, and port side to with a left-handed prop, require a little more thought. If we start off in the same way, going ahead on the forespring, the stern will still swing clear of the wall (due to the pivoting on the spring) but not so much as it will when berthed the other way round. We then cast off the spring and go astern, just the same. But this time, instead of curving neatly away to end up parallel with the wall, the stern will tend to climb away from the wall, until we end up at right angles, pointing at it. The bow will tend to drag along the wall, and we must keep a fender there all the time until it comes clear. Then we must keep going astern until we are far enough clear to be able to go ahead and motor away. See fig 124.

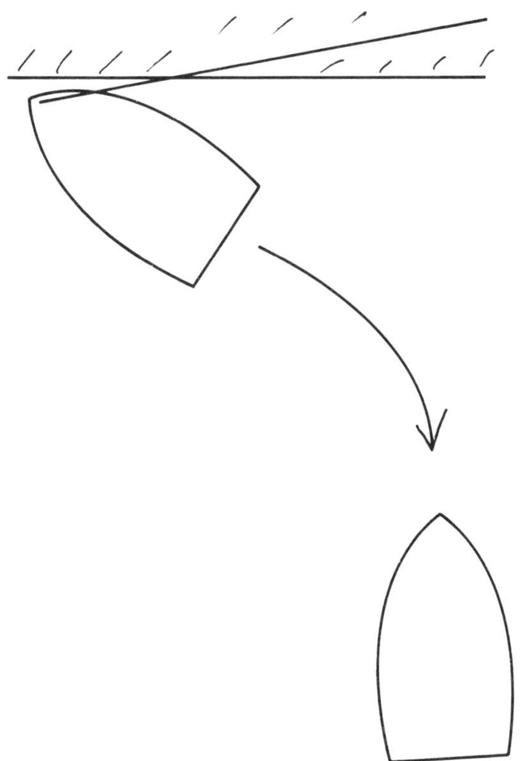

Fig. 124

Well, those are likely to be the most difficult manoeuvres we will execute under power (or under sail for that matter), and picking up a mooring or anchoring are very much easier. With these it is largely a matter of judging when to go astern in order to stop. Approach slowly (but not so slowly that you lose steerage way), aiming slightly to one side of the buoy depending on the type of prop you have. With a right-handed prop the stern will swing to port when we go astern to stop, so our bow will swing slightly to starboard. (Not so much as the stern, because the pivot point, when we are moving forward through the water, is about one third of the way back from the bow—the other way round when we are moving astern.) So keep the buoy slightly on the starboard bow and the bow will swing to it instead of away from it. Manoeuvre the other way round for a left-handed prop. As with the other manoeuvres, you cannot beat a little practice in open water to judge just how much she will swing and how much stern power you need to stop.

Turning sharp round in a confined space is another manoeuvre that can be assisted greatly by the use of the paddlewheel effect. With a right-handed prop we make the turn to port, with a succession of short, sharp bursts ahead with the tiller hard over. Each burst will kick the stern to starboard and the turn will be very much tighter than it would be to starboard. If the space is so limited, however, that we have to do a three-point turn (just as in a car), we adopt a different tactic. This time we make the initial turn to starboard, as far as we can go, then go astern. The paddlewheel effect will pull us round in a long curve, the stern going away to port, until we are facing back the way we came. For a left-handed prop everything is the other way round. See fig 125.

Using short bursts of power in order to get maximum benefit from the paddlewheel effect can be particularly useful for manoeuvering into all sorts of confined spaces, such as crowded marinas. The great attraction is that the maximum turning of the boat is combined with the minimum forward movement. With relatively high windage for'ard, this is very often the only way you can turn a sailing boat up into a strong wind without taking half the harbour over the job.

That is the basic business of handling sailing boats under auxiliary motor. Remember the paddlewheel effect, and use short bursts of power for turning sharply.

If you have an outboard, however, life is not quite so simple, unless it has an astern gear. The main things to remember about outboards is that they don't produce the same paddlewheel effect as an inboard, due to the generally smaller, higher-revving prop, and they can be a thorough nuisance if you have to keep lugging them about and attaching them to the stern every time you want a bit of power. An

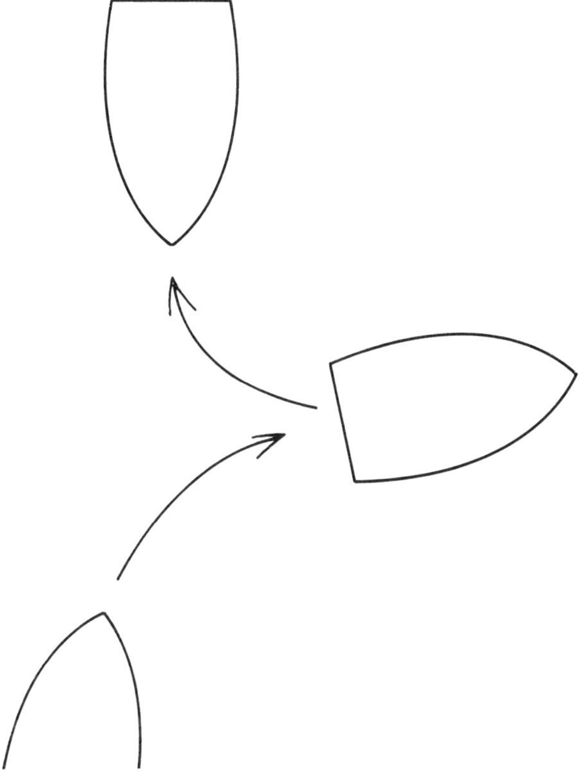

Fig. 125

outboard that lives permanently in a well at the stern is a godsend, if you have to have an outboard. The best place for an outboard is on the tender, as this can save you many a weary row ashore from a distant anchorage. On the stern of a boat they can (not always) be an unmitigated, unreliable nuisance. A properly installed little diesel inboard is , in my opinion, far and away the best form of auxiliary for the small sailing yacht. Generally powerful, reliable and economical, it will also charge your batteries for lighting, stereo, television and whatever else you may want aboard. (12 volts, that is). See figs 126 and 127.

Fig. 126 A very neat way of keeping an outboard stowed and ready for use.

Engines, of course, if you want them to run properly, need maintaining, but I don't think this is the time or place for a long technical screed on top overhauls, decoking and the like. Quite frankly, if you keep your oil topped up (engine, gearbox and reduction box if you have one—the reduction box is simply an extra little gearbox stuck on the back of the normal box to reduce the speed of rotation of the prop, and it is very often forgotten when people go

Fig. 127 A typical small inboard auxiliary. This one is petrol and fits Under the step into the cabin. Note the stern tube greaser on the right (looking like a grease gun).

round oiling their engines) with the correct grade of oil (check the engine manual); never let the engine run out of diesel (if you do the whole system has to be bled of air); keep your batteries clean, topped up with distilled water (from a chemist, not a garage—I have it on good authority that some of the less reputable ones palm you off with tap water, which won't do your battery any good at all) and your terminals tightly secured, keep the engine itself clean (easy to spot oil leaks etc when they are just beginning to develop); and make sure the wiring is kept in good condition and all terminals and pipe clips tight, you won't go far wrong. The stern tube greaser (a nipple or pump that pushes grease into the tube where the prop shaft passes through the hull) should be kept topped up with grease and given a turn or pump once a week perhaps, and every hour or so when actually motoring, in order to prevent leaks. The fan belt should be checked every now and then for correct tension (according to the manual), and all maintenance listed in the manual should be carried out (either by you or a marine engineer) religiously at the prescribed times.

If you do these few things and also treat your gearbox gently you should have trouble free running all your life. It is most important that you do look after the engine as it could be a lifesaver. The chances are that when you want it you *need* it, and there are no garages at sea, and no laybys to pull into and ring the A.A. or R.A.C. from. Your gearbox is perhaps the weakest link in the system, as it is so reliant on you pushing the lever correctly in and out of gear. The way some people do it you would never realise a gearbox is as full of cogs and gears as a watch and even more complicated. So change gear smoothly and gently. The box will appreciate it and reward you with years of reliable motoring. As will the engine—think of it as a baby, and keep it clean, fed and watered. And don't forget to clean and change the filters regularly, just as you would a nappy—the oil, fuel and cooling water inlet filters (see your manual). Dirty filters have much the same effect as dirty nappies—they cause a lot of trouble!

One final point on the use of the motor is worth mentioning, and that is the business of motor-sailing. This is, as its name implies, motoring and sailing at the same time. There are two main occasions on which this technique can be especially useful—very light winds when your progress is slow on all points of sailing, and very strong winds when your progress can be slow to windward. Running the motor at cruising revs while at the same time sailing will add a knot or so to your speed, while at the same time having the sails set and filling will keep the boat steady and reduce the rolling that one can get under power. It is worth noting that in a blow, motor-sailing beating to windward is generally much quicker, more efficient and far more comfortable than simply motoring directly into the wind.

But remember that when motor-sailing you are classed as a power-driven vessel and must keep clear of all boats under sail. It also means that you should obey the collision regulations for power-driven craft, which simply state that if the other vessel is on your starboard side you should keep clear, unless he is overtaking. As far as large vessels are concerned (coasters, fishing boats and so on) you are well advised to keep clear of them anyway. They cannot manoeuvre as easily as you can in your little boat, and it is not always easy for them to see you. Theoretically you should fly a black cone from the forestay when motor-sailing, but as this is most inconvenient if you have a jib set, and difficult to see from any distance, it is much simpler for all concerned if you pretend to be a sailing boat; everyone else does it. If your conscience needs assuaging, you can always switch off the motor on approach of a motor boat!

14 Sailing at Sea

The actual mechanics of sailing a boat through the water, as we described in the beginning of the book, remain the same whatever we are doing, or wherever we are sailing. When we leave the peaceful confines of the harbour or sheltered bay for the open sea, however, things are a little different in various respects. The most important and most noticeable difference is the fact that we encounter waves: not the little wind-blown popples we find in sheltered waters, but proper waves, if the wind is strong enough, big enough to have to sail up and over. And there is a right way, to say nothing of wrong ways, of doing it. Let us have a look at the right way.

The key to the whole thing—the secret of sailing at sea—is to treat the boat like a strong-willed child—give her her head to a large extent and simply guide her in the direction you want to go. If you try rigidly to force her in that direction, she will rebel just as the child will. You must let her wander a little, along the highways and byways of the waves, and you will find that, with firm guidance from your hand on the tiller to keep her averaging the right course, she will almost certainly pick out a better route over the waves than you can. For that is what sailing in waves is all about—picking the correct route.

Look at a mountain road next time you're near a mountain. It doesn't attempt to climb straight to the top of the mountain, it winds its way back and forth, always at an angle to the face, thus reducing the steepness of the slope it is climbing. If you feel fit enough to try it out you will almost certainly find that those path builders were not silly. They picked out the best route up that mountain, even though it was not the shortest. Sailing in waves is exactly the same. The shortest route—straight up and down the waves—is not the best. We must sail across them. If we are beating to windward and try to pinch close to the wind, we will find ourselves heading almost directly into the waves. The motion of the boat will get worse as she pitches a lot (incidentally the worst type of motion for bringing on seasickness), and this pitching will slow you down to the extent that you are quite likely to spend all day going up and down in the same spot! This may be humorous to talk about afterwards, but it is decidedly boring at the time. If we bear away a little and sail more across the face of the waves, we will get along very much faster, and the boat will be more comfortable. It is most important in waves to sail what we call 'full and bye' to windward. This means sailing perhaps a little further off the wind than we would in flat water, so that she rides the waves better, gives us a more comfortable and drier ride, and goes much faster.

There is, however, a difference between waves at sea and our mountain. There is only one mountain and, short of major seismic disturbance, it tends to stay where it is. Waves consist of a continuous succession of watery hills marching along the sea, and every one is different from the last. The normal wave pattern consists of a number of different wave trains of differing sizes and coming from different directions. So all these waves are constantly running over each other at different heights, from differing directions, and at different speeds. This produces a complex and irregular wave formation that is constantly changing, and to sail efficiently through it all we must watch the sea constantly, our main aim being to avoid a wave hitting the side of the bow flat on and knocking us sideways.

We do this basically by luffing up slightly to the face of a wave and bearing away slightly down the back of it, while maintaining an average course full and bye as we mentioned a moment ago. This imparts a nice rhythmical, flowing motion to the boat that she revels in. Luffing to the face of the wave prevents it slapping the side of the bow, and bearing away down the back keeps up the speed and momentum of the boat. And momentum is very important in waves. If we do get caught by a wave and almost stopped, it takes a long time to get going again. If we can keep her moving smoothly up and over them, she will maintain her momentum and sail fast and comfortably.

All this applies to beating to windward, when we are basically sailing against the waves. Going downwind is a little different as we have the waves behind us. In this situation we must guard against the waves catching and lifting up our stern, pushing it forward faster than the bow and screwing us round till we are almost head to wind. This is a most uncomfortable sensation. It is also not only inefficient, as it

Sometimes there are waves . . .

'. . . and sometimes there aren't!'

slows us down, but in big waves quite dangerous as the following wave is very likely to pile up and pour into the cockpit. At the very least we will get wet. At worst we could be rolled right over and sustain damage or lose something or somebody over the side. This business of being picked up by a wave and screwed round is known as broaching, and was one of the major hazards faced by the old Clipper ships as they raced through the Roaring Forties. If they broached badly in a big following sea (30, 40, 50 feet high or more!) at the sort of speeds at which they ran (anything up to 20 knots plus), they tended simply to screw round, sail right under the next wave, and never come up again. This was probably the major cause of unexplained losses among these ships.

Anyway, that is not likely to happen to us, but this business of broaching is to be avoided. We avoid it by means of a very firm guiding hand on the tiller and an eagle eye on the waves. As we see, and feel, a wave about to pick up the stern we pull the tiller over to windward so that it begins to counteract the broaching tendency a moment before she begins to go. If we do this, and catch her a moment before she goes, the wave, instead of picking up the stern and screwing it round, will tend to pick up the whole boat and push her forward. Our speed (in decent-sized waves) will probably double and we will roar off, surfing on the face of the wave. This is most delightful and exhilarating, but it does need a firm and steady hand. This is the time when you must tell the boat, through the tiller, very firmly and decisively which way to point! When she drops off into the following trough you can relax your hold and let her flow through it more or less as she wants, in order to keep sailing smoothly.

It is in conditions such as these, when the waves are mischievous and there is a fair bit of motion in the boat, that wearing a harness is absolutely vital, even sitting in the cockpit. An untimely broach (it can happen to all of us) can throw you out of the cockpit so easily, and even a bigger than normal wave catching your bow can knock you down a bit while beating. Like many things, this can be very dangerous if we do not appreciate it and prepare for it, but tremendous fun if we do. There is no thrill quite like roaring down the waves, hanging on to that tiller like the old screen heroes from the fourteenth-storey windowsill, a creaming bowwave like a speedboat foaming out from below the shrouds. I've heard staid, grown men scream with delight. I've done it myself.

The other thing we must watch for when sailing in waves with the wind dead astern is the danger of being lifted by a wave and screwed round, not into the wind but away from it. This can be a lot worse than a simple broach as it can produce a spectacular (for those watching!), hair-raising and possibly dangerous gybe. Which of course will be followed by a particularly dramatic broach. If you can get out of this in a strong wind and big waves without breaking something or somebody, you'll be lucky. So keep a very sharp eye on that burgee when sailing directly downwind. If the wind is particularly strong and the waves big (say force five or over in open water), you will be safer sailing on a very broad reach, with the wind comfortably over one quarter. If your destination lies directly downwind you can reach it by, in effect, tacking downwind: that is, reaching off on one tack for a while, then doing a controlled gybe (haul the mainsheet amidships before swinging the boat round, then ease it off steadily) on to the other tack. You then zig-zag downwind in much the same way as you do upwind when beating to windward. There are many who will say this is faster and more efficient anyway. Certainly there is little in it.

One thing you may notice if you sail off your home port all day is that the waves change every now and then. For a while they are long and smooth, then suddenly they become much steeper and shorter with pretty curly white tops as they break. The reason for this is the changing tidal stream direction. When the tidal stream is running with the wind the waves tend to be relatively long and smooth as the wind is pushing the water in the same direction as it is flowing. When the tide turns and runs back against the wind the wind blowing against the flow of the water tends to pile it up into short steep waves that break very easily. In very strong winds and strong tides this can be quite dangerous, especially if the tide is irregular and swirly, such as it might be in narrow passes and channels between islands. This is the reason why the Pentland Firth can be so dangerous to shipping. With a westerly gale blowing against a spring tide of about ten knots, even the Admiralty Pilot has to resort to poetry in order to attempt a description of the unbelievable conditions that ensue! So don't attempt the Pentland Firth in a gale against the tide, at least until you've had about 300 years experience. Don't attempt it at any time, until you've had almost as much.

And finally a few general comments on sailing out at sea. It is most important that we cultivate a sense of awareness of what is happening around us, an awareness that many will claim has been lost by civilised man since he eschewed the natural life for the cities. This, of course, is rubbish. We use exactly the same awareness today as our forefathers did, only we use it in a different environment. Instead of tramping empty, bygone country lanes listening to the dawn chorus of birds, watching the sky for rain at harvest time, or roaming the lonely sea lanes, one eye on the waves and one on the weather, we dash back and forth through high-speed, hooting city traffic, one eye on the clock and one on the traffic warden, our brains constantly hopping from work to play to household bills and so on. It is arguable that we need to be considerably more aware than our forefathers ever had to be.

All we have to do when we go to sea is transfer this awareness to a new and much slower environment. We forget about the city traffic, the work, the bills (which is largely why we go to sea in the first place!), but we don't turn ourselves into mindless morons. We must think about our position, the weather, the tide, so that all the time we are at sea we know roughly where we are, how the weather is developing and which way the tide is running. Our position comes from glancing constantly about us and checking on the whereabouts of landmarks such as our harbour entrance. There are two very important reasons for this. The first is that we then know which way to steer if a bit of mist drops down over the land; and the second is so that we do not get too far away. A constant awareness of which way the tide is taking us along the coast is also important to this end, as, of course, it will take us longer to get home against the tide than with it. If we have the children on the boat with us we have to realise that they can get bored suddenly and very easily. If we are then faced with a long slog home against the tide with a boat full of bored, squabbling and complaining children, we might find that sailing is not the delightful, relaxing pastime it should be! We might also turn the children against it, which would be a pity. Or we might simply get home just as the sailing club bar has shut—which would also be a pity.

Another point to remember with children is that they get bored far more easily if you are a long way from shore. The great seagoing romantics like Bernard Moitessier may get deep spiritual fulfilment and satisfaction from simply floating on the water for months on end (you may well find the same thing yourself to a lesser degree), but youngsters will generally be bored out of their minds after about half an hour. Much better to keep fairly close to shore where there are plenty of things for them to look at. You can teach them a bit of navigation (after you've read the next chapter!), show them the rocks and landmarks, anchor for lunch so they can get out and row the dinghy about, and so on.

So be aware when you are at sea, but most of all, enjoy yourself. That's what you go there for.

15 Basic Coastal Navigation

If we just potter about in our local harbours or off the coast from our home ports there is no great need for us to learn navigation. A chat with the harbour master will soon tell us where the rocks, sandbanks and other dangers are, where we can safely sail and where we cannot. That is how generations of sailors grew up before ever books were invented, before even navigation was invented. So there is no real reason why it should not do for us.

If we want to make a trip along the coast, however, even as far as the next harbour, we must learn at least the basics of how we go about it: how we get there and how we avoid any dangers en route. And navigation, for simple purposes like that, is little more difficult than getting the car out and driving over to your old granny's. In fact, with the complexities of modern road systems, it is very often easier.

The subject of navigation, as such, is rather like that of seamanship; one can go on learning it forever. If you intend sailing round Cape Horn backwards in a half-a-million-ton tanker singlehanded, anchoring for lunch in every little nook and cranny you can find, then you need to know quite a lot about navigation. If, on the other hand, you intend spending the weekend pottering along the coast with the family, anchoring for lunch and the night, you really need to know very little. So let us have a look at just what you do need to know.

As with taking the car over to granny's, we must first find out where our destination is and in which direction we must travel in order to reach it. We must also find what dangers, if any, lie in our path and where we must sail in order to avoid them. With a car we do all this by using a map. We look on the map to see where granny lives, then find which roads lead there. Then we simply drive along those roads, knowing that the roads themselves will lead us clear of dangers, such as ditches, rivers, other people's houses and so on.

With a boat it is not very different. We look at a map covering the area in which we want to sail, and find our destination. But then it gets slightly more difficult as there are no roads at sea, so we have to make our own. We have to find the most direct route from where we are to where we want to go, that avoids any dangers en route. Then we have to sail along it, remembering that there are no signposts or kerb stones to guide us. Doing this is called navigating, and not only is it not difficult, but it is also fun. How does it work?

Let us start by looking at the maps we use at sea. Sea maps for some reason (probably to confuse poor beginners) are known as charts, and they are produced by various Navies and nautical publishers throughout the world. Coastal charts (which are the ones that concern us here) show, naturally enough, a large expanse of sea bordered by the coast. Along the coast they show all the information that might be of use to the navigator, such as hills, churches, lighthouses, harbour entrances and so on: all prominent objects from which the navigator can find his position. On the sea we are given such information as the depth of water, positions of lighthouses, buoys, rocks and so on. Lighthouses are very tall, conspicuous buildings housing a special, very powerful light at the top, which generally flashes in a particular way so that we can tell which lighthouse it is at night. Buoys are small floating objects, moored to the seabed, often with a light on the top, which also serve to tell us where we are, especially in harbour entrances and other places where the deep, safely navigable channel is narrow and winding. The depths, known as soundings, as you will remember from chapter six, are depths below Chart Datum, so the actual depth of water anywhere is the charted depth plus the height of the tide. If the depth marked on the chart has a small line ruled beneath it, it means the seabed rises that much *above* Chart Datum, so the actual

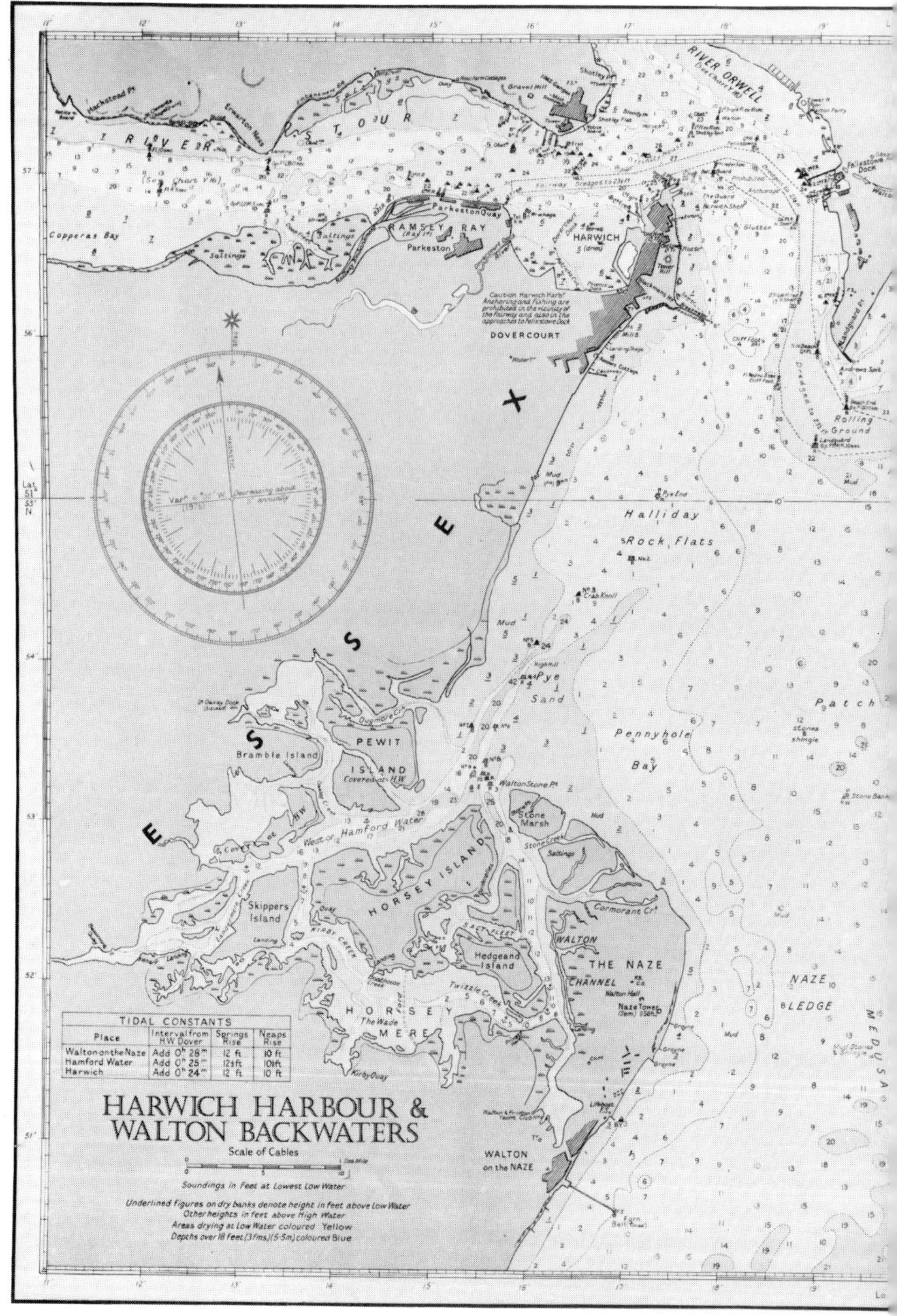

Fig. 128 *Reproduced by kind permission of Imray Laurie Norie and Wilson*

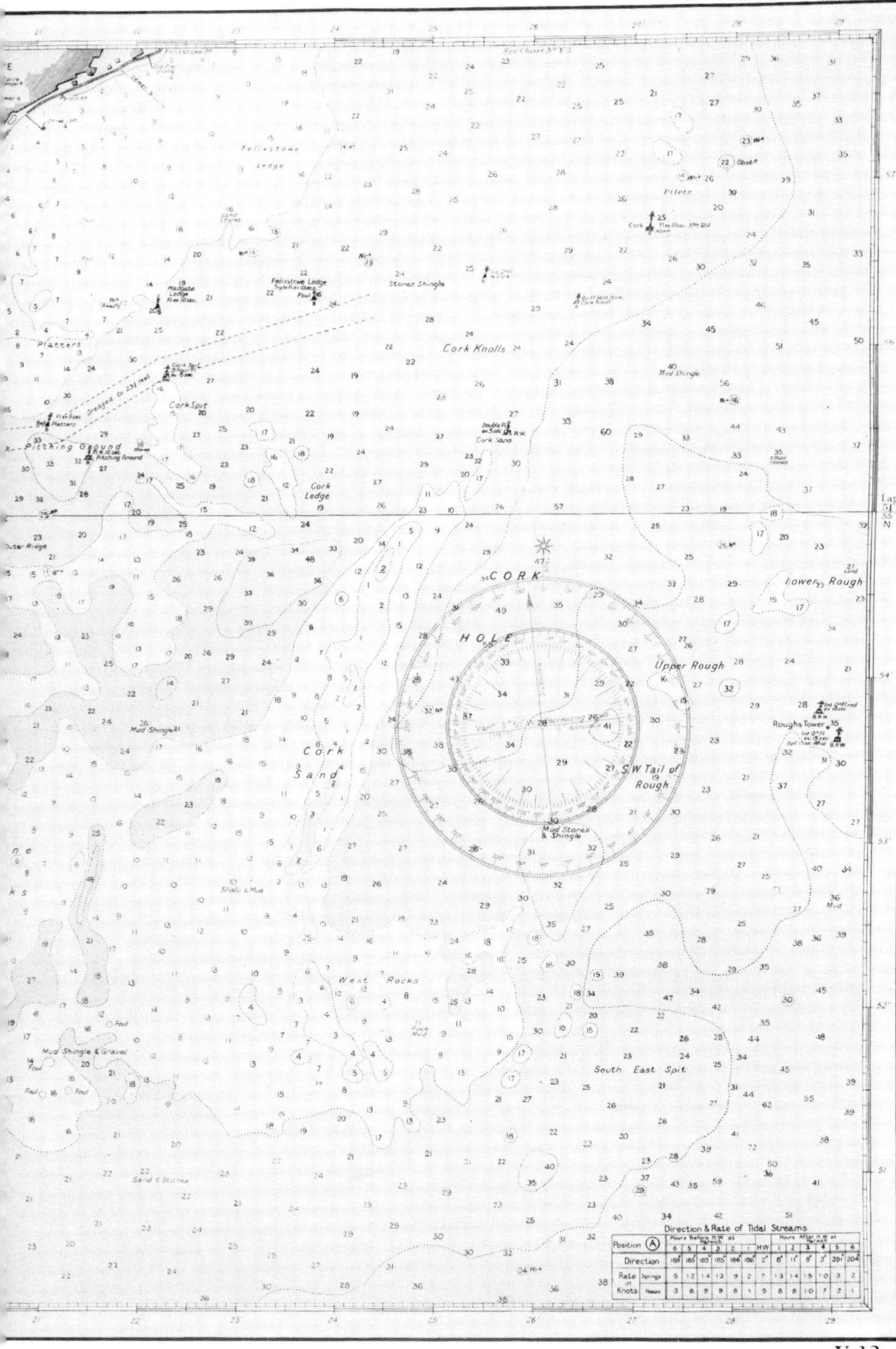

Position (A)		Hours Before H.W. at Harwich 6	5	4	3	2	1	HW	Hours After H.W. at Harwich 1	2	3	4	5	6
Direction		189°	186°	185°	185°	186°	186°	2°	8°	11°	8°	3°	351°	204°
Rate in Knots	Springs	·5	1·2	1·4	1·3	·9	·2	·7	1·3	1·4	1·5	1·0	·3	·2
	Neaps	·3	·8	·9	·9	·6	·1	·5	·8	·8	1·0	·7	·2	·1

depth of water is the height of the tide *minus* this charted amount. The diagrams in chapter six should make this clear.

Now let us take a look at one of these charts. In fig 128 we see a fairly typical example of the sort of chart that is ideal for small boat sailors. Charts are produced by various authorities around the world, but they differ only in design. The basic information they give is the same. Most charts, in fact, are based one way or another on those of the British Admiralty. This one is published in Britain by Imray, Laurie, Norie and Wilson as one of a set, and has the advantages of relatively small size (75 by 55 centimetres) and a clear, simple layout. In the bottom left-hand corner we find the title of the chart (Harwich Harbour and Walton Backwaters, in this case) and various bits of information about the chart. In this example we have a scale showing us the length of one sea mile (2000 yards, just under two kilometres), which we can use for measuring distances on the chart We also have the information shown in the blow-up in fig 129. It is most important to read this information, especially as regards the soundings, which vary from chart to chart. In many modern charts they are in metres; in this one they are in feet as most of the depths are relatively shallow; in smaller scale charts (those covering a large area) they can be in fathoms (six feet). You will see that the soundings are also taken from lowest Low Water which, as its name implies, is the lowest point to which the tide ever falls. This is not quite the same as Chart Datum, which is actually defined as a level below which the tide very rarely falls. This business of different datums for taking soundings from can be very confusing, not only for the beginner, as it means tides can often be measured above a different point from which soundings are measured below. The best way of approaching the problem is to avoid scratching around in water only six inches deeper than the boat (which is sensible anyway), approximate the depths as we described in chapter six, add (or subtract) a decent safety margin, then ignore the whole silly business. The differences are never more than a few feet anyway.

The colour-coding of the depths is a particular attraction of this

PEWIT
ISLAND
Covered at H.W.
Bramble Island
Landing
Oakley Creek
Covers at H.W.
West or Hamford Water
Skippers Island
Landermere Creek
Beaumont Quay
Wharf
Landing
Quay
KIRBY CREEK
Landing
HORSEY ISLAND
Dardenelles
SALT FLEET
Hedgeand Island
Boathouse Creek
Twizzle Creek
HORSEY
The Wade
MERE
Ford
Kirby Quay
Walton & Frinton Yacht Club
WALTON on the NAZE
TIDAL CONSTANTS
Place | Interval from H.W. Dover | Springs Rise | Neaps Rise
Walton-on-the-Naze | Add 0h 28m | 12 ft | 10 ft
Hamford Water | Add 0h 25m | 12½ ft | 10½ ft
Harwich | Add 0h 24m | 12 ft | 10 ft
HARWICH HARBOUR &
WALTON BACKWATERS
Scale of Cables
Sea Mile
Soundings in Feet at Lowest Low Water
Underlined figures on dry banks denote height in feet above Low Water
Other heights in feet above High Water
Areas drying at Low Water coloured Yellow
Depths over 18 feet (3fms)(5·5m) coloured Blue

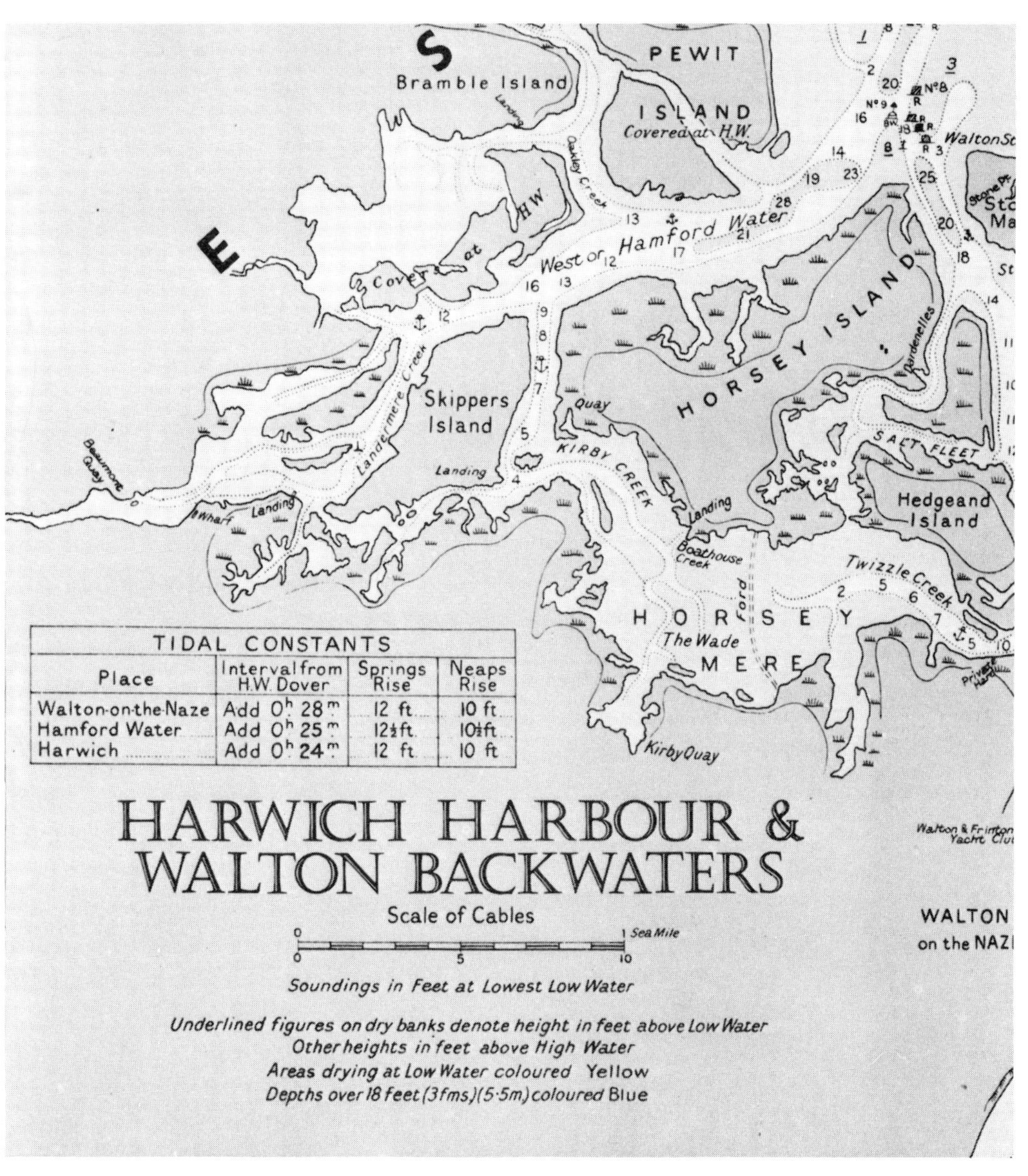

Fig. 129

chart, as it enables us to tell at a glance where the deep water is and where the dangerous shallows are. Heights, as you can see, of lighthouses, land and so on, are measured above High Water. This again varies, as strictly heights should be measured above Mean High Water Springs, which is some weird average of Spring High Water heights. For our purposes, the whole thing can be ignored, as long as we realise it is all a bit approximate.

Just above the title there is a small table headed Tidal Constants. This simply gives us the times, in relation to High Water at the port of Dover, of High Water at various places on the chart. The Spring and Neap Rises are the ranges, as we discussed in chapter six (the difference between High and Low Waters). In the bottom right-hand corner of the chart is another table, this time giving us the direction and speed of the tidal stream (at both Springs and Neaps) at various times at the spot marked with an A in a circle (about a third of the way up in the middle of the chart). Anywhere else on the chart we have to estimate the tidal stream, bearing in mind that it will basically follow the land or the deep channels, and speed up a little when going through narrow gaps, such as the harbour entrances on the chart.

The two large double circles on the chart are known as compass roses, and they indicate directions, as we saw in the chapter on weather. Only they are not marked South, North-East and so on, but in degrees from 0° (North) to 360°(North again) through 180° (South) and so on. You can see the relationship in fig 130. Degree notation is invariably used in navigation and on charts. The outer circle indicates True North and all the directions relative to it, True North being the North Pole. The inner circle indicates Magnetic North, which is where your magnetic compass actually points, being somewhere in Canada the last time I checked. This moves constantly, very slowly, so the difference between True and Magnetic North keeps changing. The difference between the two, known as Variation, and the rate of change, is shown in the middle of the compass rose.

This may seem rather complicated, but as with most things we can

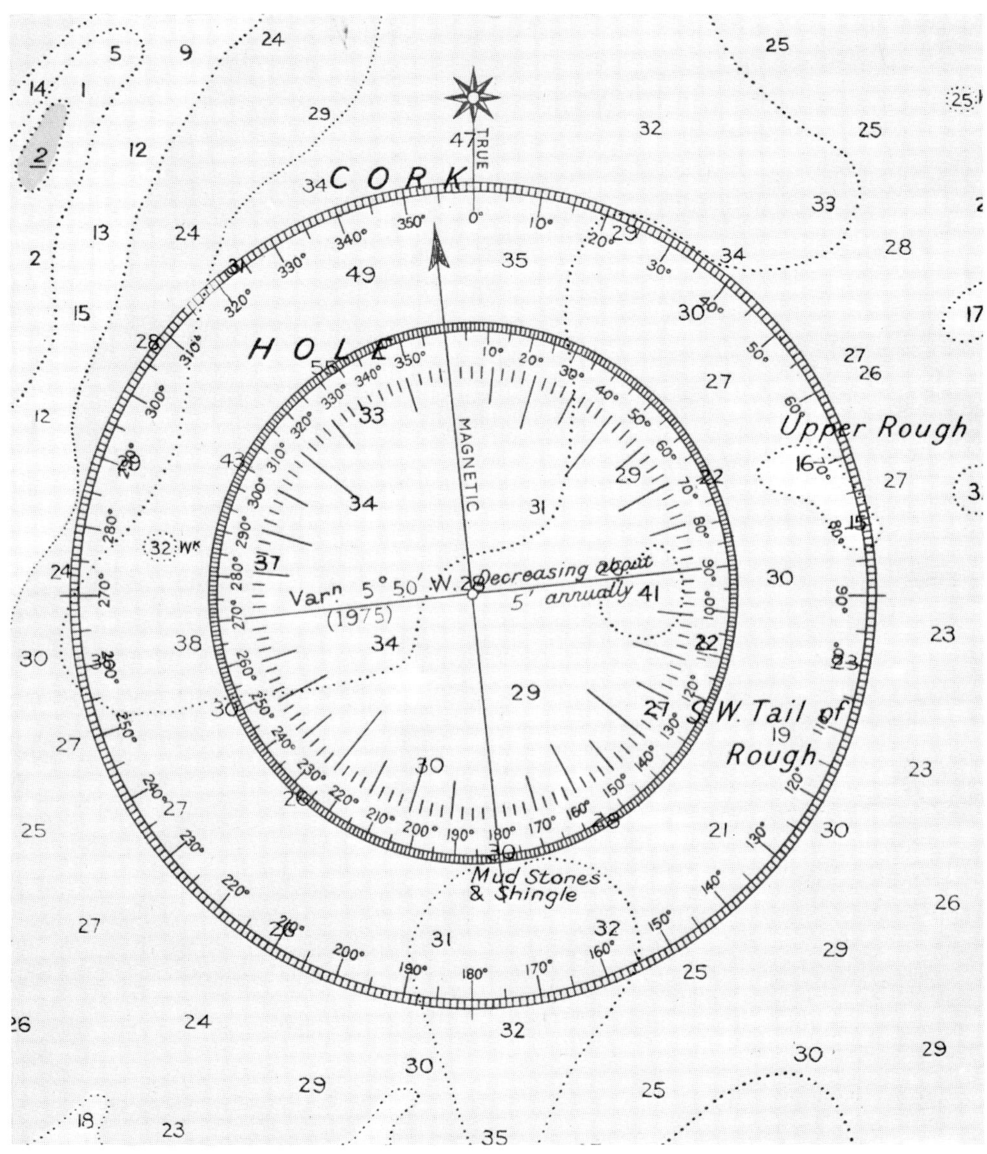

Fig. 130 *Reproduced by kind permission of Imray Laurie Norie and Wilson.*

simplify it by ignoring those parts that do not concern us: in this case, the True Compass rose. If the chart is reasonably recent, the Magnetic North direction will have only changed a negligible extent from that marked on the chart, so we can simply use the Magnetic rose all the time. If we decide to sail on a course of 340 for example, we simply line 340 on our compass with the indicator at its forward end and sail to keep it there. See fig 131. We can then plot our course on the chart simply by drawing a line in the direction of 340 on the Magnetic rose, from our starting point (just outside the harbour or wherever). All being well, and due allowances being made for tidal streams and wind carrying us to one side or the other, we will then sail along that line. If we tow a thing called a log that tells us how far we have sailed. and plot that distance along the line, using the scale on the chart, we will know where we are. That is the basis of navigation as it will concern us at this stage, with just a little more practical detail which we shall go into shortly. But now, let us go back to the chart. It is the basic tool of navigation, so we must understand it thoroughly.

Most of the rest of the information on the chart is fairly self-explanatory. The nature of the bottom (sand, mud etc) is indicated in various places, dotted about between the soundings. On some charts symbols are used for this and special charts can be obtained, often in the form of a booklet, which give all the symbols and their meanings. Charts specially designed for yachtsmen, such as this one, are

Fig. 131 *A typical yacht's compass.*

Fig. 133a *Port hand buoy with radar reflector and light.*

Fig. 133b *Starboard hand buoy with radar reflector and light.*

Fig. 134 *Middle ground buoy.*

Fig. 135 *Essential equipment for plotting courses on charts.*

Fig. 137 *A LANBY—'large automatic navigation buoy'—these are replacing light ships gradually. An idea of its size can be gauged from the fact that a man could lean comfortably on the rail round the bottom.*

Fig. 131

Fig. 133a

..g. 133b

Fig. 134

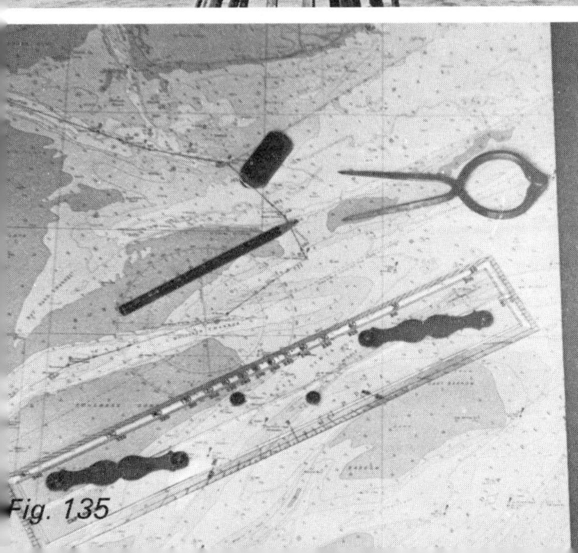
Fig. 135

Fig. 137

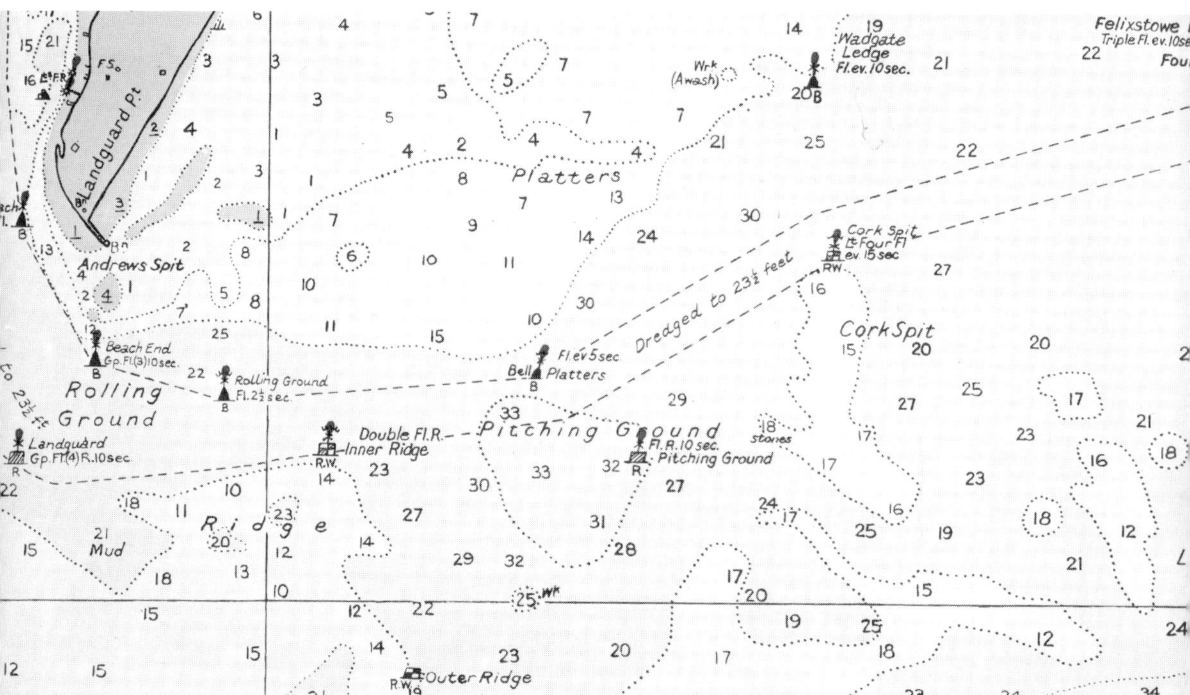

Fig. 132 Reproduced by kind permission of Imray Laurie Norie and Wilson.

generally very simply and clearly marked, with the minimum of inexplicable symbology, so they are much to be preferred. Admiralty charts, which I was brought up on, contain so many symbols that a book practically the size of a yachting magazine is necessary to explain them. I would suggest there are far more interesting things to do on a sailing boat than memorize books full of symbols.

What we must learn, however, simply because there is just not enough room on any chart to write them all out, are the details of lights and buoys. A glance at the chart, particularly at the top by the entrance to Harwich and Felixstowe, will show a number of small objects surmounted by a dark oval blob (which is actually red). These are buoys, the red blobs indicating that they have lights on them. Lighthouses also have them. Buoys come in various shapes and sizes, the commonest being shown in the blow-up in fig 132. These are marking the sides of the deep channels into Harwich, and are fairly typical. If we are going into the harbour in the direction of the flood tide, we will find on our starboard side a succession of black conical buoys; and on our port side a succession of red or red and white can-shaped buoys. These shapes are actually drawn on the chart, and the colours indicated below the buoys by the letters B, R and RW. They are also usually named or numbered, both on the chart and on the buoys themselves. See figs 133a and b.

These are the commonest buoys you will find, and they indicate the sides of a deep channel. The black conical ones should be left to starboard when entering harbour, or going anywhere in the direction of the flood tide (they often mark shoals off the coast as well as harbour channels). Red or red and white chequered ones should be left to port in the same circumstances. When going in the direction of the ebb tide, of course, we leave them on the other sides. In actual fact, it is always obvious from the chart which side of a buoy we should pass, as the danger it is marking (shallow water, rocks etc) will be clearly indicated. There are various other buoys we might come across—red and white striped round ones mark a shoal right ahead which can be passed on either side (see fig 134, Shotley Point Buoy); green ones mark wrecks and yellow ones mark sewage outfalls, both of which are to be avoided! All other types of buoy (tall pillar ones for instance) generally mark positions in mid-channel and so on, and are used as position checks. Some buoys have sound signals for use in fog, usually a bell, and this is marked by the side of the buoy on the chart.

The descriptions of lights on buoys and lighthouses are a little complex at first sight, but logical and sensible when we know the different types of lights used. For obvious reasons buoys and lighthouses near each other must have lights of differing characteristics so that we can identify which one we are looking at. There are four basic things a light can do—it can simply shine like a street lamp (known as Fixed), it can flash a series of short flashes with pauses between (known as Flashing), it can shine with a series of short periods of darkness (known as Occulting), or it can alternate equal periods of light and dark (known as Isophase). To distinguish between lights we can vary the timing, so one light may flash every six seconds (marked on the chart Fl. 6 secs) while a nearby one might flash every ten seconds (marked Fl. 10 secs). The same goes for occulting and isophase lights. A light marked Occ. 10 secs will shine continuously with a short period of darkness every ten seconds. A fixed light is simply designated FR (fixed red), FG (fixed green) or FOr (fixed orange). Fixed white are not generally used as they can too easily be confused with street lights etc. This group of buoys is known collectively as the Lateral System of Buoyage and is in use, with certain local variations, throughout most of the English speaking world.

So far, so simple. But you can probably imagine that in a complex harbour entrance there may be so many lights that we run out of ideas. So the characteristics are varied by grouping numbers of flashes or occults together, such as Gp. Fl. (3) 10 secs, which means a group of three short flashes close together every ten seconds. With Gp. Occ. (2) 15 secs we get two short periods of darkness close together every fifteen seconds, the light being on the rest of the time. This time period covers the full length of the sequence, from the first flash of a group to the first flash of the next group. Thus the time between one group of flashes finishing and the next starting may be a good bit less than this. Imagine Gp. Fl. (4) 10 secs. The flashes last about a second, so the actual time from the end of one group to the beginning of the next will be about half the stated time. Which brings us back to the isophase light. Because the total period of the characteristic encompasses the equal periods of light and dark, a light marked Iso. 10 secs will actually consist of five seconds light and five seconds dark. As long as we remember that the time is the total characteristic of the light, we will be all right.

Two other types are worth mentioning. A light marked simply Fl. will flash every second. A light marked Qk.Fl (quick flashing) will, as its name implies, flash continuously at a much greater rate than the normal flashing. Int. Qk. Fl. 15 secs means interrupted quick flashing every fifteen seconds. In other words, every fifteen seconds there will be a break in the quick flashing. If the light is of any colour other than white, this is marked in the characteristic, such as Gp. Fl. (3) R10 secs (Group flashing three red every ten seconds). Sometimes, as on this chart, the characteristics are written in a different form, such as Double Flash ev. 5 secs (Gp. Fl. (2) 5 secs) or Lt. Four Fl. ev. 15 secs (light group flashing four every fifteen seconds) and so on. As long as we understand the principles of the characteristics we can always work out what the chart maker really means! See the buoys in fig 132.

Lighthouses and lights ashore are exactly the same, except that sometimes oddities like (vert) or (hor) creep in (vertical and horizontal) as in 2FR (vert) often seen on the ends of piers and jetties, meaning two fixed red lights in a vertical line. Most other abbreviations on the chart are fairly obvious—Bn means beacon, Tr means tower, Wk means wreck and so on. If in doubt, get the book of abbreviations for the particular charts you decide to use—your chart agent or chandler should stock it. If you use the special yachtsman's charts, of which there are a number, you shouldn't need a book, as the abbreviations are invariably obvious.

You may be wondering by now what the scales around the outside of the chart are for. They are part of a sort of world-wide grid system used at sea for describing positions. The vertical one (known as Latitude) is rather like a huge compass rose around the earth passing through the North and South Poles. Positions on it are referred from the Equator, the Poles being 90 degrees North and South and the Equator zero. The horizontal line across the chart, just above the middle, is 51 degrees and 55 minutes (60 to the degree) North Latitude. The horizontal scales at top and bottom of the chart are known as Longitude and work in just the same way, nought degrees Longitude being the vertical line passing through Greenwich in London and known as the Greenwich Meridian. Longitude is measured from here either East or West, the line down the middle of this chart being One degree Twenty minutes East Longitude. By using both these measurements we can state precisely the position of any place on the earth's surface, the point where the lines on this chart cross being described, for example, as 51°55′ North 1°20′ East.

This doesn't really concern us at this stage except insofar as one nautical mile is defined as one minute of latitute. Thus we can measure distances off from the side of the chart instead of using the scale beneath the title. This, of course, is far more convenient as we can measure off any distance we need in one go, the latitude scale being much longer than the one under the title. And, in fact, if we use a much smaller scale chart (covering a larger area) we find that we must measure distances from the latitude scale, and we must measure them on roughly the same latitude as we intend plotting them. The reason for this is that the length of a nautical mile varies as we move towards the poles, due to the earth not being a perfect sphere, but actually being a bit squashed at top and bottom! So if we measure a nautical mile from the latitude scale on the Equator and plot it on the chart up by Greenland, it will not be equal to a mile. But let's not get into too much of that! Sufficient to say that we must measure distances from the latitude scale roughly opposite where we are going to plot them.

And that about describes the chart—the basic tool of the navigator. To plot our course and positions on the chart we need a few other tools—a parallel ruler (two rulers joined and pivoted so that we can lay them along the bearing we want on the compass rose, then walk them across the chart to where we want to plot the course line, thus enabling us to draw lines parallel to others anywhere on the chart); a pair of dividers for measuring off distances (special one-handed jobs as shown in the picture are worth their weight in gold as they can be adjusted in or out with the one hand that holds them); a couple of soft pencils (I would suggest 3B, and I would also suggest you keep them sharpened at both ends in case one breaks just as you are desperately trying to plot a course to take you clear of danger!); a rubber and a pencil sharpener. All the other gadgetry you may see advertised in chandlers and yachting magazines are nothing more than that—gadgetry. Generally expensive, very often so complicated you need a degree in engineering to operate them, they are to be avoided, certainly to begin with. When you are thoroughly conversant with navigating using the simple equipment I have listed, then by all means buy a gadget if you think it will make life easier. Personally, I don't like them. In fig 135 you will see a chart table adorned with all the equipment I have ever used for chartwork.

Those are the basic tools we need in order to navigate our boats on short coastal trips. How do we use them? The first thing we must realise is that out at sea we cannot stop and ask a policeman the way if we get lost. So we cannot afford to get lost. We must keep a far more accurate track of our position than we need to when driving a car along the roads. First we must work out the direction from where we are to where we want to go. Then we must calculate what course we need to steer in order to move along this route (allowing for the tide and wind that will push us off the track). Then we must be able, if possible, to check our position as we go along, to see whether we are actually adhering to the course we have plotted. Let us imagine we keep our boat at Harwich (at the top of the chart), and want to sail to the Walton Backwaters for the weekend—a short, fairly typical cruise for the beginner. How do we go about it?

Imagine we are driving over to see granny again. We can split the journey into three sections: first, from the garage along the side roads to the main motorway; second, along the motorway to a point close to granny's house; finally, from the motorway along the back roads to the house. Navigating a boat is much the same. First, we have to sail out of the harbour into open water; second we have to sail across the open water to the next harbour; and last we have to sail into the other harbour.

We begin by selecting a point just outside the harbour from which we can, ideally, draw a straight line on the chart to a similar point just outside our destination. This point should be clear of all dangers and both easy to plot on the chart and easy to identify from the boat, so that we can be certain we have accurately positioned the boat on it before setting off across the open water. Let us make the cruise from Harwich to the Walton Backwaters (all the enclosed waters around Horsey Island in the bottom left of the chart). See fig 136. There are two ideal departure points outside Harwich harbour, which one we use depending on the height of the tide at the time. In the river entrance to the right of Harwich is quite a wide expanse of shallow water with a lot of drying area close inshore. About three-quarters of a mile south, almost opposite the peninsula on the eastern side of the river entrance, is a breakwater with a beacon on the end. If the tide is high enough for us to sail safely over the shallow water, this will make an ideal departure point, and what we will do is select a point about 200 yards off the end and in line with it. 200 yards is far enough away for comfort and at the same time near enough to be fairly accurately estimated by eye. It is also one tenth of a nautical mile, and therefore easy to measure accurately on the chart, the minutes of latitude (miles) down the side of the chart being subdivided into ten. 200 yards, being clearly a convenient measure at sea for these reasons, is known as a cable, ten cables making a nautical mile.

If we calculate that the tide will be high enough for us to sail over the shallows, we take the dividers, set them to one cable using the latitude scale roughly in line with the breakwater, and measure off one cable from the beacon in line with the breakwater. We can probably do this by eye, but if we want (and there may be other times when the distance is greater) we can lay the parallel rules along the breakwater in order to be sure that we are exactly in line. We mark the spot with a small cross surrounded by a circle, and this will be our departure point. We then sail out of the harbour and over to the breakwater until we are directly in line with it and about 200 yards off. How we do this

Fig. 136 Reproduced by kind permission of Imray Laurie Norie and Wilson

Parkeston Quay
RAMSEY RAY
(Ray Id)
Parkeston
Dovercourt Dock River
HARWICH
Fairway Dredged to 23½ ft
Trinity House
Felixstowe Dock
Prohibited Anchorage
Dredged to 23½ ft
The Guard or Harwich Shelf
Glutton
Tower Hill
Blackmans Hd
Breakwater
Phœnix Dock
Patricks Cut
Caution Harwich Harbr
Anchoring and Fishing are prohibited in the vicinity of the fairway and also in the approaches to Felixstowe Dock
DOVERCOURT
Mill B.
Landing Stage
Keepers Cottage
Causeway
Water Tr
Cliff Foot
Landguard Pt
Andrews Spit
Beach End
Rolling Ground
Landguard
Mud
Pye End
Halliday
Rock Flats
Crab Knoll
High Hill
Pye Sand
Pennyhole Bay
Patch
stones & shingle
Walton Stone Pt

we will see in a moment. In the meantime let us look for the other departure point that we would have to use if there were not sufficient tide to enable us to sail over the shallows.

Clearly we would have to sail out of the harbour by the main buoyed channel over on the Felixstowe side. In actual fact the shallows extend all the way to our destination, so if we have enough water to get there, we have enough to depart from the end of the breakwater. However, not all our cruises will be from Harwich to Walton, and this will serve to illustrate the sort of considerations we must make when selecting a departure point. What we would have to do in this imaginary case is follow the deep buoyed channel until we reach a buoy from which we can draw a line safely to our destination. We can then make a departure point right alongside the buoy, which will be even easier. Technically speaking, buoys should not really be relied upon for navigation as their positions are not always accurate but for all practical purposes this is not likely to affect the small boat sailor. Do be aware of it, however, especially as buoys may be moved at short notice by harbour authorities, and this information may take time to filter down to the small boat sailor. Some yachting magazines publish regular lists of chart corrections as things are changed, and you should certainly have your charts corrected annually by the chart agent. Other than this, there are ways in which we can plot and check the positions of buoys, and we will be looking at these later.

Now, having selected a departure point, we must look for an arrival point. And we use the same criteria: ideally in line with the departure point, clear of dangers, close to the entrance and easily identifiable. At the entrance to the Walton Backwaters is a black starboard hand buoy marking the beginning of the channel in, and this is our obvious arrival point. From there on we can follow the channel by means of the buoys. So now we can take our parallel ruler and lay it on the chart from the departure point to the arrival point. We draw a line with our soft pencil and then walk the ruler across the chart until it touches the centre of the nearest compass rose. We can then read the magnetic course off directly from the inner magnetic rose. In this case, from 200 yards off the breakwater end, the course is $213\frac{1}{2}$, which is far too precise a course to steer in a small boat, so we would call it 215 which is near enough. On a short trip like this we would see the buoy long before we had drifted off the plotted course to any extent. On a longer trip we would replot the course as 215 and make an alteration en route to another conveniently steerable course that would bring us back to the arrival point.

Having plotted this line we now check over it very carefully from start to finish to make sure it does not pass over or uncomfortably close to any dangers. In this example we find that the water is very shallow, being only one foot deep in places, so we have to ensure that we make the trip when the tide is sufficiently high to give us enough water to float, with a good safety margin. The only other danger is a group of drying patches just inshore of the track about halfway along. Steering 215, which will take us slightly inshore of our track, could bring us uncomfortably close to these, so to be on the safe side we should make a bit of a dogleg, steering 210 to begin with, until we reach the Pye End buoy (a red and white striped can just above the latitude line), then alter course to 225 which will take us to the black conical buoy at the entrance. So we rub out our original course line and draw the new dogleg—210 to the Pye End Buoy and 225 from there to the buoy in the entrance. We now have a safe track from our departure point to our arrival point.

However, as we found when manoeuvring and sailing across the harbour, the tidal stream will cause us to drift from this track so we must find how much it will take us off and in what direction, so that we can calculate what course we must actually steer the boat in order to move along the plotted track. For our purposes of short, simple coastal trips, this is not as difficult as it sounds. Take a look at the bottom right hand corner of the chart and you will see a table giving the direction and speed of the tidal stream at the point marked A (middle of the chart a quarter of the way up) for each hour relative to the time of high water at Harwich. If we look up high water at Harwich in the local tide tables, and find from its height whether we are at Springs (highest high tides) or Neaps (lowest high tides) we can look in the table to find what the tide is doing during the period of our trip.

Let us imagine we are leaving Harwich about an hour before High Water, which will give us plenty of water over the shallows and also enable us to enter the narrow channel into the Walton Backwaters before the ebb starts. In a narrow channel like that the tide will run pretty strongly (because a lot of water is trying to get out through a small gap) and at half tide Springs it could be hard work sailing in there with a small boat on the ebb. Also, if we happen to run aground it will be a good bit easier to get off if we do it before the ebb starts running.

The table on the chart gives a tide running 196 degrees (bearings given on the chart like this are always true—taken from the true compass rose—and with tides they indicate the direction the tide is flowing TO. You will remember that winds are designated by the direction they blow FROM), and its speed is .2 of a knot at Springs and .1 of a knot at Neaps. At High Water Harwich (about the time we will arrive) the tide is running 002 degrees (bearings should aways be quoted in three figures like this to avoid possible confusion) and its speed is .7 of a knot at Springs and half a knot at Neaps.

Now, we are unfortunately not sailing on the spot marked A, so we must assess how the tide will be running in the area in which we will be sailing. If we look again at the figures for A we will see that, in fact, the tide is almost negligible. It changes direction completely during our passage, from down the coast to up the coast, from .2 of a knot to .7 of a knot at Springs. We can deduce from this that for the middle part of the trip the tide will be pretty well slack, only beginning to gather any sort of strength as we enter the Backwaters. Thus, for this particular example we can safely ignore the tide altogether, being aware only that we might experience a slight set into the bay as the last of the flood runs in from the sea to both the Harwich entrance and the Backwaters. As we will be heading offshore slightly during the first half of the trip, to make the Pye End Buoy, there will be no danger of this very slight set putting us on the shore, or even causing us to miss the buoy. What we will have to watch, however, is the possibility of the ebb being a bit early, or ourselves late, and this setting us offshore during the later stages, and possibly on to the drying spit to seaward of the Backwaters entrance. A glance at the chart, however, shows us a red can buoy midway between the Pye End and the black conical at the entrance. As long as we leave this to port and steer straight for the black conical, we will sail well clear of that spit. And to make certain we do not get carried over the spit we can keep an eye on the red can and the black conical and ensure that we do not get too far outside a line between the two. If we do begin to drift we must alter course further inshore to counteract it, and keep ourselves roughly on a line between the buoys.

For the moment we will leave the tide at that and continue this imaginary cruise. After we have finished it satisfactorily, without sinking, drowning or crashing into anything, we will take a closer look at the tides, how we allow for them when they are running at some strength (especially on longer trips than this), and how we can check our position as we go along.

So far we have selected departure and arrival points, plotted our course to be steered between the two, avoiding all dangers en route, checked what the tide will be doing during this leg of the trip, and made such allowance for it as necessary. The other variable we must be aware of is leeway, which we discussed in the chapter on Manoeuvring, especially if the wind is fairly strong and we are beating to windward. In all other circumstances we can ignore it, simply bearing in mind that we might experience a very slight drift to leeward. Beating to windward in fairly strong winds we might make anything up to about five degrees of leeway. In very strong winds it could be very much more in a small boat, but I trust at this stage you will be sensible enough not to go out in very strong winds! In strong winds then we can simply steer a course about five degrees further upwind than the one we want, and this should do us perfectly well for the short trips we are likely to be making, such as this one. For longer trips we will have to assess the sort of leeway our own particular boat makes, then allow for it in exactly the same way.

That completes the middle stage of the voyage. Now how do we get out of Harwich and into Walton? We call entering and leaving harbour pilotage, and it involves a slightly different technique to the relatively straightforward plotting for the middle leg. Basically we work on the principle that (except in fog, and pilotage in fog is not to be recommended to anyone bar the very experienced indeed) we can always see the next mark or buoy or bend in the channel before we lose sight of the last. Thus we can dispense altogether with plotting a course, and simply work our way around the harbour or estuary by eye, going from one mark to the next.

In this instance we would probably be moored somewhere in Harwich harbour and we would simply slip the mooring and sail out along the line of the jetties (on the corner with all the lights) and head for the buoy named GUARD, the red can with a light just to the north of the shallow area we mentioned before. If we then reckoned there was enough height of tide to take us over the drying out area close inshore on the eastern side of the peninsula, we could then head directly for the end of the breakwater and our departure point. If not, we would have to stay out in the main channel a little longer to make sure we passed well clear, so we would continue out to the next buoy, the red and white can opposite Felixstowe Dock, before striking out across to the breakwater. If we are going right out to sea, perhaps to head north up the coast, we would follow the buoys marking the main channel until we came to the departure point we had selected for our course to the north. This would very likely be the CORK, the very large buoy in the top right-hand corner of the chart. This is a special monster buoy known as a LANBY, which is beginning to replace lightships around the country. Its huge size is unmistakable. See fig 137.

There are two points to be made about this type of pilotage. First, it is a good idea to pencil in your route roughly so you don't forget it; and second, tick off the buoys, beacons or whatever as you pass them, so that you don't forget which one you are heading for next. It is easily done, especially when sailing down a long river or estuary with a succession of similar buoys, and a mistake can be most embarrassing, not to mention fraught with possible danger.

Navigation marks on the water are not the only objects we can use to guide us in pilotage. Conspicuous objects ashore can be very helpful, such as jetties, church spires, towers and so on. As an example, if we were approaching the Backwaters from the bottom right-hand corner of the chart, just below where it says THE NAZE on the bulge of land to the south of the entrance to the Backwaters, there is a large tower, 158 feet high, called the NAZE TOWER. If we steered directly towards this from the bottom right-hand corner of the chart we should pick up the MEDUSA buoy (just below the tidal position A), from where we could set a course to the PYE END buoy and then into the Backwaters. For a relatively long stretch like this we would be advised to plot a course on the chart to make sure it will take us close enough to the buoy to see it easily.

The important thing is to be aware of our position at all times, but with our kind of sailing we needn't be obsessively accurate. Just off the Naze Tower; about half a mile south of the end of the breakwater; approaching the GUARD buoy; all are perfectly adequate positions in good weather and relatively straightforward navigational situations. But do make sure you are heading for the right thing. Don't see a buoy and instantly assume it is the one you want. Direction and distance can be deceptive on the water and we must check and double-check every identification. Run the parallel rulers across the chart and see what direction the next buoy you want is from the one you are about to pass. Then turn the boat until your compass heading is the same. The buoy should be right ahead. Check its shape and colour, and assess its distance. This latter is the most difficult, and there are many techniques and dodges for estimating it, none of which I have ever managed to remember in all my years at sea, so I see no reason to expect you to do so! The best answer to this is practice and experience. Whenever you are out on the water, even sitting on the mooring, make a point of looking about and seeing what objects look like at known distances. This is well worth putting a bit of effort into, as the ability to judge distances by eye is one of the greatest navigational assets of all. It is rather like spelling. There are dozens of rules for spelling, none of which anyone ever remembers, but if you read a lot you will find you spell instinctively, knowing that if a word is spelt correctly it will look right.

The same goes for identifying objects and places ashore. It can be surprisingly difficult to translate the vertical picture of the chart into the horizontal one you actually see. Once again the answer is practice. When you are taking tea in the cockpit on the mooring, get out the chart of the area and look for the objects about you. Compare them with their counterparts on the chart, so that you learn what they look like in real life, particularly from the low horizontal viewpoint on a small boat. See how the general lie of the land appears to you, how obvious the spire (conspic) actually is. Can you actually see that water tower half a mile inland, or is it hidden behind unmarked trees, and so on. In fig 138 is a photograph of the eastern side of the Harwich peninsula, past which we will sail to get to the Walton Backwaters, taken from a point to the south east of the end of the breakwater. See if you can identify the features on it and make a rough estimate of your position (where the picture was taken from). I'll give you a clue—the breakwater end in line with something ashore will give you the line you must be on, and we are in shallow water (checked from the echo-sounder and the position of the channel buoys). Remember, objects that appear conspicuous on the vertical plan of the chart (such as the breakwater) will not be so from the low horizontal position of a boat. Conversely, those vertical objects that do not look obvious on the chart are the ones you will see clearly from the boat. They are often

Fig. 138

marked (conspic) as a help to you. At the end of this chapter you will find the answers.

Well, we seem to have been sitting off the CRAB KNOLL buoy for rather a long time, waiting to get into the Backwaters, so let's go in. The procedure basically is exactly the same as for leaving Harwich, except for two things. Leaving Harwich we were sailing out against the direction of the flood stream so would leave starboard-hand buoys (black conical) to port. Here we are entering in the same direction as the flood stream so we leave them to starboard. Second, as we don't keep the boat on a mooring here, we must first, before we can sketch our route in, decide exactly where we are going to go. Assuming we are going to anchor, we must bear in mind what we said in an earlier chapter about selecting a spot to anchor—shelter from the wind and waves, enough room to swing, and, ideally, a position not too far from the nearest landing place if we intend going ashore. If the wind is blowing off the land we can go more or less anywhere where there is sufficient water and swinging room. If we look at the chart, in fact, we will see a number of little anchors drawn in various places—the chart makers have done our work for us! Those anchors will be in the most suitable, not the only, places for anchoring—probably where the bottom provides the best holding ground for the anchor, and there are no moorings.

So which little anchor do we head for? If the wind is off the land we can pick one at random, being prepared to move elsewhere if the place is too crowded. If the wind is from Felixstowe, say, blowing right into the harbour entrance, then we would take the left hand creek going towards the Naze as the shelter would be better, or possibly the little creek between Skippers Island and Horsey island, at the inland end of the Backwaters. The latter, being further from the entrance, would probably be quieter with fewer boats. Wherever we decide to go we must be prepared to change plans and move on if we find it very crowded.

Thus we can negotiate the main entrance channel by following the buoys, leaving the requisite one on the requisite side, after which we must make our way slowly down the middle of whichever channel we decide to take (in this case the channels are more or less midway between the land on either side, so we simply keep midway between the banks), running the echo-sounder so we can keep a check on the depth. Have the anchor ready for letting go, and enter under power (until we are more experienced, or know the area). Count the islands or estimate distance run to find out how far along the channel you are, as the log should be brought aboard before entering confined waters.

Haul it in by slipping the loop of the line off the machine, then pull in the rotator while allowing the line to drop into the water, until you are holding the rotator and all the line is trailing in the water. This will prevent an unbelievable mess as the rope otherwise will twist and kink dramatically. If your log is of the non-trailing type you have no problem and can use it in confined spaces without fear of it fouling up. Remember that if the tide is flooding and carrying you up the creek the distance your log shows will be less than the distance you have actually gone, and vice versa if entering on the ebb. So do look around for landmarks, buoys and so on that will help to indicate your position. Don't anchor too close to other boats, whether moored or anchored, keep an eye on your echo-sounder, find a spot with sufficient water that you like the look of (or simply where there happens to be enough room—with the number of boats about these days you cannot often afford to be choosy about where you anchor!) and anchor the boat.

If there are permanent moorings in the harbour you may be able to borrow one for the duration of your stay, but don't just pick up the first empty one and clear off ashore—the owner might come back, and he will be justifiably annoyed. Ask the local club ashore, or the fellow on the next mooring, when the owner is due back and whether he would mind you borrowing the mooring. Some far-sighted owners leave a board on the buoy saying 'Please borrow the mooring, but I will be back on Saturday night. Maximum size boat five tons', or something similar. In which case accept his kind offer, make a note to do the same with your own mooring, and ensure that you are away well before he is due back, even if you have to go off and anchor for a while. If he makes a fast passage and is home early, he will appreciate it, as you would if the situations were reversed.

To go home again we simply reverse the whole process. And there it is—our first cruise. Not difficult: just requiring a modicum of knowledge, some commonsense, a little attention to detail, and a tremendous amount of fun and satisfaction. And now, in case we take a cruise during which the tide will have a noticeable effect on us, let us take a closer look at the question of making allowance for the tide.

Tides, as we saw in the chapter on Manoeuvring, are fairly simple things—the water flows here and it flows there and it takes us with it. By using tide tables to find their time and height, and tidal stream tables such as the one on this chart, or tidal stream atlases (small booklets containing maps of the area, on which arrows and numbers indicate the direction and speed of the stream, a separate page giving the situation for each of the six hours before and after high water at a convenient local place) to find the rate and direction of the stream, we can calculate fairly easily how far and in what direction the tide will take us during a trip. Basically we then aim for a point that same distance in the opposite direction from our destination, and the tide will then carry us, during the trip, right to our destination. Despite the complicated mathematical formulae and diagrams one generally sees interspersed among writings on the subject, it really is as simple as that. Let us take an example.

In fig 139 we have a section of a smaller scale coastal chart, covering a much larger area of coastline than the harbour chart we have been working on. This section covers from Harwich to the entrance to the River Blackwater, a distance of some twenty miles from one river mouth along the coast to the next—the typical sort of cruise you might want to undertake when you have mastered sailing in the harbours and rivers, and short trips such as Harwich to the Backwaters. Let us imagine we intend cruising from Pin Mill, which is up the River Orwell from Harwich, to Brightlingsea, which is up the River Colne on the north side of the entrance to the Blackwater.

As we did before, we will split the navigation into three sections: from Pin Mill to a departure point off Harwich; from this to an arrival point off the mouth of the Blackwater; from here to an anchorage at Brightlingsea. The first thing we notice is that the chart is too small a scale to give information for the river from Pin Mill to Harwich, and the same for the leg from the Blackwater entrance to Brightlingsea.

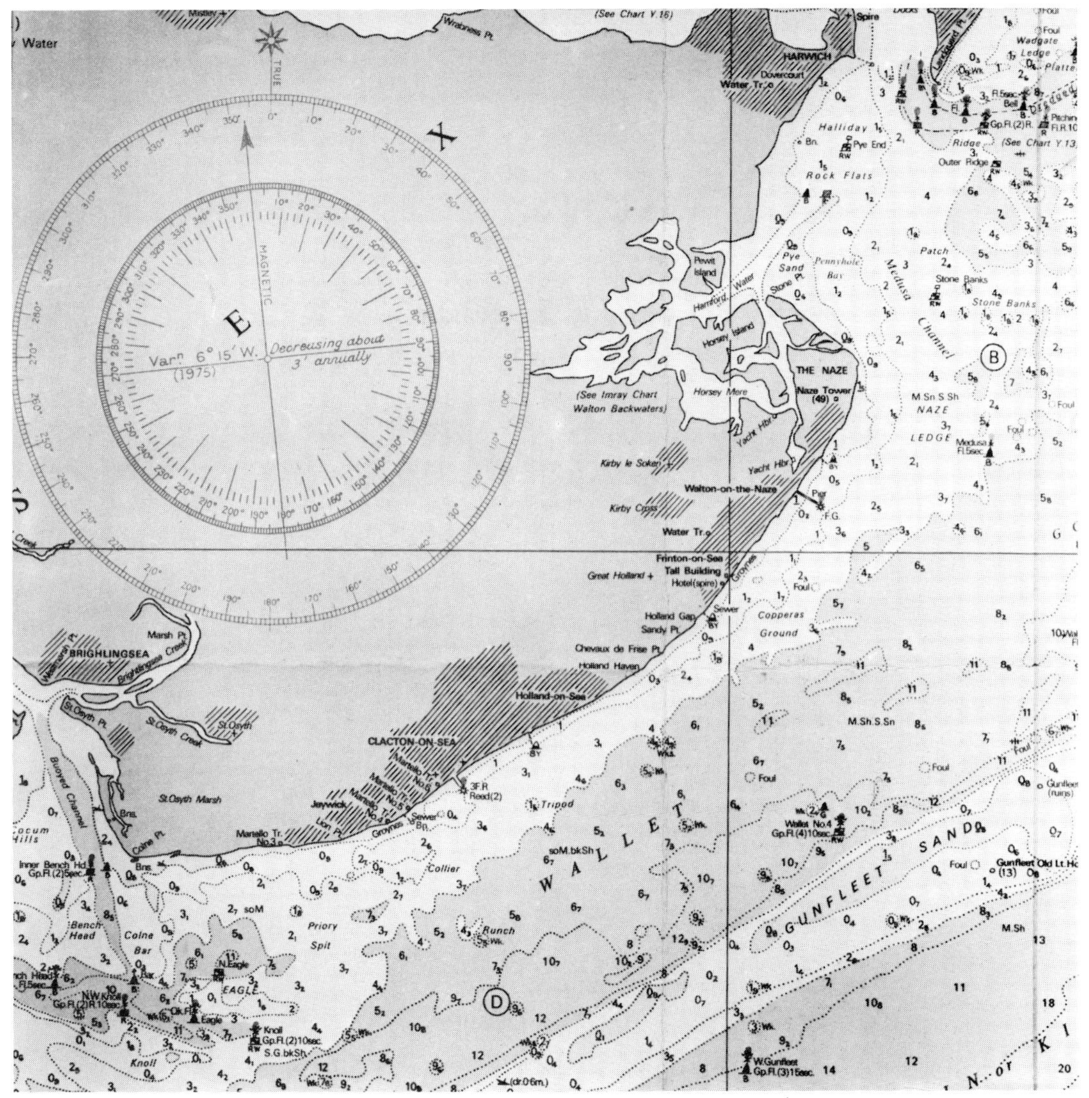

Fig. 139 *Reproduced by kind permission of Imray Laurie Norie and Wilson.*

Written on the chart by these rivers, however, are the legends—(See Chart Y16) and (See Chart Y15), so we must obtain these charts as they will give us larger scale details of the two rivers. See figs 140 and 141.

In this particular case then we would use the harbour chart Y16 to sail down and out of the River Orwell, the coastal chart Y6 to sail the passage leg, then the harbour chart Y15 to sail up into Brightlingsea. If we look at chart Y16 we see that the passage down the river is actually very simple as there is a straightforward deep channel running down the middle, well marked by port and starboard hand buoys. All we have to do is sail down between the buoys, marking off each one on the chart as we pass it, so that we always know where we are. The tide will simply run up and down this channel, so if we are leaving around high water (see the table of tidal constants on the chart) we will have the tide running with us, so will get down the river quicker. The encircled letter D in the channel near the mouth of the river will tell us, by reference to the table at the top right-hand corner of the chart, precisely how fast and in what direction the stream will run at hourly intervals from high water at Harwich. This can be quite important to check, as in light winds there may be many occasions when the tide might run faster than we can sail; so we have to 'work our tides'—in other words only sail when the tide is running with us. We try to take the ebb out of the river and the flood into the next one, regardless of the tide outside on the coast as it is invariably in confined spaces such as rivers that the tide runs the strongest.

We make our way thus to a departure point outside Harwich that we have selected, just as we did for the short trip to Walton. The point in this instance will depend on whether we have sufficient tide to enable us to sail over the shallow water off Walton. We must estimate how fast we are going to sail and thus how long it will take us to cross the shallows; then check how far the tide will fall during this time, if we have left Pin Mill on the ebb. If we calculate that there will be plenty of water, remembering to leave a good safety margin, especially on the ebb, we can use the same departure point that we did before, or

BRIGHTLINGSEA
Lower Fm.
Quay
Farm
Hurst Green
Brightlingsea Creek
Flag Creek
Cindery Islands
Saltings
St Osyth Park
St Osyth
St Osyth Creek
Priory
St Osyth Stone Pt.
Tower No. 1
Water Tr
Blockhouse Wick
Mill Dam
To Clacton-on-Sea
Sandy Pt.
Brightlingsea Reach
Batemans Tr & Two Trees in one
Lee Wick
Wigborough Wick
White Ho.
Saltings
Ray Creek
Ballast Bn
Tower No. 3
Saltings
Colne Pt.
Lion Pt.
Inner Bench Head
Gp. Fl. (2) 5sec.
Fishery
Bench Head
Bar
Priory Spit
N. Eagle
Bench Head
Fl. 5sec.
Bar (Refl.)
Eagle
NW Knoll
Gp. Fl. (2) R 10sec.
Qk Fl.
Eagle
Knoll
Knoll
Gp. Fl. (2) 10 sec.
KNOLL SWA

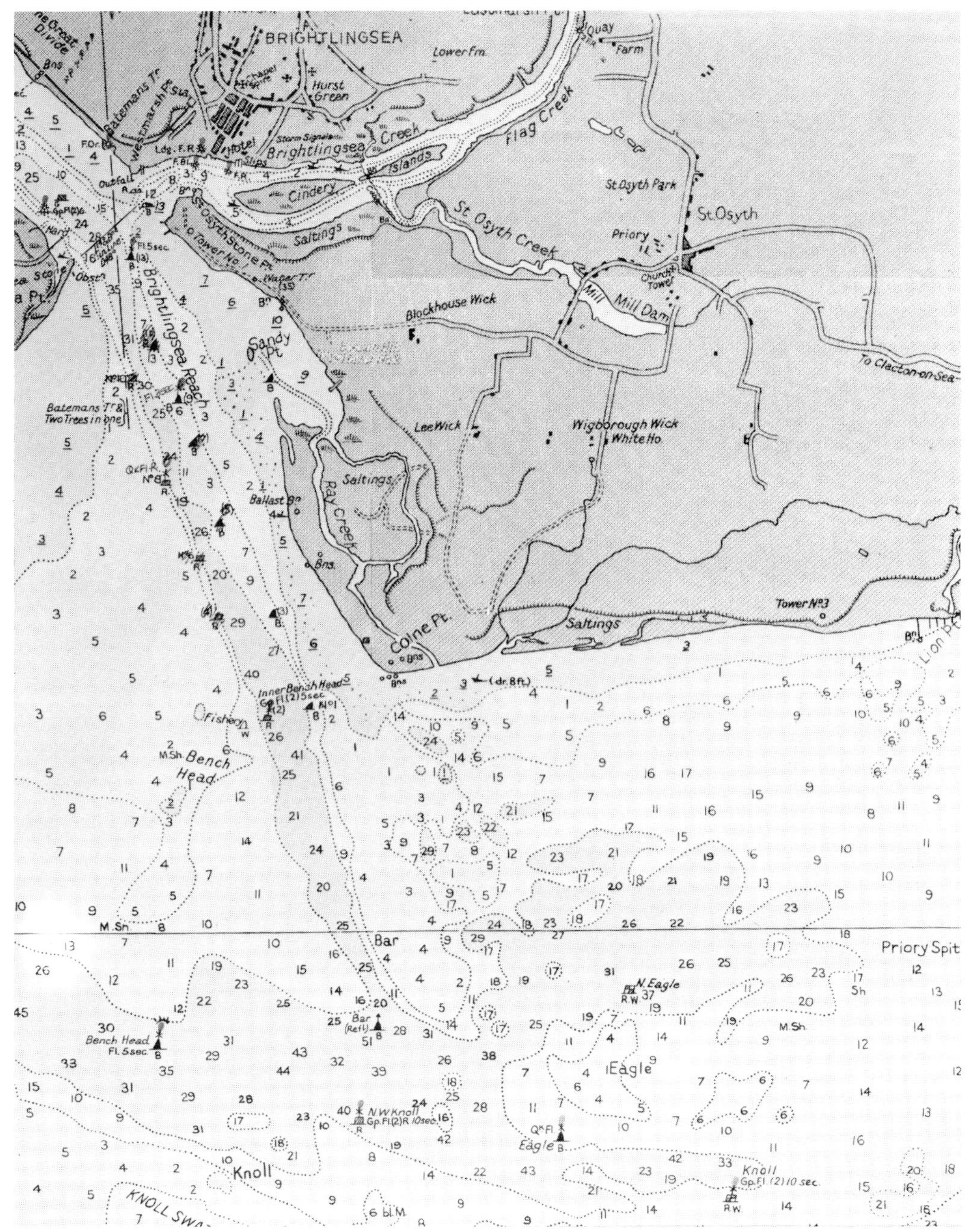

Fig. 140a

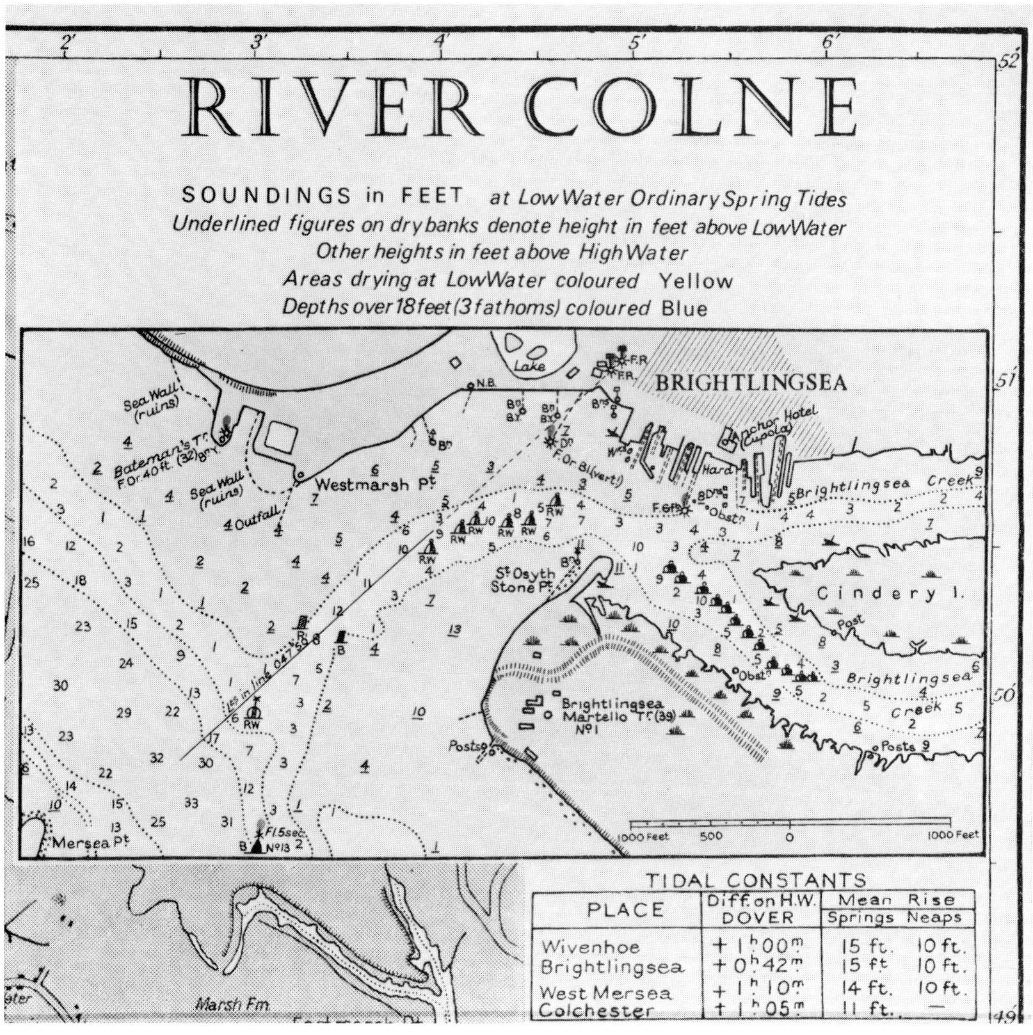

TIDAL CONSTANTS

PLACE	Diff. on H.W. DOVER	Mean Rise Springs	Mean Rise Neaps
Wivenhoe	+ 1h 00m	15 ft.	10 ft.
Brightlingsea	+ 0h 42m	15 ft.	10 ft.
West Mersea	+ 1h 10m	14 ft.	10 ft.
Colchester	+ 1h 05m	11 ft.	—

Fig. 140b

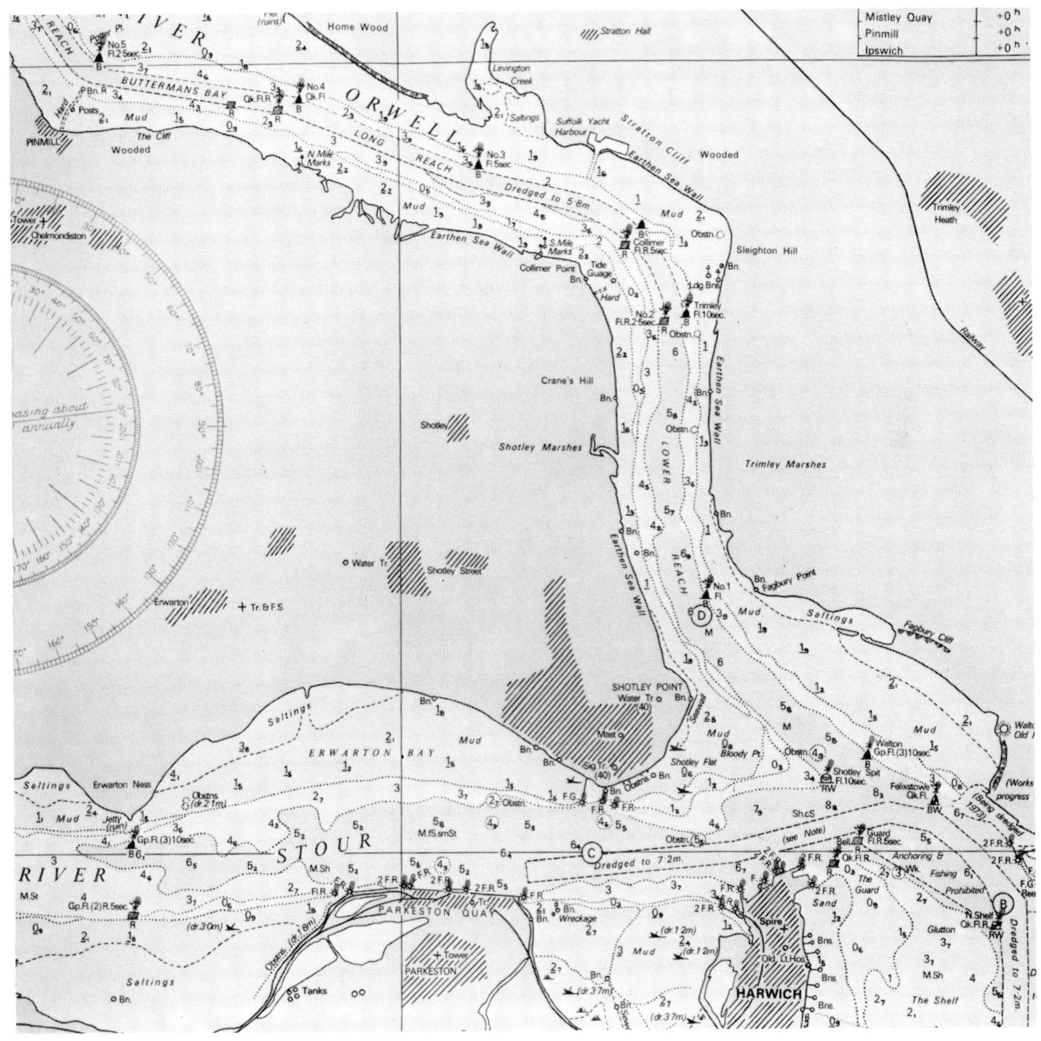

Fig. 141

we can simply strike off from one of the channel buoys, such as the Cliff Foot or the Landguard. It is not crucial so long as it gives us a course to the next mark through deep and safe waters, containing no rocks, wrecks or what-have-you.

And it is here that this longer trip differs from the short hop to Walton. We cannot lay a straight course to our destination; we have to go round a few corners. But all we do is select an easily identifiable turning point at each corner, then lay a series of courses from point to point until we arrive at our arrival point. If any course leads us through shallow or dangerous water we find another turning point somewhere along the course that will lead us clear, and steer a dogleg via that. Suppose for example we needed the height of tide plus a sounding of two metres in order to be certain of not grounding. A look at the chart will tell us that we could not set a course from the end of the breakwater as before, because of the shallow water over the Cliff Foot rocks and the Halliday Rock Flats. We would have to follow the main channel out further to sea. At first glance it might seem that a course from the Landguard buoy out to the Medusa buoy (our obvious turning point off the Naze) would be safe. A closer look, however, shows a number of shallow patches very close to the course—far too close for comfort. If, on the other hand, we carried on out of the channel to the next buoy—the red and white checked Inner Ridge, then set a course from there to the Stone Banks (the red and white unlit checked buoy in the middle of the Medusa Channel), then from there to the Medusa buoy, we would pass clear of all the shallow patches without the necessity for going miles out to sea and right round the Cork Sand. On the way from Stone Banks to the Medusa we will pass a large letter B in a circle, which, by referring to the tidal stream table on the chart, will tell us what the tide is doing out there. And it is here that we must apply a little thought.

In the river all our marks and guiding points ashore are in sight so we can simply allow for the tide by eye as we discussed in chapter five. Out here everything is much further apart—two-and-a-half miles from the Inner Ridge to the Stone Banks is a long way to see and identify a buoy for certain—so we must allow for the tide by calculating how far off our course it will set us during the time it takes us to reach the next turning point. And we must do it fairly accurately so that we don't get carried on to one of the shallow patches we pass close to. We start by finding the nearest tidal stream letter to our course and looking it up in the table on the chart. We must then estimate as accurately as we can (by checking our speed on the log and measuring the distance we must travel) what time we will leave the Inner Ridge and what time we will arrive at the Stone Banks. And we must do it, of course, before we get to the Inner Ridge so that we can set the correct course immediately we arrive. We then see from the table what the tide will be doing during this period, whereupon we have to do a little juggling. If the tide is with us, for instance, it means that the leg will take us less time, so the influence of the tide will be reduced. Vice versa if the tide is against us.

Now, there is a mathematical way of calculating this which you will find in the navigation book recommended for further reading at the end of this book. However, for small boat sailors coastal and harbour sailing, the method I am going to describe is, I feel, far more practical and less prone to calculating errors. Although, as I said before, the distances between marks when coasting are greater than when sailing in the harbour or river, they are almost never so great that one cannot home in on the turning mark, as described in the manoeuvring chapter, after sailing a relatively short distance. Thus our tidal calculation need not be mathematically and absolutely accurate. When once we can see and positively identify our next mark, we can simply sail to keep that mark on a steady bearing. This bearing, and not our course, is the track along which we will move, and laying the bearing off on the chart back from the mark will enable us to check whether we are in safe water or not. We can keep the mark in line with a shroud or something convenient on board and check its actual bearing by using a small handbearing compass, which is simply a compass that can be held in the hand to take bearings with. See fig 142.

Conversely, of course, we can do exactly the same thing with the mark we are sailing away from. If we sail to keep it on a steady bearing, and that bearing, checked frequently with the handbearing compass, is the same as the course we must move along to the next mark, we will move along that course. Thus if we can rely on seeing the next mark before losing sight of the last, we need never do any tidal calculations at all. A check of the tidal stream table to determine whether the tide is setting us to port or starboard of our track will tell us which side of our track to steer in order to counteract it. The amount we must aim off is controlled automatically by keeping the object on a steady bearing which is identical with the track we want to maintain. The only problem with this is knowing which way to turn if the bearing drifts off, but there is an easy way to remember. If the object is ahead on a bearing and it draws to the right (say, from north to 010), we must alter course to the right (starboard) until it comes back to the correct bearing. We must then hold a course slightly more to starboard than we were, in order to keep the bearing steady. If it draws to the right as we look at it (looking astern), we must move the boat to the right in order to regain the bearing: that is, to our right as we are looking astern at the mark. In other words, we must actually alter course to port, as the boat is going in the opposite direction, in order to achieve this.

Once we are sailing steadily with the buoy, lighthouse or whatever astern on a steady bearing, we can check the main steering compass and see what course we are actually steering through the water. Then, if we do lose sight of the buoy astern before seeing the mark ahead, we can simply continue sailing on that course, knowing it will make correct allowance for the tide and cause us to move along the required track to the next mark. When we can see and correctly identify the next mark (and don't assume that because it is ahead it is the one we want—check shape, colour and so on) we can then sail to keep that on the required steady bearing.

Navigating like this we can make our way simply and safely from the Inner Ridge buoy outside Harwich harbour to the Stone Banks in

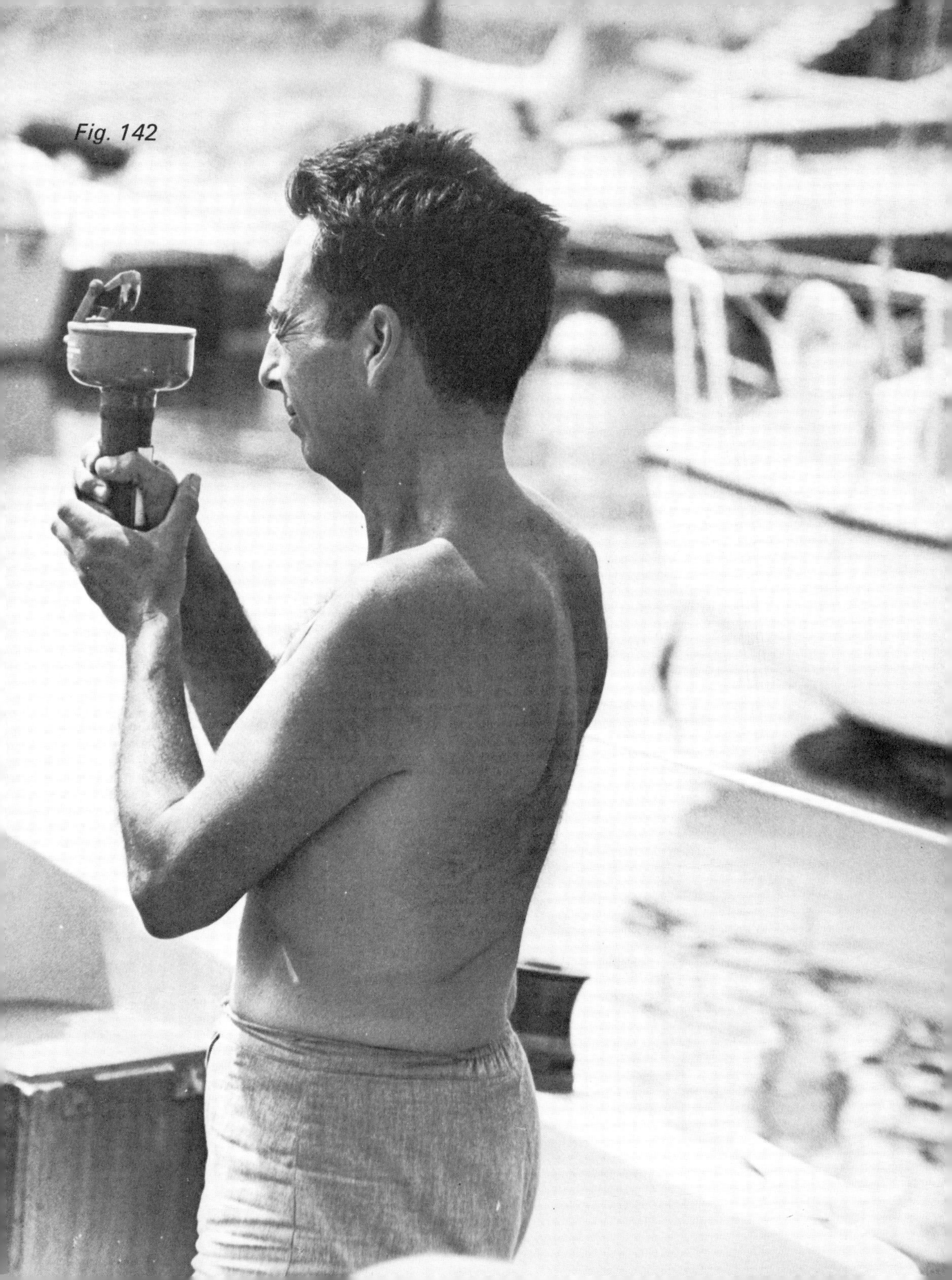

Fig. 142

the Medusa Channel, to the Medusa buoy itself, then to the Wallet No. 4 by the Gunfleet Sand, and on to the Knoll buoy outside the entrance to the Blackwater, noting that the tide for the leg down the Wallet comes under the letter D in the tidal stream table. Remember to tick each buoy off on the chart as you pass—it is surprisingly easy in a well-buoyed channel to forget which one you have just passed.

When we reach the Knoll buoy we change from the coastal chart to the harbour one, Y15 covering the River Colne. We can then make our way up to Brightlingsea in exactly the same way as we came out from Pin Mill, by following the buoys to keep in sufficiently deep and safe water, navigating and allowing for the tide by eye. However, we come to a slight snag—there are no anchors on the chart to mark the anchorages, and a relatively large place like Brightlingsea is bound to be absolutely full of moored craft. So where do we go? We don't want to pick up any ground chains with our anchor, nor do we want to anchor in the fairway where big ships might steam back and forth. Well, there are books available known as 'pilots' or 'Sailing Directions' and these give us all the information we need to know about harbours and ports: where to anchor; where not to anchor; whether any buoys are available; name and phone number of the Harbour Master; what stores and water are available; where to land in the dinghy; local yacht clubs that will welcome visiting yachtsmen and so on. With charts and pilots of the area you intend sailing in, you will have all the information you need for safe and simple coastal navigation. At the end of this book there is a list of recommended pilots and books for further study should you wish to undertake more ambitious cruises for which more advanced knowledge is required.

Figs 143 and 144 show the features mentioned earlier on the Harwich shoreline. See from the numbers how the features depicted on the chart appear in real life.

Fig. 143

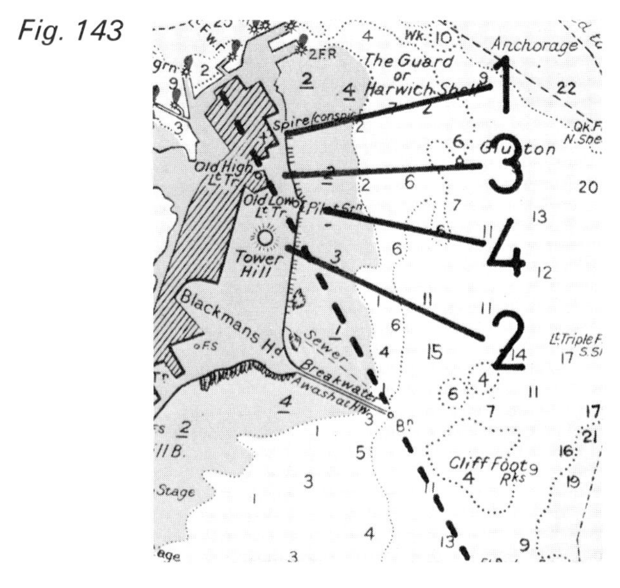

Fig. 144

2 3 1 4

Changes in the Buoyage System

Beginning in April 1977 the buoyage system round the coasts of Britain is to be gradually changed to a simpler and more logical form. The Dover Strait is the first area to be altered, followed in 1978 by the North Sea; the English Channel and Western Approaches in 1979; and the whole country is expected to be completed by 1980. It is hoped by the powers that be that the rest of the world will follow suit one of these dark and stormy days. The changes that will affect the information given in the previous chapter are as follows:

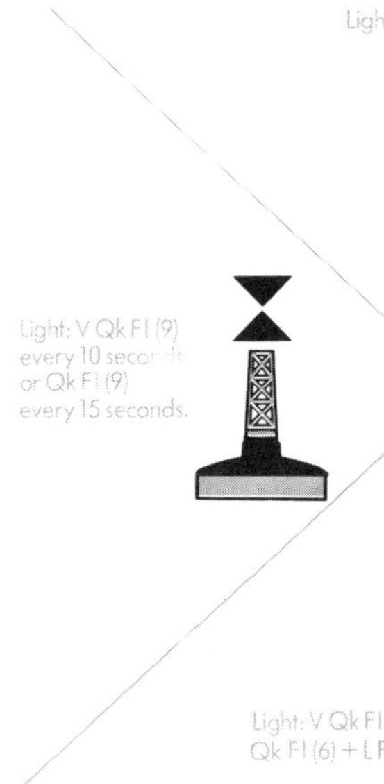

Fig. 145

1) All starboard-hand channel buoys to be changed from black to green. The buoys will then be the same as sidelights on a boat—red to port and green to starboard. Shapes of buoys stay the same.
2) Lights on channel buoys will change from white to red on port-hand buoys, green on starboard-hand buoys, thus maintaining the colour code of red to port and green to starboard.
3) There will no longer be chequered buoys, black and white or red and white. All port-hand buoys will be red with red lights; all starboard-hand green with green lights. The differing timing characteristics of lights will be retained to aid identification.

UOYS

KS

pass, the deepest water in an area or
nel.

. Fl.

Light: V Qk Fl (3) every 5 seconds or Qk Fl (3) every 10 seconds.

10 seconds or
nds.

arks are always fitted.
bout 120 flashes per minute.

CAUTION:
Buoys are an aid to navigation but should not be used without reference to a navigational chart.

OTHER MARKS

ISOLATED DANGER MARKS

Use:	To mark a small isolated danger with safe water all around.
Topmark:	2 black spheres, one above the other.
Colour:	Black, with one or more horizontal red bands.
Shape:	Pillar or spar.
Light:	Colour – white. Rhythm – group flashing (2).

SAFE WATER MARKS

Use:	Mid-channel or landfall.
Colour:	Red and white vertical stripes.
Shape:	Spherical, pillar or spar with spherical topmark.
Topmark:	(If any) Single red sphere.
Light:	Colour – white. Rhythm – isophase, occulting or 1 long flash every 10 seconds.

SPECIAL MARKS

Use:	Not to assist navigation, their purpose may be determined from the chart.
Colour:	Yellow.
Shape:	Optional, not conflicting with navigational marks.
Topmark:	(If any) Single yellow X.
Light:	Colour – yellow. Rhythm – not conflicting with white navigational lights.

4) All middle ground (spherical with horizontal stripes to mark shoal in centre of channel) and wreck buoys are to be eliminated, their job being done by a new system known as the Cardinal System. (Ordinary channel buoys are known as lateral marks as they indicate danger laterally displaced either to port or starboard of the buoy).

In the Cardinal System buoys indicate danger in a particular compass direction from the mark, although the buoys are actually named after the direction they are from the danger. This is, in fact, a modified form of the system already in use on the Continent. Where a starboard-hand buoy must be left to starboard (when travelling in the direction of the flood stream) because the danger is to starboard of it, a North buoy must be passed to the north (left to the south) as it marks the northern side of the danger. It is, in fact, a simple and easily remembered system as it is not influenced by the direction of the main flood stream.

The system comprises four buoys, North, South, East and West, which must be passed to the north, south, east and west respectively. All are pillar-type buoys coloured in black and yellow horizontal stripes, a different arrangement of the striping being used for each buoy. Lights are white. See fig 145 for full details.

The only other buoys in this new, simplified system are shown in the diagram, and they mark as their names imply. The Isolated Danger Mark shows solitary rocks and suchlike, beacons sometimes being placed on the rocks with the same markings as shown for the buoy. Safe Water Marks will indicate the centres of channels etc where there is safe water all round, while the Special Marks will mark sewage outfalls, Naval exercise areas, submerged pipelines etc. In general, things that are useful to know rather than navigationally essential.

This sytem is to be known as the IALA buoyage system (International Association of Lighthouse Authorities), and is intended to be a truly international system covering the whole of Europe, and replacing the many different existing systems.

16 The Domestic Side of Things

Well, I think we have had enough of the technicalities of navigation and suchlike for a while. Let us have a look at the domestic side of living on board a small sailing boat, for it is very different from living in a house ashore. If you can imagine stepping down from a five-bedroom mansion to a tiny bedsitter, then imagine stepping down an equivalent degree from the bedsitter, you should begin to get some idea of the problems of living on board a small sailing boat. If you can imagine this perched on top of a roller coaster at the funfair, with all the doors and windows open and a strong wind blowing sheets of rain in through all the nooks and crannies, while the family crouch in wellington boots and oilskins round a small bucket being travel sick for hours on end, then you can begin to get some idea of what it CAN (not always—so do please read on) be like at sea on a small sailing boat, especially if you haven't heeded the advice in chapter ten of this book!

It is not always as bad as that—look at the picture on the cover—but it is always cramped on a small boat. The kitchen (we call it a galley for some reason) on a twenty-five-footer will almost certainly be smaller than your airing cupboard at home, while the total living space will be about the size of a small suburban bathroom! On the other hand, you will have a different view every weekend (every five minutes when you are actually sailing), a view that you can select yourself and vary at will, a view that will almost certainly be more attractive than the one from your frosted bathroom window. So, as with most things in life, there are pros and cons. Hundreds of thousands of families have spent days and weeks on end living quite happily aboard small, cramped sailing cruisers, so there is no reason why you shouldn't do the same. All it requires is a good deal of organisation and a modicum of tolerance and patience. And they can't be bad attributes to have to encourage.

You can see the sort of space we are talking about from the photographs, and it won't take a great effort to realise that one of the most important factors going towards efficient and comfortable living aboard a small boat is tidiness. A boat is a mass of very cleverly designed drawers and cupboards, fitted into the smallest and most inaccessible places to take maximum and most efficient advantage of the limited space available. And ALL your gear must be stowed tidily in these lockers and drawers, and wedged securely. They must be tidy so that you can find them again when you want them, and they must be secure so that they do not get thrown about when the boat heels and pitches on the sea. And they must always be put back in the same place, in case you need anything in a hurry. This particularly applies to safety equipment such as lifejackets, harnesses, flares, engine spares and so on. Best of all is to label each locker and drawer with a list of the contents.

Close after tidiness comes cleanliness. This has nothing to do with morality or godliness, but a lot to do with the prevention of seasickness and low morale on board. Especially in bad weather you will find there is nothing more depressing, and nothing quite so likely to induce seasickness, as a galley sink full of greasy, dirty plates. So make a habit of always washing things up as soon as they are finished with, and keeping the whole boat, but especially the galley area, as clean as you possibly can. It will do wonders for increasing morale and reducing the chances of seasickness.

Seasickness, while we are on the subject, probably generates more homilies, half-truths and complete untruths than almost any other nautical subject. It can be a problem; it can be a terrible problem; it is certainly a most unbelievably unpleasant experience, a hundred times worse than car sickness. The first time I ever went to sea, I was sick

Lunch in the cockpit.

A galley—note the cramped space and the elastic holding the grill pan down.

solidly and continuously for about ten hours, during which time I quite genuinely wanted to die, and certainly swore blind I would never set foot on a boat again as long as I lived! The second time I went to sea I was rather unwell most of the time, but I wasn't sick. Since then, apart from an unfortunate experience putting to sea in a fishing boat at three o'clock in the morning into a full gale after a friend's pre-wedding stag night, and being told to cut up rotting, three-day-old dogfish for bait, I have never been sick at sea. The moral of all this is that the vast majority of people are sick the first couple of times they go to sea, and after this they are not. There are pills available to prevent seasickness, but they generally make you drowsy, so tend to be a mixed blessing, and if you take them all the time you will never find out whether you actually need them or not! My advice is not to take them and see how you get on after the first two or three trips. If your stomach adjusts and copes with the sea, then fine. If not, then by all means take the pills; but do try and manage without them, you will feel much better for it.

How, apart from taking pills, can we ward off seasickness? Well, the first thing is to try not to think about it. Keep busy, keep warm and keep well fed. If you start feeling a little low, get on deck and do some steering, or trim the sails or do a little maintenance. Keep out of the cabin, and especially the galley, as the atmosphere below can tend to bring it on. Keep away from the engine as the smell of oil and fuel can bring it on. Keep off greasy foods, beginning the night before, and keep off alcohol. When I was at sea in the Navy we had a cook who could be relied upon to produce greasy pork chops the moment the weather began to get rough! Believe me, don't ever eat pork chops at sea, or for a day or so before sailing. They play absolute havoc with the stomach! One final factor I have always found interesting in connection with seasickness is the proper stowage of gear below. The sight of a fish slice swinging from the deckhead (ceiling) hypnotically in time with the motion of the boat can have grown men rushing for the lee rail, hand over mouth! So keep all gear stowed securely so that

A nice chart table with flexible light and bookshelf.

none of it moves at all, whether in sight or merely rattling in a locker. The rattling will be rhythmical and will draw attention to the motion of the boat. This will then communicate itself to your stomach, and it may well rebel. The same thing applies on deck. Keep everything securely lashed and stowed, and never watch the mast swinging back and forth across the horizon! If you follow these simple rules, there is an excellent chance that you will never be troubled with seasickness, especially if you can endeavour to sleep aboard the boat the night before sailing, as this will get your body used to being on the water.

If you are seasick, drink plenty of water as you will be dehydrated, eat dry biscuits, keep warm and out in the fresh air. Find a job to do and concentrate on it. If others on board are seasick, don't whatever you do, commiserate with them. The worst thing a seasick person can do is feel sorry for himself. You must joke and laugh about it, draw him out of himself, and keep him out of himself by chatting and generally obliging him to talk and do things. Anything to take his mind off being seasick. I remember the first time I went to sea, the only thing that kept me from jumping over the side and putting an end to it all was a Petty Officer who kept popping out of the galley with a bacon sandwich stuck in his mouth and asking me if I wanted one! I couldn't help laughing, and it made me feel immediately better.

Well, I think that's enough of seasickness for a while! Let's have a look at cooking. Not pork chops, but simple, nourishing meals that cook quickly and easily in one pan. Sandwiches and flasks of coffee are all right in a car, but no use to anyone on a boat. Fresh sea air makes you amazingly hungry and you really need decent meals—good hot stews or proper salads, depending on the weather, and plenty of them. With a little ingenuity and a browse through the cook books, you can always come up with something that is prepared quickly and simply, thrown into a pan and left to brew while you get on deck and back to the sailing. That is the secret. And if you don't like cooking, remember that it is traditional on board boats that the cook never does the washing up. So you pays your money and you takes your choice!

Many people think they will have problems keeping perishable food like milk and butter on board ship without a fridge, and often go to the expense and bother of iceboxes, or even 12-volt fridges. For relatively long cruises in large boats the latter are probably a good idea if you don't mind the expense, and the weather is very hot. But it is amazingly cool down in the bilges (the very bottom) of the average boat, even when the actual weather is very hot. In a hot British summer for example, the sea temperature never gets very high, and the bottom of the bilges, surrounded by all that cool water, will keep milk and butter fresh for days, certainly over a weekend's cruise. It is an excellent place to store the beer too, and will keep it cool enough for the most fastidious tastes. In many years of sailing in temperate

In very small boats you will not have the luxury of a chart table.

climates I have never found it necessary to buy special food or specially packed food of any kind. Get hold of a plastic milk crate and secure it in the bilge—you will have a very neat, compartmentalised stowage for bottles, cans, packets of butter, meat and so on, in which they will keep for as long as you are ever likely to need them.

Apart from these few comments, cooking on board the boat is much the same as it is in your kitchen at home, with the very big difference that the boat is constantly moving and lurching about, especially in any kind of a sea. With cramped conditions and a gas stove this can produce the very real possibility of burns and scalds unless you are extremely careful. The stove should have rails round the edges to keep the pots and pans in place, and you must keep yourself very firmly wedged in the galley, near to but clear of the cooker. Don't make any attempt to stand in front of the stove and sway to the movement of the boat the way sailors do on the television. Not only does it require considerable practice, but it is very tiring and not nearly so comfortable as wedging yourself and simply going with the boat when she rolls. This latter technique is also less likely to bring on seasickness, so is to be particularly recommended for the cook!

The possibility of burns and scalds, of course, brings us to the question of first aid. If you are simply pottering around a harbour you are, quite frankly, no further from a doctor than you would be at home, so there is really no need for any more elaborate first aid equipment or knowledge than you have at home. When you go out to sea, however, things are a little different. You can be a very long way from a doctor even only a few miles offshore, so you must be equipped a little more thoroughly. I am not going to tell you what you should carry on board and what you should know, but at the end of this book is a list of books that I recommend you should carry on board. One of them is a first aid book and it will tell you all you need to know, and give you a comprehensive, but sensible, list of the things you should carry in a clearly-marked, white-painted box carrying a large red cross. Stow it in a dry, obvious place so that you don't have to search for it when you need it.

It is not reasonable to expect the average sailor to remember a detailed selection of first aid procedures, so don't try. Apart from mouth-to-mouth resuscitation, which you should know thoroughly as it is likely to be needed in a great hurry, if you have a good book on board and know roughly where to find the information on various ills, you won't go far wrong. The point to remember about mouth-to-mouth resuscitation is that it is probably the quickest, simplest and most efficient way of getting air into a drowning person's lungs, and therefore oxygen to his brain, and approximately two minutes without oxygen will leave him with permanent brain damage. So you must act fast. Anyway, it is all in the first aid book. Read it, learn the resuscitation, and keep the book handy on board, near to or in the first aid box.

Finally, it is important to realise that first aid is not a substitute for a doctor—it is simply a means of preventing further damage occurring to the patient while he is taken to a doctor. So don't try to be too clever. If you are out at sea and need a doctor urgently, fire off a red flare. It is an emergency, and that is what the emergency services are for. But be sensible. It takes time for emergency services to be alerted, then to put to sea and reach you. If you can get to shore in a reasonable time, then do so, and call the doctor from there. If there is a big ship nearby you can use your white flares to attract his attention; he might have a doctor on board. If not, he will have radio and will be able to radio for advice, or for a doctor to come out if the situation is sufficiently serious to warrant it. And that means a life in danger—not just someone in pain or discomfort. As with most of the things we have discussed in this book, it is largely a matter of keeping calm and applying commonsense to the situation.

But sailing is not one long saga of accidents and dramas. It is living on board your boat, visiting new places, meeting new people, and enjoying a whole new way of life. You will be delighted to hear that life at sea is very different from life on the roads in your car. If you are broken down, people don't roar past ignoring you. At sea we generally discover our hidden qualities of helpfulness and courtesy; we help one another and we are friendly towards one another, so it might be an idea to mention one or two specific ways in which this works. The newcomer to sailing cannot be expected to realise immediately what is expected of him, what is appreciated and what is not, in a strange and unfamiliar environment. But it is important to know for example, what to do when we berth in a strange place. Very often we will have to tie up alongside another boat. Even if we have been instructed to do so by the Harbour Master, it does no harm to hail the boat on approach and ask if he minds you berthing alongside. If he is rude and says he does mind, you can then simply tell him you have been told to do so, but it very rarely happens. Make sure you put plenty of fenders out, and secure yourself properly, and put head and stern ropes to the shore, or piles, as well as on to your neighbour. You cannot expect his lines to take the weight of your boat as well as his, and if he wants to slip out in the middle of the night, he can do so with the minimum of inconvenience. When you go ashore, walk as quietly as possible over his foredeck, so that you do not intrude into his cockpit. Privacy is hard enough to find on a small boat, and it is most important that we all respect it.

If you find someone becalmed outside a harbour and you have a motor, offer him a tow in. Don't charge him a fat fee, simply accept the drink he will offer you, enjoy the fact that you have done someone a good turn, and remember that it might happen to you one day. And that, basically, is what courtesy at sea is all about. Simply imagine yourself in the other fellow's place, and behave as you would like him to. If that sounds a bit trite in this day and age, remember that life at sea runs far more slowly than that ashore, and there is time for these little niceties. Enjoy them.

17 Sailing at Night

Sailing at night is one of the most exciting and rewarding of experiences; a time when the sailor feels closest of all to the sea and the sky, the stars and all the elements with which he shares his boat. It is a time when the workaday cares and strife of the civilised shore seem most removed from his little floating kingdom; when the plankton rise from the depths to paint phosphorescent streamers about his passage through the dark and mysterious seas. It is a time that stirs even boring old yachting writers to poetry—a time of complete magic.

It can also be jolly cold and very tiring. So let us look at some of the ways in which we can ensure the minimum of discomfort and the maximum of magic. But first let me say that sailing at night is not to be undertaken lightly. It is dark, the wind seems stronger and the waves bigger, the coastline has to be interpreted purely from its lights, other ships' movements have to be assessed from the lights they carry, sails have to be trimmed and the boat sailed largely by feel; in short we need a reasonable amount of experience before sailing off into the sunset.

Let us imagine you have been sailing your boat a fair bit and have got to know her thoroughly, so that you feel confident to handle her in the dark. You have made a simple coastal passage (the same one) a few times so that you know the landmarks, where the lights are and so on. The time is ripe for a night passage, so let us go through the necessary preparations. The first thing we need is a set of lights so that other boats can see us. These are little more complex than lights on a car as it is important that they show other boats which direction we are heading in. To achieve this we have a red light on the port side of the boat, which shows only from right ahead to just abaft the beam. On the starboard side we have a green light showing over the same arc, and at the stern we have a white light that fills in the gap. These three lights can be replaced by a single tri-colour lamp at the masthead, which has the great advantage that only one bulb is used for all three lights so a more powerful one can be used without draining the battery too much. Also, being higher up, the lights are more easily seen. When we are motoring we must also show an extra white light above the sailing lights, which is displayed from just abaft the port beam through for'ard to just abaft the starboard beam. In effect, it covers the same arc as the port and starboard lights together. See fig 146 and fig

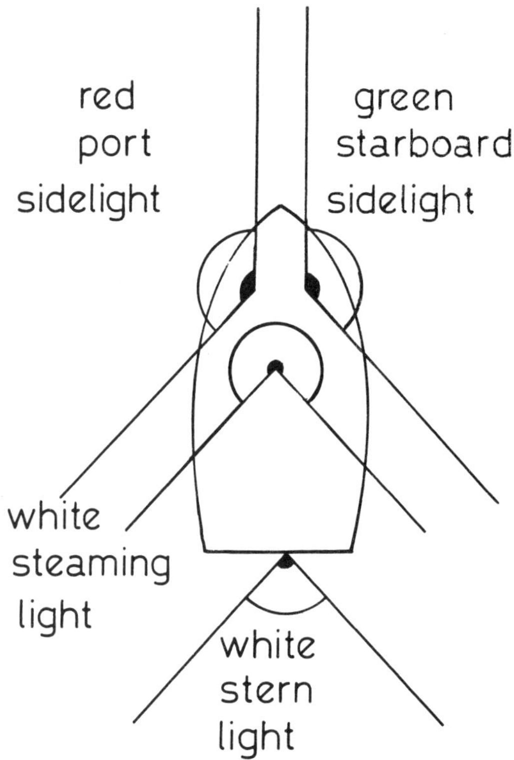

Fig. 146

Fig. 147 A typical set of electric side lights fitted to the pulpit of a small cruiser.

147. One more light we must have is a white one showing all round that we can hoist about halfway up the forestay to show we are anchored. Paraffin lamps are quite good for this if they are designed not to blow out (hurricane lamps, for instance), or you can obtain small electric lights with long leads that can be plugged into sockets inside the forehatch. Permanent anchor lights on the masthead are too high, and can be very confusing to someone approaching an anchorage.

Apart from the navigation lights, which should be as bright as possible, and a couple of really powerful heavy-duty torches for emergencies, all lights in the boat must be dim, or capable of being dimmed. This is because your eyes take nearly half an hour to adjust fully to the darkness after being in bright white light. For about five minutes you are almost completely blind, after which you can see, but it will be almost half an hour before you see *properly*. This is clearly a very dangerous situation, so it is vital we keep all lights as dim as possible. There will be a light in your compass which almost certainly has a dimmer switch on it. If it hasn't, fit one, and keep the compass light as dim as you possibly can. There is no need to peer at it all the time; in fact you shouldn't. Steer on a star, lighthouse, buoy or something, or simply by the wind, with just occasional glances at the compass to check the course. You will sail better, enjoy it more, and be less prone to seasickness and cold.

Down below you want a dim light over the chart table and one over the galley, so that you can navigate and brew up without losing your night sight. Try dim red lights. They are very much less harmful to night vision than white ones if your eyes are good enough to see by them. And talking of eyes—make sure you are not colour blind to white, red and green! If you are, then ensure there is always someone with you who isn't.

It can get very cold sitting in a cockpit steering at night, however hot the day has been, so make sure you have plenty of warm clothing on board. Two or three thin shirts and jumpers are better than one thick one, as they create air layers that are very effective at keeping out the cold. An oilskin or sailcloth smock will keep out the wind, and short rubber boots and thick socks will keep your feet warm. The inner man, or woman is best served with hot drinks and biscuits.

Keep a powerful torch handy in the cockpit for checking the burgee and the trim of the sails, as well as any emergencies, but keep its beam well clear of your eyes or you will lose your night sight. And always wear a harness at night, even sitting in the cockpit, with the line secured such that you cannot go right over the side. Even a lifebuoy with a light attached can be extremely difficult to see at night, and if you are on your own in the cockpit you will stand no chance of being found by the time those below, probably asleep, realise what has happened. With two or three, or even four, aboard you will obviously have to spend time sailing alone while the others sleep, changing over every two or three hours so you each get your fair share of sleep and sailing. We call this routine watchkeeping and, although not really necessary during the daytime on short coastal hops, it is essential at night so that we all get some sleep. The traditional watch is four hours, but this is too long for a man alone in the cockpit of a small boat, too long even for two of you, so cut it down to three hours, or two if the weather is rough. You'll find that quite long enough. Finally, get up in good time for your watch and make a hot drink for yourself and the person you are taking over from. It will be very much appreciated, and will give him or her a chance to fill you in on what is happening—the course you are steering, buoys, lighthouses etc in sight, any ships about and what they are doing, where you are and so on.

Avoiding other ships at night involves exactly the same procedure as doing so in daytime, except that you cannot see the other ship, only his lights. So you must work out which way he is headed, and what tack he is on if a sailing boat, from his lights. Take a look at fig 146 again. If you see, for example, a red light all on its own you can deduce immediately that it is a sailing boat's port side. A motor boat would have a white light above it showing over the same arc, and he, of course, must keep clear of you, unless by any chance you are overtaking him, in which case you would see not his red side light, but his white stern light. If you are going fast enough to overtake the average motor boat anyway, it must be blowing a gale and you shouldn't be at sea at all. It is a very unlikely situation, so let's go back to the sailing boat.

Knowing which side of him you can see and knowing the wind direction, you can work out what tack he is on, and therefore who has right of way. You then take a bearing of him, or simply line the light up with a shroud, and see whether he is moving ahead or astern of you, in which case there is no problem. Keep checking till he is well clear, in case he alters course. If he is on a steady bearing you alter course away from him (go under his stern) if it is his right of way, and hold your course if it is yours. But watch him to make sure he does alter away. He might have fallen asleep, or just not have seen you; so be prepared for the possibility of a last minute avoidance.

Big ships pose a slightly different problem. In open water they should keep clear of you, but even with radar, small sailing boats are extremely difficult to see at night. And quite frankly, many big ships do not seem to keep as good a lookout as they should, and even if they do see you wait till the very last moment before altering. My advice is simply to keep out of the way of all big ships, especially at night. Big ships invariably carry two white steaming lights on their masts, the for'ard one being lower than the after one, so you can tell from a very long way off which way they are going. See fig 148. A check on the bearing will tell you if you are on a collision course, in which case you can alter course only a few degrees while he is a long way off, and sail well clear of him. But, particularly in coastal waters near headlands or harbours, watch him and keep checking till he is well clear. You'll know if he begins to alter course because his steaming lights will draw together or open out, and the direction he alters is the direction his lower (for'ard) steaming light moves. Don't bother about his

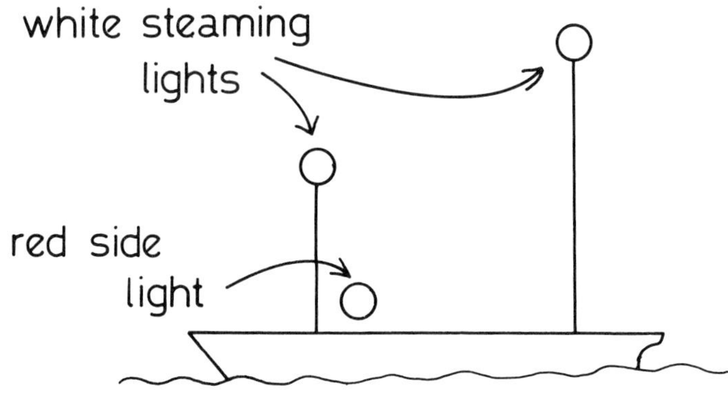

Fig. 148 big ship - port side

sidelights, they will not be visible at anything like the range of the steaming lights, and are usually well obscured by deck or cabin lights anyway. If you can see a big ship's sidelights he is almost certainly too close for comfort.

The other kind of vessel we must watch for at night is the fishing boat. Fishing boats have right of way over you, and they show special lights which I won't confuse you with as you can never see them through the mass of powerful working lights they have all over the deck. If you see a great mass of white light, or a number of them dotted about, and they appear to be stopped or moving very slowly, they are fishing boats as sure as this is a book. Keep well clear of them as they may have long nets out.

Navigating at night is exactly the same as navigating in the day except that all we see is a collection of lights—flashing, fixed, occulting, isophase, red, white, orange, green, all of varying characteristics as we explained in chapter fifteen. The problem is to sort through them and find the ones we want—the lighthouse or buoy that we are heading for. A well-marked harbour approach can look very confusing with its profusion of lights, but it is not difficult to find the ones we want so long as we go about it methodically. First we memorise the characteristics of the lights we want and find from the chart the approximate bearings they should be on. We then look out on that bearing and methodically check each light in the vicinity in turn till we come to the one we want. We then take an accurate bearing of it and steer directly for it (assuming it is navigationally safe to do so—we haven't got any corners to go round), and ignore all the others. But be very careful you have got the right one; if there are any waves the lights could be disappearing from time to time and giving the impression of having different characteristics.

The real problem at night is getting into an anchorage. If you look at fig 149 you will see how confusing an anchorage can look at night. This is the Walton Backwaters. So for your first few trips make the night passage back to your home port where you know precisely the layout of the boats, and where you know there is a buoy you can go straight to and pick up, or a marina berth you can go straight into. When you've done this a few times, try a quiet spot that you know well for your first strange night anchorage. You'll soon build up your confidence and ability to cope with restricted waters at night.

Sailing at night really is the most wonderful experience, but I must stress again that you should wait until you know your way around your boat thoroughly and have some experience and confidence under your belt before trying it. Everything is more difficult at night than it is in the daylight; you tend to be less alert as your system takes time to adjust to nighttime routines, and the general geography of land and other ships, even when you know the land, can seem strange and confusing. Familiarity should breed confidence, but never let it breed contempt where the sea is concerned. She doesn't like it; and she has her ways of letting you know. Always treat her with respect, and she will reward you with a tremendous amount of pleasure and satisfaction.

Fig. 149 A crowded anchorage at night can be very confusing with a mass of anchor lights showing.

18 Elementary Maintenance

Maintenance, even for a fibreglass boat, is a big subject and I do not propose to go into it in any depth here. At the end of the book I recommend further reading which you should do before attempting a winter refit or any major maintenance jobs, but in the meantime let's take a look at the important aspects of running maintenance that you should be aware of. These can be likened to the simple jobs you do all the time on your car, such as topping up the windscreen washer bottle, checking the oil and water and tyres and so on.

While we are on the subject of the car let's begin with the auxiliary engine, as the routine is more or less the same. Once a week (before you sail on a Friday night) check the oil—engine, gearbox and reduction box (if fitted); check there is plenty of grease in the stern tube greaser and give it a couple of turns; check the cooling water header tank and the fuel tank; check the battery; and have a quick check round that all pipe clips and electrical connections are tight. Have a look round for any oil or water or fuel leaks, and get them attended to as soon as possible (fuel leaks immediately!) You should have a handbook with the engine which will give you details of all the servicing to be done and when. Stick to it religiously, do the routine jobs we have just mentioned, and your engine will serve you well.

On deck, check that all the bottlescrews are secure, and keep the threads, and all your shackle pin threads, lightly greased with lanolin or something similar. Check bilge pumps are clear and working properly. Check gas bottle for secure stowage, and make sure all connections are tight. After changing a bottle check for leaks by rubbing soapy water over the connection. Check, above all, for any signs of chafe. If the sheets or sails are rubbing against bottlescrews or shrouds, they will be worn to shreds in no time. Split plastic tube wrapped around bottlescrews and stays will prevent this, but try to lead your sheets so that they do not rub against anything. Rope is very expensive, and once it starts to chafe it will lose its strength very quickly. Sails are even more expensive so look after them. Modern synthetic sailcloth is very resistant but the stitching is prone to chafe as its stands proud of the cloth. At the first sign of wear put a few stitches in to reinforce it. When you lay up for the winter you can send them to a sailmaker for a thorough check over. Synthetic materials generally do not like strong sunlight, so keep your ropes stowed below and a cover on the mainsail, especially if it is coloured, as it will fade.

If you have any varnished woodwork around the boat, have a pot of varnish and brush on board. Any scratches or scrapes can then be varnished over quickly as soon as they happen, and this will prevent the wood discolouring and making a major revarnish job necessary during the winter. The same with a wooden mast. These are very prone to chafe from the halliards, so always rig frapping lines to hold them clear of the mast when you are not sailing.

One of the best things you can do for the maintenance of your boat, especially if she is wooden, is to ensure you have good ventilation throughout the boat. Ideally you should have a vent right at the very stern and one right in the bow, but one in the forehatch and one in the mainhatch will certainly suffice to keep the air fresh and clean in a fibreglass boat, where you haven't got the rot problem that a wooden boat has.

Fibreglass boats really are almost maintenance free, certainly when compared with wooden boats. The only problem is that, because you don't have to keep painting them, they tend to get rather scruffy-looking, so try to wash off any stains—tea leaves carelessly thrown over the side, scum from the water, and especially oil from dirty harbours—as soon as you can. A simple rub over with sea water will shift most dirt if it is done soon enough, and a bit of washing up liquid will help if it isn't. Oil can be removed with petrol, but use it sparingly and don't splash it about. Once a year, at the beginning of the season, you can give the hull a thorough cleaning with one of the proprietary cleaners available, then a good coating of fibreglass polish will help to keep it clean and smart. All these products should be available at your local chandler.

Under the water all boats are treated with a special paint called 'antifouling'. This slowly releases poisons into the water which prevent marine growth such as weed and barnacles from attaching themselves to your bottom. There are various types and they all work best in certain conditions, so ask your local chandler for the one best suited to conditions around your cruising area. With a good one you should need to do it only once a season, just before launching in the spring, as anti-fouling does not as a rule like being left out of the water for long. Ask your chandler for advice and read the instructions. A book such as the one I recommend in the appendix will give you fuller details, but for the moment it is useful to realise roughly what it is all about, so you can watch out for a build-up of fouling if your local area is particularly bad for it, and have the boat hauled out for a scrub if necessary, or simply dry her out on a fairly hard beach and scrub her there. Alternatively you can lean her against a wall and let her dry out as the tide goes away. It all depends on the type of boat you have and the local facilities available. A twin keel boat will dry out easily anywhere, but a single keel boat really needs laying against a wall or posts, or hauling out on a cradle. Drying out can be quite a tricky operation so let's look at it in a little detail. Not only is it necessary for scrubbing off and underwater work, but it can also be very useful when cruising, if you want to visit a small harbour that dries out at low water.

The first thing we must do is find a suitable wall where the water is deep enough at high water to get alongside, but dries out completely at low water. We can calculate this from the tidal heights and the soundings on the chart. For it to dry out it must have drying soundings alongside it (those with a line underneath them) that are greater than the height at low water. At low water then the tide will fall below the level of this ground. We must then check that the bottom is flat and clear of rocks or rubbish, and that it is fairly hard. The only certain and safe way of doing this is actually to go and look at it when it dries out. If you have posts in your harbour that are specially designed and built for drying out against, you will have no problems, but with a strange harbour wall you cannot be too careful. A boat dried out against a wall is fairly delicately balanced and it does not need much to cause her to fall over—very embarrassing and very expensive!

When we have selected a suitable spot we must select a suitable date, almost certainly at Spring tides, when the range of the tide is sufficient both to float us on and dry us out, and with a good margin for floating on. If we cut it very fine, a slight increase in atmospheric pressure, or a strong wind in the wrong direction, could lower the height and we could find ourselves stuck there for a fortnight or more. It is best to go on while the tides are making up (getting bigger), then we know the next day's tide will be a bit higher and that should allow for any variations.

When we have chosen place and time to our satisfaction, and made arrangements with the owner of wall or posts to use them, we can go ahead. There are two basic things we must remember before actually going on. First we must heel the boat over slightly towards the wall, to ensure that she lays comfortably against it with lots of big fat fenders (car tyres are excellent but you will have to lay a piece of old sail or something between them and the hull to prevent rubber marks). We can do this by piling weights on that side of the deck—anchors and chain, gas bottles and so on—and as an extra safety measure we can take a halliard from the masthead to a strong point well inshore from the wall and haul it tight when she grounds. Don't heel her over too much or it will put a lot of strain on the topsides: she only wants sufficient list to ensure that she leans that way on grounding. And try to place your fenders against strongpoints inside, such as bulkheads. The second main point is that, unless you are very experienced indeed and know the wall, you must watch her go down and keep adjusting the mooring lines to hold her against the wall. If she drifts out a little as she grounds she will stick like glue and end up listing far too much, so this point is very important. And don't clear off to the pub the moment she grounds, you must watch her right until the water has gone away so far that there is no chance of her lifting a little and maybe pivoting on the keel to assume a bad angle with the wall.

Finally, make sure the wall is sheltered from wind, waves and strong tides if possible. Check the weather forecast so that you can be certain the weather will remain quiet while you are on the wall, and berth facing up the beach, not down, as she will sit far more comfortably. It can be a tricky operation, but if you heed this advice carefully you should be all right. Try to get someone who has done it before to accompany you the first time; you will find it reassuring.

A lot of the worst scrubbing can be done afloat, however, as the waterline tends to pick up weed more than the hull below water. Just go round in the dinghy with a scrubbing brush and scrub it off. This is worth doing as it is amazing how much the stuff slows you down. It is an ideal job for mischievous children when you want to relax and savour the peace and tranquillity of a quiet anchorage.

That about sums up the running maintenance necessary to keep your boat in good condition, unless you have an old wooden boat, in which case I refer you to the book in the appendix. Do carry a reasonable set of tools (and keep them dry—a tool box with an oily rag draped over the tools works well) for dealing with any minor problems that may crop up, particularly with the engine, and some sail needles and thread for any odd stitches the sails may need.

19 Buying a Boat

How do we set about buying a boat? There are so many to choose from these days, and so many different specifications and prices, that it can be a very difficult job deciding what boat to buy, whether to buy new or secondhand and so on. My advice is quite simply—don't buy a boat at all. Not until you've done at least a little sailing: enough to get a reasonably clear idea of your requirements, anyway. Buying a boat is not like buying a car; it is a great deal more complicated, and it really is impossible to gauge your needs properly until you've been in and seen a few boats about, so that you have some idea of what boats are, and what an advertiser means when he says 'four comfortable berths'. Remember how the estate agent described your house to you before you saw it? Boat salesmen are much the same. 'Roomy and spacious' for instance, has quite different connotations to a sailor than it would have to a non-sailor!

Having glibly told you not to buy a boat, I'd better make some suggestions as to how you can get sailing. The easiest way is to scrounge a few trips with a friend who has got a sailing boat, but failing this, there are many sailing schools about where you can have a week's sailing with tuition for a very reasonable price, and I would recommend this very strongly before you think about buying your own boat. A week at a reputable sailing school will not only give you the chance to see and experience boats and sailing, and get the general feel of the whole thing, it will also surround you with experienced and helpful sailors who will be happy to talk boats with you, discuss the sort of boat you personally want, and give you some ideas to start you

P
300

off. A little experience like this will be worth its weight in gold before you start to look for your own boat. Addresses of recognised and reputable sailing schools can be obtained from the controlling yachting authority of your country (see appendix) and from various publications (see appendix).

When you do start to look for a boat try to see at least pictures and details of as many different boats as you can, so that you get some idea of what is available, before you actually go to a yacht broker and give him your requirements. The photographs show a typical selection. Read all the yachting magazines, which contain many illustrated advertisements, plus the various publications that are available that list all the production small yachts that are on sale (see appendix). There are a tremendous number of small sailing yachts on the market these days, but your experience at the sailing school should give you a fair idea of what you want. You will then be able to draw up a short list from those available which you can take to a reputable broker (look through the advertisements in the yachting press), then discuss with him the pros and cons of each one. You can also discuss with him the advantages of buying new or secondhand.

Let us have a look here, however, at the question of new or secondhand, and also at some of the main points you should consider before drawing up your short list. The problem of buying new or secondhand is more difficult than it is with cars, as boats do not depreciate in the same way: in fact, a good boat will appreciate in value, so buying new is not necessarily the financial burden it might seem. You will also almost certainly get more advantageous credit terms on a new boat. On the other hand, a very large proportion of the expense in buying a boat lies in the ancillaries, such as anchors, warps, extra sails, bunk cushions, engine, boathooks, dinghy etc, etc, many of which are not included in the new price of a boat, but which, of course, will be thrown in with a secondhand boat, together with a lot of other useful and expensive gear. This also will save you the bother of working out precisely what extra gear you need, buying it, and

installing it. A secondhand boat, assuming it is in good condition, and a proper survey by a qualified surveyor (which is an absolute must before buying secondhand) will check this, will also be tried and tested; any little problems will have been discovered and corrected; the rig probably balanced and tuned; the engine run in and settled down; and, even gear stowed in suitable places that the previous owner has discovered from trial and error to be best.

There is a lot to be said for buying your first boat secondhand, as long as you employ a reputable broker and good surveyor. Both are to be found advertising in the yachting press, but if you find a good broker he will arrange the survey for you anyway. If you do want to buy new for any reason, then make sure it is a well-tried and long-running design. You would be surprised how many new designs appear on the market long before they are sorted out properly, and how much rubbish manages to stay on the scene for a few months before folding up. Buy a badly designed boat and you are in trouble. It will probably cost you a fortune to put it right (assuming it is possible), by which time word will have got round about it, and you'll never be able to sell it. Clearly this does not apply to well-established reputable firms, but even they have their occasional gambled off-moments, the odd design which for some unknown reason does not work. It may suit you, but no one else, and you must think of the possibility that after you have sailed her for a season or two, your ideas will have developed and changed, and you will want a different boat. So resale value for your first boat is an important consideration. New, experimental designs are fine for the experienced yachtsman who knows exactly what he wants, but they spell terrible trouble for the beginner. Tell your broker that you want a popular, well-established class of boat that will resell easily. When you have had more experience you can take a flier, but not now.

Now let us have a look at some of the things you should consider before selecting your boat. None of them are technical, structural, or in any way nautical: that side of it is what you pay the broker and

SM

surveyor for. What we are interested in is the domestic side of things—number of berths, type of motor, space and so on. Inevitably, the first thing you must consider is the number of berths, depending on the size of your family and/or the number of friends you intend sailing with. And it is not quite as simple as it sounds. If you want a modicum of comfort you must realise that you won't get it in an 18-footer with four berths. Designers can cram a lot of berths into a small boat these days, and we need to be a little wary. Only if we intend mainly day sailing with perhaps the occasional night aboard, would a small boat around the twenty-foot mark be adequate for a family with two children. These would have to be small enough to be happy in the miniscule cots you will find up for'ard, and there will be space for two adults.

If, however, you intend to take longer cruises, even short weekend jobs, you would be well advised (if you can afford it) to go for something around twenty-five to thirty feet. A boat of this size will give comfortable accommodation for four (luxurious by some sailors' standards!) with enough room and temporary berths to take two more. And it will be far more comfortable all round, especially at sea.

And so on up the scale; but that should give you a basis to work on.

The next thing you must decide is whether to have twin keels or a single keel. The latter will generally perform better, but needs deeper water to sail in and can only dry out temporarily against a wall; it must lie on a mooring where it floats all the time. If the area in which you intend sailing dries out extensively at low water you might be well advised to go for a twin keeler as it can be left on a mooring that dries out every tide without coming to any harm. It will also sit upright, so can be dried out anywhere that you want to visit without any discomfort for those on board, so long as you are certain the bottom is clear of rocks or obstructions. A twin keeler draws less water than a similar size single keel boat, so it can be sailed in shallower waters, which can be quite an important consideration in many places. Discuss this in detail with your broker when you have decided where to keep

CR
822
CR
822
SCILLA
SCILLA

your boat. And see the next chapter.

The next thing we must consider is whether to buy a fibreglass or wooden boat. A wooden boat is without a doubt a beautiful thing; but it can be a real labour of love to keep it in good repair. Unless you are sufficiently dedicated to want to spend hours and hours and hours rubbing down, painting, varnishing and Heaven knows what else, you shouldn't even think about buying a wooden boat. A good quality fibreglass boat requires hardly any maintenance at all, and is therefore a clear favourite for the man who wants to spend his free time sailing rather than 'messing about in boats'.

The final major factor we must consider (and this really only applies to boats over about 30 feet) is whether we want a true sailing boat with auxiliary power, or what we term a 'motor-sailer'. The latter generally has a much bigger engine than the normal sailing boat and less sail. It is likely to be bigger for its length, and thus more spacious and comfortable, but will not sail so well as a pure sailing boat. On the other hand, if the weather is dreary and wet you usually have some sort of covered wheelhouse and can potter about in reasonable comfort under the big engine, which will drive you over adverse tides much faster than the sailing boat's auxiliary. In calm weather you will be able to make much faster passages. If you intend making a lot of longish cruises, like a bit of comfort (they don't normally heel over so much either), aren't averse to a bit of noisy motoring, are more interested in 'being on the sea' than pure sailing, then it could be the boat for you. Discuss it with your broker.

Those are the main points we must consider before selecting our boat. After that you will probably find your bank balance determines the final choice from the short list. But do check exactly what you are getting for your money. A better equipped but more expensive boat may prove to be cheaper in the long run, by the time you have bought all the bits and pieces for a cheaper one. And you must consider the question of running costs. The bigger the boat the more expensive will be mooring and harbour dues, and these can constitute a large part of

ARCO

955 Y
55 Y

your annual costs. And a motor-sailer will cost more in fuel and engine maintenance than a sailing boat with a little auxiliary. Discuss it with your broker.

I hope any brokers reading this (hopefully none—as they are generally experienced yachtsmen in their own right, which is why you should discuss your requirements with them) aren't cursing me for these exhortations to 'discuss it with your broker', but that is what they are there for. There is no point in my telling you all the minor points you should look for in a boat, as they will probably go straight over your head. If you can understand the major factors that we have listed, you will be in a good position to select, in conjunction with your broker, exactly the right boat for your requirements.

20 Getting Afloat

Actually getting from your armchair in front of the television on to a boat on the water is not always quite as simple as it sounds. It requires a certain amount of investigation and organisation, so let us have a look at how we go about it.

The question of how to get away for a sail before you think of buying your own boat is, as far as I am concerned, very simple if you live in Britain—you join the Island Cruising Club. But first perhaps I should declare an interest—I worked there as a skipper for a couple of years, and am still a member. I love the club and think it is a wonderful place for a beginner to make his first tentative steps into the strange environment of the sea. So, admittedly, I am biased. Equally, I know the place well, so am reasonably qualified to comment on it. So I shall. If you don't live in Britain, or you don't like my biased opinions, then write to your national yachting association (listed in the appendix), and ask them to recommend a sailing school to suit your particular requirements. And this goes for any country. Simply write to the main yachting organisation for your area.

If you don't mind biased opinions, let me tell you a little about the Island Cruising Club. Set in Salcombe, South Devon, the Club members jointly own something like thirty-odd dinghies, four small cruising yachts and four very large ones. All the staff are members of the Club, and everyone is a joint owner of all the boats, so there is a very friendly, non-commercial atmosphere about the place. It exists solely, in the words of the Secretary Ted Pearce, 'to get as many people afloat as possible, from all walks of life, as cheaply as we can', and it does that very thing extremely well.

If you want a high-powered, solid instructional course you can take it in dinghies with experienced and qualified instructors, while living afloat in the Club's converted Mersey Ferry. If you prefer a more relaxed approach you can take a cruise in one of the big boats, in which the instructional aspect is less organised, and you can learn as much or as little as you want. You will be handsomely looked after by a skipper, mate and cook, all of whom will be happy to talk boats with you and, as I said in the previous chapter, help you make up your mind about the sort of boat you want. Mind you, after a cruise with the ICC you might decide it is not worth the hassle of buying and owning your own boat, when membership of the club enables you to sail anything from a 13-foot dinghy to an Olympic racing keelboat, or 35-foot cruising yachts, or 50-foot, 40-year-old racing cruising yachts, or

A typical marina—crowded but convenient.

a 50-ton Grand Banks type schooner, or a 78-ton converted sailing trawler! If you want further information write to Ted Pearce, the Secretary, Island Cruising Club, Salcombe, Devon, TQ8 8DR.

If you do decide, however, to buy your own boat, and there are undeniable advantages, especially if you have young children, then you have to decide where to keep it and sail it. In Britain, the simple answer to that problem is to purchase a copy of BOAT WORLD (see appendix B). This volume lists all the sailing centres in Britain, with full details of facilities, launching sites, moorings, who to contact and so on, for each place. They are arranged geographically around the

A peaceful mooring in the saltings is more attractive and tranquil than a marina, but not so convenient. This one dries out, and is a long way from facilities.

coast, so it is a simple matter to find the one nearest you that sounds suitable. You can then write to or ring the Harbourmaster to ask whether a mooring would be available, floating or drying out, how much it costs and so on. You can go down and see the place and meet him, and talk over your requirements. He will probably be most helpful in assisting you with your choice of boat (twin or single keel, maximum draft for the local waters and so on).

The other thing you can do is look through the list of Marinas in BOAT WORLD and find one near you. Marinas have tremendous advantages over a simple mooring in a harbour. Your boat lies alongside a floating pontoon all the time, probably with water and mains electricity laid on, and there will probably be a good selection of facilities such as chandlers, engineers, boatyard, fuel, and perhaps a club. They are, however, invariably crowded, and tend to be far more expensive than simply mooring in a harbour (you pay for the convenience, of course), and sometimes there are limitations in relation to working on the boat or buying and selling a boat. Some marinas (not all, let's be fair) like to get their grubby little fingers into everything, and you might find yourself obliged to use their boatyard and their engineers and their brokers—so read the small print very carefully.

You pays your money and you takes your choice. If you want to drive down Friday night, step aboard and sail off with no effort, the marina is the place for you. If you like a quiet life and don't mind rowing about with stores, and doing a bit of work yourself, save your money and hire a mooring in a harbour. If you can put up with the inconvenience of drying out on the mooring (limits the times you can sail to when the tide is up) these are invariably very much cheaper than floating ones. Discuss it with the Harbourmaster. You might find the tide is invariably up when you want to sail.

And that about covers how to get afloat, and finishes the book. I hope you have enjoyed it, I hope you have learned from it, and I wish you very good sailing in the future. It's a beautiful place, the sea.

Appendix A
Basic Equipment Lists

Pottering in harbour, estuary etc
anchor and warp
mooring warps
buoyancy aids
hot or cold drinks and sandwiches etc
lifebelts near cockpit
fenders
boathook
dinghy with oars, crutches and bailer
auxiliary engine (inboard or outboard)
harnesses for very small children
deck scrubber
bucket
boarding ladder

Day sail at sea
All harbour equipment plus:
flares
lifejackets
harnesses
liferaft or good rubber dinghy
food
water
engine spares
spare shackles, lashings, etc

fuel
warm clothes
oilskins and boots
compass
chart of area
parallel rulers
dividers
pencils
rubber
handbearing compass
radio for weather forecasts
first aid kit and manual

A typical radar reflector secured high up on the back stays.

Short Coastal Cruise

All day-sail equipment plus:
charts for complete area, harbour and coastal
2 or 3 complete clothes changes
spare food and water
spare fuel
sleeping bags
radar reflector (see photo)
tide tables
pilot books

Appendix B
Recommended Reading

Books to keep on board

Reed's Nautical Almanac: published annually and available at all chandlers and nautical book shops. The bible for the coastal sailor, this book contains more information than I could possibly list. The main features, however, are a complete tide table for British and European ports; tidal atlases; excellent first aid section; details of all buoys, lights etc in British and European ports; phone numbers of Harbour Masters; distress procedures; radio-beacons; a nautical glossary in five languages; weather information; and much, much more.

Boat World: published annually by Sell's Publications, this is another all embracing volume like Reed's, but is particularly suited to the man who trails his boat to the water. Its main feature is a complete list with full details of all sailing centres in Britain, arranged both alphabetically and geographically. For each area there are tidal constants from Dover, list of charts covering the area, list of sailing clubs, and detailed information on all the local ports. It also contains a very comprehensive list of brokers, suppliers and manufacturers of boats and equipment, a list of marinas with brief details of each one, a tide table for Dover together with constants for the rest of the country, and many useful articles on safety, first aid, electronics on board, weather forecasts and so on. Together with Reed's, it constitutes a most comprehensive reference library for your boat.

The Cockpit Book: written by Pim Zandvoort and published by Adlard Coles, this is a cheap and slim reference book containing details of such things as rules of the road; sound signals; buoys and lights; port symbols; forecast symbols and wind scales and much more. It also has an excellent engine fault-finding chart, and makes a most useful little instant reference book to keep on the chart table or in the cockpit.

Books to read

The Long Way: written by Bernard Moitessier and published by Adlard Coles, this book tells the story of the author's experience in the first single-handed round the world race. After circling the world he decided not to return to Europe and its civilisation after all, so he carried on halfway round again to end up in Tahiti. It is beautifully written by a sailor who is sensitive and poetic as well as seamanlike, and if you want to delve into the real magic and mystery of the sea, it is a must.

Boat World Guide to Sailing Cruisers: published by Sell's Publications, this lists all the sailing cruisers on the market, with an index in order of size. Photographs, accommodation plans and full details of each boat are given, and it is a very useful book indeed when you are contemplating buying a boat.

Bristow's Book of Yachts: compiled by Philip Bristow and published annually by Navigator Publishers, this is similar to the above, but gives prices and also a list of secondhand prices for popular classes.

More Fun From Your Boat: written by Charles Jones and published by the Nautical Publishing Co., this is a delightful little book that tells you how to do anything but sail. Lobster potting, photography (above and below water), sea fishing, trawling and skin diving are all dealt with in a simple manner to encourage the average sailor during a weekend potter, or a quiet day on cruise.

Owning a Boat: written by Hugh Marriot and published by the Nautical Publishing Co., this friendly book is very good on buying, selling, and the general problems and joys of boat ownership.

The Sea-Wife's Handbook: written by Joyce Sleightholme, wife of the editor of *Yachting Monthly*, the well known sailor and writer, Des

Sleightholme, this is published by Angus and Robertson and is an excellent book on the whole domestic side of boating, ranging widely from cooking to crewing to coping with the captain. Full of useful information, it should find a place in the saloon bookshelf.

Fitting Out: written by Des Sleightholme and published by Adlard Coles, this little book is a good, simple guide to the basics of maintaining and fitting out your boat. If you have major work done in a boatyard, this book will give you all the information you need for the little jobs you want to tackle yourself.

The Boat Owner's Maintenance Manual: written by Jeff Toghill and published by David and Charles, this is a complete and very comprehensive manual that covers just about any job you are ever likely to do on board. If you are a keen D.I.Y. man this is the book for you.

Handling Small Boats in Heavy Weather: written by Frank Robb and published by Adlard Coles, this chatty, down-to-earth book tells you all about how to cope if caught out in bad weather. The author packs a lot of very useful information into a fairly small book, and has the knack of explaining the procedures, the weather and the waves in such a way that the reader can actually understand what happens and what he should do in his own boat when caught in similar circumstances—a pleasant rarity in these days of glossy, expensive productions that may look very nice on your coffee table, but too often communicate only money to the author's bank!

Safety and Seamanship: written by John Chamier and published by Adlard Coles. The author is a well-known yachting journalist and his breezy, journalistic style is perfect for a book on a subject that is all too often treated with such gravity and dreariness that no one ever reads about it. As John Chamier says, safety is nothing more than good seamanship, and he goes into the related subjects very efficiently. A most worthwhile book that tells how to cope with the disasters, minor and otherwise, that can befall you at sea, and best of all, how to avoid them in the first place.

Practical Yacht Navigator: written by Kenneth Wilkes and published by the Nautical Publishing Company, this is a very well presented book that attempts to teach navigation rather than simply describe it. It is well illustrated, and not particularly cheap, but I think it is probably the most suitable of a fairly large selection of books on the subject, especially for the beginner. If, however, you can cope with something slightly more academic in approach, and very much cheaper, then I would suggest you try:

Coastwise Navigation: written by G. G. Watkins and published by Stanford Maritime. This is a paperback containing a very solid and extensive run-down on coastal navigation. Not so glossy and not so artistically presented as the Kenneth Wilkes book, it is almost a quarter of the price, and contains everything you need to know.

Outlook: another excellent paperback from Stanford Maritime, this one, written by G. W. White, is all about the weather and how to interpret and analyse the shipping forecasts. It is not as technical as it sounds, and if you want to learn more about the weather (which you should if you intend anything more than pottering) I would recommend this little book very strongly.

Modern Rope Seamanship: written by Colin Jarman and Bill Beavis, and published by Adlard Coles, this book deals with ropework from the point of view of the modern seaman, and the synthetic materials he has to work with. The authors are both experienced yachtsmen and nautical journalists and they handle a subject that, to the beginner, all too often flies off into the realms of fantasy, in a practical and realistic way.

Appendix C

Glossary of Basic Nautical Terms

Astern—behind.

Ahead—in front of.

Anchor—specially shaped piece of metal that digs into sea bottom. A line from this to the boat holds the boat in one place—anchored.

Aweigh—the anchor is aweigh when it is lifted just off the bottom.

Aft—towards the stern, as 'he went aft'.

Amidships—in the middle of the boat.

Athwart—across, as 'the dinghy was caught athwart the bow'.

Athwartships—across the middle of the boat.

Anticyclone—region of high pressure marked on weather map.

Aground—stuck on the bottom with insufficient water to float.

Aloft—up the mast, as 'he went aloft'.

Bow—the front end of the boat.

Bowline—knot forming a large loop, used for mooring.

Breastrope—short mooring line going directly ashore at right angles to the boat.

Bollard—wide metal or concrete post to which boats moor.

Backstay—wire from top of mast to stern of boat.

Buoy—floating canister of varied shape to mark sides of channels or dangers. Often carries lights.

Backspring—mooring line from stern leading right for'ard along jetty, to prevent boat surging back.

Block—pulley through which rope runs to make a purchase or change its direction.

Beaufort Scale—a system of numbers known as Forces, by which wind speeds are referred for convenience.

Burgee—small triangular flag flown from top of mast to show wind direction.

Boathook—pole with a hook on the end for catching buoys etc.

Broach—when a wave catches a boat's stern and pushes it round so that she screws up into the wind, she broaches.

Buoyancy aid—slim PVC waistcoat filled with foam.

Broad reach—sailing with the wind on the quarter.

Beam reach—sailing with the wind on the beam.

Boom—length of wood along the bottom of a sail to hold it straight.

Batten—thin length of wood or fibreglass inserted into pocket on after edge of sail (leach) to hold it stiff.

Boom Vang—tackle running from a point along the boom to the foot of the mast, to prevent the boom lifting into the air.

Backing the jib—holding the jib by its sheet on the wrong side of the mast, so the wind blows on the wrong side and pushes the bow round.

Barometer—instrument that measures air pressure. Very useful for foretelling the weather.

Bottlescrew—device with two threads for tightening stays.

Below—down inside the cabin.

Bermudan rig—set of sails in which the mainsail is triangular and set on single tall mast.

Beating to windward—sailing as close as possible to the wind.

Bulkhead—wall or partition in a boat.

Bilge—the very bottom of a boat.

Cleat—T-shaped fitting round which ropes can be secured.

Clew—lower after corner of a sail.

Crutch—support for boom; U-shaped fitting in which oars rest when rowing.

Cable—200 yards (one tenth of a nautical mile); also used when referring to anchor chain—anchor cable.

Coachroof—cabin top that stands above the deck.

Centreboard—wooden plate that sticks out from the bottom of a boat to prevent sideways drift. It pivots up into a case when not needed.

Centreplate—as above, but metal.

Closehauled—sailing as close to the wind as possible.

Course—the direction in which a boat is sailing.

Cockpit—well at the stern in which the crew can sit.

Close reach—sailing with the wind forward of the beam, but not quite closehauled.

Chart—a map of the sea.

Coaming—raised surround to a cockpit etc.

Cheek block—a block that screws flat on to a surface.

Compass—instrument that indicates direction by means of a revolving magnet that always points to magnetic north.

Chainplate—strip of metal fastened to side of boat to which stays are secured.

Clew outhaul—line that adjusts the position of the clew.

Cast off—let go of a line or mooring.

Chart Datum—an imaginary line below which the tide very rarely falls. Soundings on charts are measured below it.

Draft—the depth of a boat below the waterline.

Deckhead—ceiling of a boat (underside of the deck).

Double sheet bend—knot for joining two ropes.

Dividers—instrument for measuring distances on a chart.

Depression—area of low pressure on a meteorological chart.

Dipping the eye—passing the eye of one mooring line up through the eye of another already on a bollard. This enables the first one to be removed without disturbing the second.

Dredging—pronounced 'drudging'—hauling the anchor line up short so that it drags. The boat is then carried away by the tide but retains steerage way as the dragging anchor causes water to flow over the rudder.

Dropping moor—strictly a way of mooring with two anchors, but often used to signify dropping the anchor when stopped and falling back on it.

Deck—the surface over the top of a boat on which you walk.

Dinghy—small open boat.

Drying height—sounding on a chart with a line beneath it, signifying that it shows that much above Chart Datum or Low Water.

Drag the anchor—when wind and tide are so strong that the boat pulls the anchor out of the bottom and drags it along.

Echo-sounder—electronic instrument for measuring depths.

Ebb tide—the tide flowing out of a harbour and falling in height.

Eyebolt—bolt with an eye built in to the end. Used for tying things to.

Equinoctial Spring Tides—spring and autumn Spring tides that are the highest of the year.

For'ard—slang for forward—towards the bow (opposite of aft).

Flood tide—tide that flows into harbours and up in height.

Forestay—wire from top of mast to stem, to hold mast up.

Foresail—triangular sail set on the forestay.

Forespring—long mooring line leading from for'ard back along the jetty to prevent boat going forward.

Fairlead—circular device through which a rope is led to make it lead fair.

Full and bye—sailing slightly off closehauled. Often used in waves to give the boat extra speed.

Forehatch—hatch into the boat through the foredeck.

Fender—soft plastic sausage that cushions the boat when lying alongside something.

Frapping—passing a rope round another at right angles and pulling to tighten the other.

Frapping lines—lines passed round halliards to haul them tightly away from the mast to stop chafe and noise.

Fathom—six feet. Falling out of use with the advent of metric charts.

Figure eight knot—a knot put in the end of a rope to stop it passing through a fairlead.

Foot (of sail)—the bottom edge.

Gunwhale—pronounced gunnel—the top edge of the side of a boat.

Gybe—to turn a boat so that the wind swings across the stern.

Galley—a boat's kitchen.

Goosewing—to sail directly downwind with the mainsail on one side of the boat and the jib on the other.

Guardrail—wire rail running round the gunwhale of a boat a couple of feet up, to stop you falling over the side.

Go about—to turn the boat through the wind, the bow passing across the wind, in order to go from one tack to another. Also known as tacking.

Gooseneck—universal joint by which the boom is attached to the mast.

Gudgeon—one of the fastenings that attach a rudder to the stern of a boat. Similar to a garden gate fitting, the gudgeon has a hole into which the pintle (a long pin) slots, enabling the rudder to pivot.

Half hitch—simple hitch with a rope that forms the beginning of many knots. Also nautical slang for stealing.

Hounds—fitting on the mast to which stays are fastened.

Head (of sail)—the top corner.

Harness—webbing structure that fastens round the body with a line which can be attached to strong point on boat to prevent you falling overboard.

Heave to—back the jib and let the mainsail flap with tiller lashed to leeward. Boat will look after herself and move very little.

Hove to—past tense of above.

Heeling—when a boat lays over due to the pressure of the wind.
Halliard—rope or wire used for hauling sails up stays or masts in order to set them.
Half tide—halfway between high and low water.
Half ebb—halfway from high to low water.
Half flood—halfway from low to high water.
Head wind—wind blowing from right ahead.
Hand—to hand sails is to get them down and stow them.
Headrope—mooring line from bow to jetty.
Headboard—stiff piece set into head of sail to hold it out.
High Water—when the tide is at its highest.
Head to wind—lying pointing directly into the wind.
Harbourmaster—official in charge of running a harbour.
Helmsman—person steering a boat.
Helm—sometimes used to refer to the tiller or wheel.

Inboard motor—engine set inside a boat with a shaft passing outside to rotate a propellor.

Jib—in small boats, the same as foresail. In large boats often means a sail set for'ard of the foresail, flying from the mast without a stay.
Jib sheet—the rope controlling the position of the jib by passing through a fairlead on the gunwhale.

Keel—part of boat that extends down through the water and acts as a centreboard to counteract leeway. In cruising boats it is made of iron or lead to prevent capsize.
Ketch—sailing boat with two masts, the after one generally being small and carrying only one sail, similar to the mainsail, called a mizzen.
Kicking strap—see Boom Vang.
Knot—one nautical mile per hour of speed.

Lee—you are in the lee of something when it stands between you and the wind.

Leeward—the lee side of a boat or object.

Leadline—a line marked in depths with a weight on the end. It is dropped over the side to measure the depth of water.

Luff—the forward edge of a sail.

Luff (verb)—to luff is to swing the boat into the wind.

Leech—the after edge of a sail.

Leeway—drift to leeward caused by wind pressure on sails.

Lifejacket—a device to keep the wearer afloat in the water. Sometimes has permanent buoyancy; sometimes is inflated.

Liferaft—special rubber dinghy carried for emergencies. Thrown into the sea it automatically inflates, and has a canopy for protection.

Lighthouse—tall building with a special light at the top for guiding sailors.

Landmark—conspicuous object ashore for guiding sailors.

Lee helm—when the boat swings away from the wind on letting go of the tiller, it is said to have lee helm.

Lanyards—lashings of small line often used to tighten stays of small boats instead of bottlescrews.

Low Water—the time when the tide is lowest.

Mainsail—the sail set on the after side of the mast.

Mainsheet—the rope that controls the position of the mainsail.

Mooring—buoy permanently attached to the sea bottom to which boats can tie up safely.

Motor-sailer—boat that is a combination of sailing boat and motor boat. Has a large motor and less sail than equivalent sized sailing boat.

Motor-sailing—sailing along under motor and sail together.

Millibars—units by which air pressure is measured on meteorological charts.

Marlinspike—tapered length of steel used for opening shackles and splicing.

Mouse—mousing a shackle consists of securing it with thin wire so it cannot come undone.

Mizzen—small sail like a mainsail set on the after edge of the mizzen mast, which is the after mast on a ketch.

Mizzen staysail—sail similar to a foresail set from the front side of the mizzen mast.

Navigation—the art of finding your way from A to B on the water.

Nautical mile—one minute of latitude—around 2000 yards.

Neap tides—fortnightly tides with least water movement. The high tides are fairly low and the low tides fairly high.

Outboard motor—very compact motor unit that has propeller built in. The whole unit is fitted to the stern of a boat.

Painter—line permanently attached to bow of dinghy for mooring up.

Parallel rules—a pair of rulers fitted together so that they can be moved apart while remaining parallel. Used for transferring courses and bearings from the compass rose on a chart.

Pinch—to sail too close to the wind.

Paddlewheel effect—the tendency of a propeller to climb sideways through the water, thus pushing the stern to one side.

Port—the left-hand side of a boat looking forward.

Pulpit—metal structure around the bow of a boat to enable one to work for'ard without going over the side.

Pushpit—exactly the same thing round the stern of a boat.

Port tack—sailing with the wind on the port side.

Pintle—pin which fits into a gudgeon to enable the rudder to swing on the stern.

Quarter—the after corner of a boat.

Round turn and two half hitches—knot for securing rope to any object, especially rings and buoys.
Reaching—sailing on any point except closehauled and running.
Running—sailing with the wind directly astern.
Reef knot—knot for tying parcels and reefs in sails.
Reduction box—extra gearbox behind the main one to reduce the revolutions further before turning the propeller.
Reefing—reducing the sail area of a mainsail by rolling it round the boom.
Running moor—strictly a method of mooring with two anchors, but often used to denote anchoring by dropping the anchor while still under way, and laying out the cable as you run forward.

Sheet—rope for controlling angle of sails.
Shackle—U-shaped metal fitting closed by a small threaded rod to join things together.
Sheet bend—knot for joining two ropes.
Stern—back of boat.
Spinnaker—large, balloon-type sail often set when running.
Stanchion—post to which guardrails are attached.
Shipping forecast—special weather forecast for shipping.
Set of tide—direction tide is running.
Shrouds—stays from the mast to the sides of a boat.
Sloop—boat with one mast, one mainsail and one jib.
Stay—wire running from the top of mast to deck to hold up mast.
Starboard—right-hand side of boat looking forward.
Shoal water—shallow water.
Stern gland—gland through which the propeller shaft passes through the hull—watertight.
Stem—the bow where it enters the water.
Sea room—used to denote room to leeward when storm comes.
Synopsis—the general weather situation given in a forecast.
Shackle key—device for opening shackles.

Standing part—the part of a rope that is attached.

Shock cord—very strong thick elastic with hooks on the ends.

Stern rope—mooring line from the stern to shore.

Starboard tack—sailing with the wind on the starboard side.

Sail tiers—short lengths of line or webbing or material used to tie up sails on to booms.

Slack water—when the tidal stream is slack at high and low water before changing direction. Also used simply to mean water that has no tide pushing it.

Spring tides—fortnightly tides when the high water is very high and the low water very low.

Sounding—the depth of water shown on a chart. It is measured below Chart Datum. Thus the actual depth of water is this plus the height of tide.

Spreaders—metal rods extending from the sides of a mast to hold the rigging out, thus improving the angle at which it pulls on the masthead.

Sole—the bottom of a cockpit, or the floor in a cabin.

Tackle—a collection of blocks through which rope is led to create a purchase (pronounced taykel).

Tack—the for'ard lower corner of a sail.

Tack tackle—a small tackle used to haul down on the tack of a sail, and thus tighten the luff.

Tiller—stick that fits into the top of the rudder to steer with.

Tacking—see going about.

Tender—small dinghy carried by a yacht for ferrying crew and equipment about.

Topping lift—line that hooks into the end of a boom to hold it up when the sail is off, or when reefing. Sometimes fixed to the backstay; sometimes adjustable from the masthead.

Trysail—small, heavy triangular sail set in place of the mainsail in very strong winds. Not used much in small boats these days.

Tide—a flow of water created by the pull of the moon and the sun. The level of the water rises and falls as the tide flows hither and thither.
Tidal stream—refers to the horizontal flow of the tide.
Topsides—the sides of a boat.
Transom—a square stern seen on many small boats.
Tide tables—tables tabulating the times and heights of high water.
Tidal stream atlas—collection of small maps showing the strength and direction of the tidal stream during all the period of the ebb and flow of the tide.
Twelfths Rule—a simple rule for calculating the height of the tide.
Tripping line—a line with a buoy that is attached to the crown of an anchor, so that it can be pulled from the opposite side of the cable if the anchor catches under a chain or other obstruction.

Under way—a boat is under way when it is not attached to the land by ropes or anchor. It does not have to be moving.

Variation—the angular difference between the direction of True North (the North Pole) and Magnetic North (a point somewhere in Northern Canada).

Windward—towards the wind; the side of a boat facing the wind.
Weather side—side of a boat facing the wind.
Wind force—denoted by a number from the Beaufort Wind Scale. Each number covers a small range of wind speeds, and is simply a form of shorthand.
White horses—when waves break with little white foaming tops, these tops are known as white horses.
Waggoner's hitch—a knot used by lorry drivers for securing loads, and very useful on board a boat for lashing down dinghies.
Working end—the free end of a rope which is being used to tie a knot or whatever.

Whipping—a lashing of very small twine put around the end of a rope to stop it unravelling.

Warp—a rope. Generally applied to anchor warps and mooring warps. Also used as a verb meaning to move a boat about by pulling on ropes.

Weather helm—the normal tendency of a boat to swing up into the wind if the tiller is released.

Windage—a boat is said to have a lot of windage if she presents a lot of surface, such as a high cabin top, to the wind. The more windage she has, the more easily will the wind blow her sideways.